GEORGE WHITEFIELD
WAYFARING WITNESS

GEORGE WHITEFIELD
WAYFARING WITNESS

Stuart C. Henry

ABINGDON PRESS
New York • Nashville

GEORGE WHITEFIELD: WAYFARING WITNESS

Copyright © MCMLVII by Abingdon Press

Library of Congress Catalog Card Number: 57-10273

SET UP, PRINTED, AND BOUND BY THE
PARTHENON PRESS, AT NASHVILLE,
TENNESSEE, UNITED STATES OF AMERICA

FOR

Pearl Frances Stuart and Charles Aubrey Henry

MY MOTHER AND FATHER

whose deep wisdom and Christian charity
would have recognized Whitefield's worth
and forgiven his faults

Preface

BETWEEN the summer of 1736 and September of 1770, George Whitefield preached no less then eighteen thousand times. He preached in churches and fields, in foundries, courthouses, and barns —from wagons, balconies, horseback, boats, and windows. Men flocked to hear him in vast throngs. It is impossible to say for what countless thousands his creed became their creed and his faith their faith.

George Whitefield was an ordained priest of the Church of England. He was also the goad and companion of the fops at Bath, confidant of the outcasts who peopled Hogarth's lusty London, idol of "awakened" Christians on two continents, and the bane of bishops within his own communion. For more than three decades he exhorted the British Isles. He visited America seven times, and he improved the occasions of his transit by preaching on the high seas. In his full life he published pamphlets, directed charity drives, instituted schools, and founded an orphanage. His remarkable personal history is the context for the presentation of his message.

The manner, no less than the matter, of his preaching made Whitefield a pivot of controversy. His message was variously received. He was styled saint and devil. Some took him for a knave; others called him a fool. There was no unanimity regarding him in the Christian community. Bishops wrote against him. Commissaries railed at him. Ministers denied him their pulpits. Whitefield met his opposers head on, waited on authorities, and charged boldly into the strongholds of his enemies. His own spirit was not always above reproach, for he made telling use of irony and offered invective in a professed meekness. And all the while many called him "blessed."

Dispute over Whitefield was not confined to the Christian community. The polite and frivolous world of Bath and the literary world of London were as strongly impressed by him as the colliers of Wales, though in a different way. Fascinated by Whitfield, the eighteenth century invited him to preach in its ballrooms, wrote of him in letters and literature, depicted him in idealized paintings and cruel cartoons. Walpole accused Whitefield of encouraging crime in order to have a dramatic setting for eleventh-hour conversions. Samuel Foote lampooned the cross-eyed preacher as Dr. Squintum. Richard Graves made him the butt of gentle, restrained satire. The poet Cowper wrote of him with admiration. Though often baffled by Whitefield's message, his world never ignored it.

It is impossible to analyze the man's appeal without knowing something of the man himself. His personality is meaningless without his message. But his message is shorn of significance when considered apart from its reception. Men who have written of him seem, for the most part, eighteenth century in attitude if not in fact. That is, they have seen Whitefield as one to be championed or attacked. This evaluation, it is hoped, points below the surface contradictions of a turbulent career and indicates the secret of the man's personality which was at once the reservoir of his power and the source of his appeal.

Whatever light the following pages shed on the religious revival of the eighteenth century as such is reflected from the figure of the fabulous preacher. Consideration of the Great Awakening has been important but not central in the investigation. Like Methodism, it was part of the rich setting in which Whitefield played his part. The revival was a force in the milieu of which he was—in a measure—both creator and product.

The present work is divided into two parts: "The Man" and "The Message and How It Was Received." Concern with Whitefield as a focal point of investigation was not primarily biographical, but consideration of the near-legendary record of his astonishing career was essential to the research.

Materials of the first part were carefully chosen and included only as they seemed to add some new dimension to the character of Whitefield. Notice is not made, for example, of a trip to Holland, because it throws no additional light on the wellspring of his action. The chapter titles in the first part indicate not only something that

Whitefield did; they also suggest something that he was. They do not summarize, but describe the high points of the divisions which they introduce.

The second part sets forth the content of Whitefield's message and tells how his world received it. As a nobody who sprang from menial obscurity to international prominence, he preached a theology of the sovereign, electing grace of God that could redeem the lowliest and set him on high places. As a figure of a great religious revival in which thousands accepted the promises of God, he lived by the faith of man's ability to set his face to the light. He decried the human ability while exhorting men to good works.

This study of Whitefield would not have been accomplished without encouragement and help from many sources. It is not possible to mention all whose labor and consideration assisted in bringing the work to completion.

I am grateful to the staff of Duke University's excellent library, who have been consistently courteous and helpful. I am indebted to Mr. Thomas M. Simkins, the Curator of Rare Books, for considerations beyond those normally expected. Miss Florence Blakely, Mr. William Chalker, Mrs. Gus L. Ford, Mr. Tom Gilcrest, Mr. David L. Mueller, and Mr. John N. R. Score aided me in various ways. Dr. David Ruffin and Dr. Elizabeth Buckingham read proof. Certain improvements were made on the advice of Dr. Gusta B. Nance, who read the manuscript with scholarly eye and friendly interest. Miss Doralyn Hickey prepared the index with understanding and skill, assisted in compiling the bibliography, and made valuable suggestions —especially that of including a chronology. Mrs. Joyce Lockhart Farris, who typed the final copy, was unfailingly efficient, and the form in which the material is here rendered owes much to her intelligence and imagination. Mr. Donn Michael Farris read the final copy with sympathy and care. He offered valuable technical assistance at many points and was always encouraging. Especially I want to thank Dr. H. Shelton Smith, professor of American religious thought at Duke University. It was he who first saw the possibility of the present work and who from the outset was confident that it could be accomplished. I am more grateful to all these friends than this brief notice suggests.

Last of all I am indebted to Whitefield himself for being the colorful character that he was and so affording me interesting paths to follow. The long titles of his works (and of those by his eighteenth-century contemporaries) have been shortened. The erratic use of italics and capitals, however, and the impulsive punctuation and spelling have been retained. For that reason there is in the pages that follow as much variety in the spelling of words as there is in the estimate of the controversial figure whom they describe.

STUART C. HENRY
Southern Methodist University

Contents

PART I

The Man

Chapter I

Out of the Inn

EXACTLY at six o'clock on Sunday morning, September 30, 1770, George Whitefield "fetched but one gasp, ... stretched out his feet, and breathed no more." [1] He made no comment, but—in fulfillment of his own prediction—died "silent." [2] This was a singular circumstance in the career of one who for more than thirty years had improved every occasion (especially death and disaster) to declare the gospel. Yet death alone was able to still the powerful voice of the trumpeter whose preaching had galvanized sinners on two continents to repentance and spurred innumerable thousands to persevere in proving their election. Indeed, he had preached his last sermon less than twenty-four hours before he died.

On the preceding Saturday he had been riding toward Boston, traveling from Portsmouth. And though he was already ill, when he was but fifteen miles along the route, he was stopped by a multitude who had heard that Whitefield was passing by and who were insistent that he should preach. He mounted a hogshead and spoke to them for two hours in the fields of Exeter. Though he was "then much troubled with asthma, yet the charms of his rhetorick and oratory were surprising." [3] He went that evening to be the guest of the Rev. Jonathan Parsons, Presbyterian minister at Newbury Port, who had met him on the way. While he was at supper, townsfolk who were eager to hear him collected before the manse and pushed into the hall. Whitefield, candle in hand, paused on his way to his bedroom and gave a final exhortation as he "lingered on the stairway, while the crowd gazed up at him with tearful eyes, as Elisha at the ascending prophet. His voice, never perhaps, surpassed in its music and pathos, *flowed on until the candle which he held in his hand burned away and went out in its socket!*" [4] It was the next morning that he died.

By noon the news was spreading fast. A "stranger was seen" riding along the main street of Portsmouth, "halting at the different corners, and in a clear but subdued voice crying out, *'Whitefield is dead! Whitefield is dead!'*" [5] This intelligence had been given to Whitefield's followers more than once during his turbulent career; on occasion his friends had heard that he was a victim of poison,[6] or again that he had been taken prisoner by the Spanish.[7] Whitefield himself had expected and professed to wish for death for many years and once confessed amazement at not having "been measured for a coffin long ago!" [8] But now it was true, and the solemn fact "stunned the whole population."

No sooner had the "news of this melancholy event" been brought to Boston than

a respectable number of Gentlemen of the south church set out for Newbury Port, with a view of bringing the corps [there] for interment, knowing it to be Mr. Whitefield's desire, . . . in so much as to request the favour of a particular tomb; but, to the surprise of these Gentlemen, upon application for the body to the Reverend Mr. Parsons, . . . they were totally defeated . . . Mr. Parsons absolutely refusing to permit the corps being buried but from his own house, and before his own pulpit! [9]

The inhabitants of Georgia showed no less concern:

All the black cloth in the stores was bought up; the pulpit and desks of the church, the branches, the organ loft, the pews of the governor and council, were covered with black. The governor and council, in deep mourning, convened at the state-house, and went in procession to church, and were received by the organ playing a funeral dirge. Two funeral sermons were preached.[10]

On the same day that the news of Whitefield's death reached London, the Georgia assembly, doubtless ignorant of the experience of the Bostonians, was appropriating funds to defray the expense of "bringing the Remains of the Reverend Mr. Whitefield from Newbury Port, in the Massachusetts Government, to be deposited at the Orphan House" and planning for public-financed mourning and a "proper Monument." [11]

Funeral sermons "were preached in the principal cities of America";[12] and in his native land the attitude of those who looked on Whitefield's death in terms of a personal loss was typified by the sincere, if indifferent, poetry of Charles Wesley:

> AND is my WHITEFIELD entered into rest,
> With sudden death, with sudden glory blest?
> Left for a few sad moments here behind,
> I bear his image on my faithful mind.[13]

In England the official funeral sermon for Whitefield was preached by John Wesley. Indeed, he preached it twice—once at the chapel in Tottenham Court Road and once in the tabernacle at Moorfields.[14] In both places sanctuaries were adorned with mourning which was not to be taken down for six months. Pulpit and galleries were draped with "fine black baize" for the solemn occasion. That was on November 18.[15] Five days later Wesley was requested to repeat the sermon at the Greenwich Tabernacle. He did so, and the house could not "contain the congregation." Even as late as January 2, 1772, Wesley preached a "kind of funeral sermon for Mr. Whitefield" at Deptford, because he wished "to show all possible respect to the memory of that great and good man." [16]

By the following spring there were indications that forces were working on both sides of the Atlantic to manufacture a Whitefield legend. In May a young man preached successfully at the Tottenham Court Road Tabernacle, seemingly recommended by the fact that he looked "somewhat like Mr. Whitefield in the face." [17] A Negro slave girl published a rhapsodic eulogy on the evangelist and called for America to "drop a Tear upon his happy Urn." [18] Less than a year after Whitefield had died, two enterprising ladies were exhibiting a wax figure of him in Boston "readily brought to such Perfection . . . as amazed Spectators of all Ranks." [19]

Nothing in the circumstances of Whitefield's birth augured the spectacular character of his meteoric career. He was born on December 16, 1714 [20] (a year notable for the death of Anne and the coming of the Hanoverians to England), in the Bell Inn at Gloucester. When he wrote of this some years later, Whitefield did so in questionable taste that betrayed an inclination—if not an effort—to see a rather particular providence in his personal history. His artless account is unblushing, though no doubt sincere:

My Father and Mother kept the Bell Inn. The former died when I was two years old; the latter is now alive, and has often told me how she endured fourteen Weeks' Sickness after she brought me into the World; but was used to say, even when I was an Infant, that she expected more Comfort from me than any other of her Children. This, with the Circumstance of my being born in an Inn, has often been of Service to me in exciting my Endeavours to make good my Mother's Expectations, and so follow the Example of my dear Saviour, who was born in a Manger belonging to an Inn.[21]

When Whitefield wrote this, however, he did so from the vantage point of a popular success which might well have turned older and wiser heads than his. Only twenty-six years old, he had already preached to crowds estimated at sixty and even eighty thousand people. The fact is that his origin was so inauspicious, and that he knew it to be such, that it is one of the prime factors in explaining Whitefield's tenacity in holding to a doctrine of election. He was dazzled by the consideration that he, George Whitefield, who had been born in an inn, had preached to great throngs of people, had seen his name frequently in the public press, and had become the uneasy companion of men who were nobly born. His success intoxicated him till his dying day.

The Bell Inn in Gloucester stood in Southgate Street, near the church of St. Mary de Crypt.[22] Here Whitefield passed the childhood years that he later referred to as profligate beyond description. He said of himself, "I can truly say that I was froward from my Mother's Womb"; he remembered "early stirrings of Corruption."

Standing in the community of Oxford Methodism he looked back on his youth with a severe eye and wrote the following lurid description of what was doubtless a relatively normal childhood:

> I was so brutish as to hate Instruction, and used purposely to shun all Opportunities of receiving it. . . . I soon gave pregnant Proofs of an impudent Temper. Lying, filthy talking, and foolish jesting I was much addicted to even when very young. Sometimes I used to curse, if not swear. Stealing from my Mother I thought no Theft at all. . . . Numbers of Sabbaths have I broken, and generally used to behave myself very irreverently in God's Sanctuary. . . . Often have I joined with Others in playing roguish Tricks. . . .
>
> It would be endless to recount the Sins and Offences of my younger Days. They are more in Number than the Hairs of my Head.[23]

Perhaps Whitefield was the monstrous child, precocious in vice, presented in these autobiographical confessions, the only available records of his early years. Certainly there was a calculated risk in exposing a child to the rough environment of the lusty, eighteenth-century inn, of which Thomas Brown, who was no prude, offered the following description:

> A *Tavern* is a little *Sodom*, where as many Vices are daily practised, as ever were known in the great one; Thither *Libertines* repair to drink away their brains, . . . *Aldermen,* to talk Treason, and bewail the loss of Trade; *Saints,* to elevate the Spirit, hatch calumnies, coin false News, and reproach the Church; *Gamsters,* to shake their Elbows, and pick the Pockets of such Cullies who have no more wit than to play with them; *Rakes* with their *Whores,* that by the help of Wine they may be more Impudent and more Wicked, and do those things in their Cups, that would be a Scandal to Sobriety; . . . Thither *Sober Knaves* walk with Drunken Fools, to make cunning Bargains, and over-reach them in their Dealings, where, . . . they will tell more Lyes about a hogshead of Tobacco, than *Tavernier* in his Travels does about Mount *Aetna:* Thither *Young Quality* retire to spend their Tradesmens Money, and to delight themselves with the Impudence of Lewd Harlots, . . . Thither *Bullies* Coach it to kick Drawers, and invent new Oaths and Curses, . . . Thither run *Sots* purely to be Drunk. . . . Thither *Beaux* flock to shew their Vanity . . . Thither *Cowards* repair to make themselves valiant by the strength of their Wine; . . . *Maids* to be made

otherwise; *Married Women* to Cuckold their Husbands; and *Spend-thrifts* to be made Miserable by a ridiculous Consumption of their own Fortunes.[24]

If such a description even approximates the truth, then the youthful Whitefield was fortunate to sustain no more serious moral injury than he did. Surely petty theft and a childish tendency to repeat oaths overheard from his elders were a modicum of turpitude under the circumstances. But there were evidences in Whitefield's childhood, even by his own self-castigating confession, that the latent Savonarolan passion was striving to actualize itself at an early age. He tells of "some early Convictions of Sin" and of how after being teased he went alone to his room and "kneeling down, with many Tears, prayed" about his enemies. Rather a curious conceit for a depraved child! But the detail that he offers which renders all the protestations of aggressive wickedness suspect is the record of a pronounced and early bent toward the ministry:

I was always fond of being a Clergyman, and used frequently to imitate the Ministers reading Prayers etc. Part of the Money I used to steal from my Parent I gave to the poor, and some Books I privately took from Others, for which I have since restored fourfold, I remember were Books of Devotion.[25]

The chances are that Whitefield was, if not an ordinary child, certainly not an unusually outrageous one, and that his childhood and youth assumed their sinister character only under the examination of an overly sensitive conscience which sought (even though unwittingly) to magnify the grace of God by enlarging the object of its beneficence.

Good or bad, however, Whitefield was a born actor. In this respect the child was definitely father to the man. The lad who was later to give "churchgoing America its first taste of theatre under the flag of salvation" [26] was "very fond of reading Plays" and was truant "from School for Days together to prepare" for them. Young George was so successful an actor that the master of the school, in composing a play for the entertainment of the visiting Corporation, provided a piece in which Whitefield played a girl's part. It was in reference to this experience that the actor turned divine wrote,

"The Remembrance of this has often covered me with Confusion of Face, and I hope will do so, even to the End of my Life." [27]

Oddly, it was while Whitefield was "reading a Play" to his sister (a singularly specific detail in an account much given to generality) that he made the dramatic announcement: "God intends something for me which we know not of." [28] From that time his energies were collected and pointed to purpose. The techniques that he employed were various, and personal sense of success was often indifferent, but his goal was constant. He was responding to a challenge of destiny. Whether he was deluded in his sense of mission is a question to moot. There is no question, however, that he thought himself called from that hour or that he was thereafter ever able to look on any circumstance of life without remarking, "God . . . sweetly prepared my Way." [29]

When he was twelve years old, Whitefield was placed in the grammar school of St. Mary de Crypt—"the last," he says, "I ever went to." [30] Two years earlier Mrs. Whitefield—a widow of some eight years—had in a marriage to a Mr. Longden (an ironmonger of Gloucester) [31] effected "what the World would call an unhappy Match as for Temporals." [32] It was shortly plain to George that his mother could not continue to finance his education, and he resolved to spend no more time studying Latin, which—as he said—"would spoil me for a Tradesman." By his own account he soon became, not a tradesman, rather a common tapster in the tavern:

> But my Mother's Circumstances being much on the Decline, and being tractable that way, I from time to time began to assist her occasionally in the Public-House, till at length I put on my blue Apron and my Snuffers, washed Mops, cleaned Rooms, and, in one Word, became professed and Common Drawer for nigh a Year and a half.[33]

For a while George's fortune went from bad to worse. Mrs. Longden left the inn, which was taken over by one of her sons. The younger Mrs. Whitefield, who was commended by Fielding for the "prudence and wisdom of her temper," [34] was, nevertheless, a woman with whom George "could by no means agree." [35] He left the inn, but after a short stay at Bristol, where he was meticulous in personal devotions, he was back in Gloucester disporting himself in the reading of plays and, as he darkly described it, "abominable secret Sin." [36] At this juncture Whitefield's mother saw the possibility of George's going to the University when she received a visit from one of her son's schoolfellows who explained the servitor's situation whereby a student might work for his expenses. Whitefield's record of his mother's vision and his own happiness reads like a scene from a play of the period: "Upon that my Mother immediately cried out, 'This will do for my Son.' Then, turning to me, she said, 'Will you go to Oxford, George?' I replied, With all my Heart." [37]

In a week he was back with his old schoolmaster, preparing for Oxford. Although he did considerably better at his studies than he had formerly, he got "acquainted with such a Set of debauched, abandoned, atheistical Youths" that his distinction was achieving a "great Proficiency in the School of the Devil." Yet he persisted in his spiritual quest. Forsaking (and even informing on) his degraded companions, he began a rigorous pattern of personal religious life that included "receiving the Sacrament monthly, fasting frequently, attending constantly on public Worship, and praying often more than twice a Day in private." [38] When at eighteen he came to Oxford, recommended to the master of Pembroke College by his friends, it was to George Whitefield clearly an evidence of Providence that he was, "contrary to all Expectations, admitted . . . immediately." [39]

Chapter II

The Methodist Servitor at Oxford

WHITEFIELD'S first days at Oxford were rewarding. His tavern training served him well. Whether by efficiency or by attitude it is difficult to say, but by some means he soon ingratiated himself "into the Gentlemen's Favour so far, that Many, who had it in their Power, chose" him for their servitor. The situation reduced his expenses considerably, for servitors were excused lecture fees. It also gave him firsthand opportunity to observe—as he did with unsympathetic eye—"young Students spending their Substance in extravagant living." [1] Yet the vengeful nemesis of satanic power, which Whitefield believed dogged his steps till his dying day, never walked closer to him than at this time of his life. The problem of evil companions (a former pitfall) was shortly dismissed, for when the giddy students who solicited George to "join in their Excess . . . perceived they could not prevail," they quickly left him "alone as a singular, odd Fellow." [2] His temptations, which were real, were of subtler variety.

Certain *that,* but not *for what,* God had called him, Whitefield was powerless to respond to the frantic immediacy of heaven's challenge. Writing of the ordeal later he said that Satan began then to "sift" him like wheat. Nor was that the worst. Before conversion resolved his difficulty, Whitefield believed himself a victim of demonic attacks in which Satan "transformed himself into an Angel of Light, and worked so artfully" that in an effort to do what he "imagined the good, and not the evil, Spirit suggested," the struggling Whitefield was actually following the guidance of the devil. [3]

Yet during this trying season the postulant at heaven's gate did not doubt the possibility of religious assurance—if for no other reason—because of the eloquent witness of John and Charles

21

Wesley. By the time Whitefield entered Pembroke, these brothers and their friends, seeking in community to vitalize their personal religion, had been united three years in a group which less dedicated residents at the University laughingly called the "Holy Club." Whitefield had already heard of these earnest folk and for some time had admired the regular pattern and careful piety of their lives. When he knew them better, he learned that his own spiritual problems were not unique. Having esteemed the "Methodists" before he came to Oxford, he defended them so "strenuously," once he was there, that he became suspect to his fellow students, who predicted that he "in time should be one of them." [4] He was. It happened in this way. Not long after his arrival at the University, he heard of an unfortunate wretch who tried to cut her throat. Considering the situation one to which Charles Wesley might speak aptly, Whitefield, accordingly, sent him word of it by an apple-woman, taxing her with the responsibility (which she betrayed) of withholding from the Methodist the name of his informant. This led to an invitation for the servitor to have breakfast with the tutor, an opportunity which Whitefield "thankfully embraced." [5]

Thereafter Whitefield was increasingly identified with the band of Methodists and "began, like them, to live by Rule, and to pick up the very Fragments of . . . Time, that not a Moment might be lost." [6] By his association with them Whitefield was subjected to the contempt of his fellow students and became the object of their derision. He lost pay as well as face by his friendship with the Wesleys, for some refused him his servitor's wages because of his Methodist connection. But Whitefield did not find peace, even at this price. There was little joy in his life. His "Soul was barren and dry." He felt himself like a "Man locked up in iron Armour." He suffered "heavings" of the body. The nights he spent groaning on his bed were countless, and "Whole Days and Weeks" were passed "lying prostrate on the Ground, and begging for Freedom from . . . proud hellish Thoughts." [7] Years later, in one of his farewell sermons on the eve of his last departure from England, Whitefield referred to these dark days and the futility of trying in outward religious conformity—however diligent—to take heaven by storm. He learned then, he said, that a "man may go to church, say his prayers, receive the sacrament, and yet . . . not be a Christian." He added,

"I am now fifty-five years of age, . . . I tell you, brethren, . . . I am more and more convinced that this is the truth of God." [8]

Before he found release, Whitefield had tried more than living "methodically." He has left a record of an asceticism which spares few details:

Whilst my inward Man was thus exercised, my outward Man was not unemployed. I soon found what a Slave I had been to my sensual Appetite, and now resolved to get the Mastry over it by the Help of Jesus Christ. Accordingly, by Degrees, I began to leave off eating Fruits and such like, and gave the Money I usually spent in that way to the poor. Afterward, I always chose the worst sort of Food, though my Place furnished me with Variety. I fasted twice a Week. My Apparel was mean. I thought it unbecoming a Penitent to have his Hair powdered. I wore woolen Gloves, a patched Gown, and dirty Shoes; and though I was then convinced that the Kingdom of God did not consist in Meats and Drinks, yet I resolutely persisted in these voluntary Acts of self-denial, because I found them great Promoters of the Spiritual life.[9]

The determination implicit in this confession would be impressive coming from anyone. The latter part of it is particularly telling coming from Whitefield, who was subsequently rather fastidious about his dress, especially in his later years. "He was neat to the extreme in his person and everything about him. . . . He said he did not think he should die easy, if he thought his gloves were out of their place." [10] Asceticism had not brought him the assurance that he sought.

It was not until he was twenty years old that freedom of spirit finally came for Whitefield. He had tried the method and the literature of the group at Oxford. He had attempted to renounce himself in a rigid asceticism of inflexible pattern and unattainable goal. All this he had done in an effort to answer the challenge of an imperative from God. Nothing availed. And then it happened. He received an assurance that made it impossible for him ever again to be uncertain.

The episode is brief, as it is contained in *A Short Account of God's Dealings with the Reverend Mr. George Whitefield,* but it is of paramount importance to the understanding of the man. His emergence from the chrysalis of conviction dictated the nature of his work. His telling of the experience offers the framework of his theology and the focal point of his faith. Whitefield now understood his mission. It was to tell men the truth—truth that he knew neither from books, nor from man, but from his experience of God. It was a lofty conception of destiny, yet it could hardly have been otherwise in one who described his conversion in the following words—words that occasioned caustic and incredulous comment from those who were less certain of the young prophet's rapport with heaven than he was himself:

About the end of the seven Weeks, and after I had been groaning under an unspeakable Pressure both of Body and Mind for above a Twelvemonth God was pleased to set me free in the following Manner. One Day, perceiving an uncommon Drought and a disagreeable Claminess in my Mouth, and using things to allay my Thirst, but in vain, it was suggested to me, that when *Jesus Christ* cried out, "I thirst," His sufferings were near at an End. Upon which I cast myself down on the Bed, crying out, I thirst! I thirst!—Soon after this, I found and felt in myself that I was delivered from the Burden that had so heavily oppressed me! The Spirit of Mourning was taken from me, and I knew what it was truly to rejoice in God my Saviour, and, for some Time, could not avoid singing Psalms wherever I was. . . .

Thus were the Days of my Mourning ended. . . . Now did the Spirit of God take Possession of my soul.[11]

It was three years, therefore, before Wesley's heart grew strangely warm that Whitefield felt himself to be born again, and the shocking egoism in his account of it cannot obscure the obvious earnestness of the youthful importunate. Moreover, once he had solved the riddle of his existence, he lost no time in sharing the secret with the world.

Whitefield had been converted seven weeks after Easter in 1735.[12] As early as June 12 of that year he began to write about the "pangs and pleasures of the new birth." [13] And earlier than he wrote thus of regeneration—or more correctly, earlier than there is available record of his having so written of it—Whitefield began to teach and to tell his joy. In the spring of the year of his conversion Whitefield went to Gloucester for a long vacation that lasted until the following March. A well-meaning physician had sent him home in the vain hope that he might be diverted from too intense an application of religion. The prescription illustrates only how little the doctor knew his patient.

God had spoken to Whitefield, and he had no choice but to prophesy. He was by no means idle, therefore, during his Gloucester holiday. Rather he set out on his mission at once, initiating a pattern and variety for his ministry from that time on. After "importunate prayer" he went to call on a woman of his acquaintance to whom he "had formerly read Plays, Spectators, *Pope's Homer,* and such-like trifling Books." He found her an eager pupil, and she "soon became a Fool for *Christ's Sake."* Inevitably there was the formation of a small society that "had quickly the Honour of being despised at *Gloucester."* When he heard that the strolling players were coming to town, Whitefield, remembering what an "egregious Offender" he had been in his earlier days, addressed himself to the situation. Never averse to using an idea or an expression because it had been used by another, Whitefield extracted portions of Law's *The Absolute Unlawfulness of the Stage Entertainments* and persuaded a printer to "put a little of it in the *News* for six weeks successively." He spent many days, "almost always upon my Knees," he said, studying sacred books and especially the Bible. Although the conditions of jails were so unspeakable at this time that frequently "chaplains held aloof" from them, Whitefield visited the prisoners and preached to them. He called on the sick.[14] With a self-authenticating sensitivity to the spirit world that operated early he reflected on his activity and could not deny that the devil had a "particular spite against weekly communion," or question that the Holy Spirit was "moving on the hearts"[15] of some of his hearers. Even at this date financial matters created pressures but no problems.[16] When he needed material assistance, he followed the "example of Professor Frank" and "pleaded the Scripture Promises for the Things of this life."[17] His emphasis was already on "being justified . . . by *Faith only."*[18] And in the midst of his activity he moved in a growing throng of friends who were convinced of his special worth and—to that end—urged him to take holy orders.[19]

These were authentic Whitefieldian attitudes and actions. They were characteristic of him for the rest of his days. The same themes recurred with endless variation in detail but with a constant fidelity to form. His lifework is not unlike a river in which the eddies and backwash sometimes give a deceptive appearance of the direction in which the water is flowing, but the sweeping trends of the stream that carry the river to the sea do not vary. There was always in Whitefield a fearless, almost arrogant prophecy delivered to a society that could revere or despise, but never ignore, its spokesman; a religion that preached faith and demanded works; a private life secure in the protection and maintenance of heaven; and a personal existence guided, "even in the minutest circumstances," [20] by the word of God. The message that Whitefield preached and the frenzy with which he pursued his way sprang from the conversion experience of being born again; for him nothing could compare with the new birth, and without it there was no meaning in existence.

The circumstance of Whitefield's birth may have been commonplace, but there was nothing ordinary in the beginning of his career. Even discounting the melodramatic quality of the autobiographical *Short Account,* the stark facts are impressive. Whitefield was certain about his conversion. It did not necessarily follow for him, however, that he should become a clergyman. His friends entertained no doubts and urged him to take the step, but he was not thoroughly convinced and hesitated until Providence left him no choice in the light of the following incidents.

One afternoon Martin Benson, Bishop of Gloucester, chanced, while taking a walk, to meet Lady Selwyn, who recommended Whitefield for ordination. A few days later, as young George was coming from cathedral prayers, one of the vergers summoned him to speak with the bishop. It is impossible to put an unflattering interpretation on the bishop's words to the young student: "Notwithstanding I have declared I would not ordain any one under three and twenty, yet I shall think it my duty to ordain you whenever you come for holy orders." After this unexpected commendation the startled youth received a present of five guineas from his lordship.[21] The only question about Whitefield's ordination now was when it would be effected. That he would be ordained was a foregone conclusion. The ceremony took place on Sunday, June 20, 1736, in Whitefield's twenty-first year.

The cathedral of Gloucester was impressive. It was hallowed by the memory of Osric, "sub-regulus" of Ethelred, King of Mercia, and of John Hooper, Protestant prelate and martyr.[22] Whitefield was properly impressed by the setting of his ordination and the communion of the saints whose goodly fellowship he now entered. But he was equal to the occasion, and in his own way he was impressive too. He "rose early, and prayed over St. *Paul's* Epistle to *Timothy,* and more particularly over *that* Precept, '*Let no* man despise thy Youth.'" [23] It was about noon that he was "solemnly admitted by good *Bishop Benson* before many witnesses into holy orders, and was, blessed be GOD, kept composed both before and after imposition of hands." [24] When Whitefield went to the altar, he could "think of nothing but *Samuel's* standing a little Child before the Lord"; and when the bishop placed his hands on George's head, the candidate's "Heart melted down." [25] When ever afterward he referred to his own ordination—or to that of anyone else—he centered the sanctity and the validity of the rite in the postulant's profession of being "inwardly moved by the Holy Ghost" to take the solemn step.[26] Throughout the service Whitefield "endeavoured to behave with unaffected devotion." [27] During the week following his ordination the degree of Bachelor of Arts was conferred on him at Oxford.[28]

Reluctant as Whitefield may have been to enter the ministry precipitately, he showed no hesitation in speaking with authority, once the step was taken. "I shall displease some," he wrote as he prepared his first sermon, "being determined to speak against their assemblies." [29] Nevertheless he spoke boldly and forcefully against those social gatherings for the "sake of conversation, gallantry and play," which were called *assemblies* and which formed a regular feature of fashionable life in the eighteenth century.[30] The man who stood up to preach in St. Mary de Crypt had been a common tapster in the adjoining tavern five years before. There is the ring of authenticity in Whitefield's comment that "curiosity . . . drew a large congregation together upon the occasion." [31] It was in this period that he was sometimes called the "boy parson" and brought shopkeepers, gaping, to their windows to see one so young in gown and cassock as he passed along the street.[32] What the sensation seekers who attended his first sermon saw was a man whose

person was graceful, and well proportioned: his stature rather above middle size. His complexion was very fair. His eyes were of a dark blue colour, and small, but sprightly. He had a squint in one of them, occasioned either by ignorance, or the carelessness of the nurse who attended him in the measles, when he was about four years old. His countenance was manly, . . . He was always very clean and neat, and often said pleasantly "that a minister of the gospel ought to be without spot." [33]

What they heard was a sermon that set their ears to tingling. It was the "Necessity and Benefit of Religious Society," [34] and it realized the determination to speak against the assemblies. "But this leads me," he said,

to warn persons of the great danger those are in, who either by their subscriptions, presence, or approbation, promote societies of a quite opposite nature to religion.

And here I would not be understood, to mean only those public meetings which are designed manifestly for nothing else but revellings and banquetings, for chambering and wantonness, and at which a modest heathen would blush to be present; but also those seemingly innocent entertainments and meetings, which the politer part of the world are so very fond of, and spend so much time in: but which, notwithstanding, keep as many persons from a sense of true religion, as doth intemperance, debauchery, or any other crime whatever.[35]

These were bold words, and of doubtful acceptability to those who heard. Whitefield, though, was not displeased with the result. "The sight at first awed me," he wrote. Not, however, for long. For as he proceeded, he "perceived the fire kindled" till at last, even in the presence of those who knew him in his "infant childish days," he was able to speak with "some degree of gospel authority." When some mocked, and others reported that fifteen were driven mad by his first sermon, the bishop, to whom they complained, expressed the hope that the "madness might not be forgotten before next *Sunday*." [36]

What measure of madness the power and effect of his preaching contained was a question never settled for the satisfaction of partisans or opponents during Whitefield's lifetime, or since. But whatever it was, the power was growing, and by a geometric progression. The newly ordained deacon went to London in the first week of August to officiate as curate in the Tower of London during the absence of the incumbent.[37] While he was in the city, he was invited to preach in the Bishopsgatestreet Church. The ability of the young speaker to catch and hold an audience, the powerful effect of his sermons on his hearers, and his conviction that this constellation of circumstances was occasioned by a divine providence are plainly shown in his own account of that memorable first appearance in London. He wrote of that afternoon:

> I preached at Bishopsgate Church, the largeness of which, and the congregation together, at first a little dazed me; but by adverting to God . . . my mind was calmed, and I was enabled to preach with power. The effect was immediate and visible to all; for as I went up the stairs almost all seemed to sneer at me on account of my youth; but they soon grew serious and exceedingly attentive, and, after I came down, showed me great tokens of respect, blessed me as I passed along, and made great enquiry who I was.[38]

It was not long until such inquiry was needless.

Whitefield remained in London, preaching regularly in prison and in churches when he was asked, until mid-November, when he went to the parish of Dummer to supply in the absence of the Rev. Charles Kinchin. It was in this "poor and illiterate" parish, while Whitefield thought of his Oxford friends and "mourned for the lack of them as a dove that has lost her mate," that he decided to go as a missionary to America.[39]

The proprietary colony of Georgia had been begun as a philanthropic enterprise, largely through the efforts of General James Oglethorpe, who envisioned a place of asylum for debtors and distressed folk in the new world.[40] The colony was established, but life within its borders was not idyllic. Indeed, certain aspects of life in Georgia were crude, and certain colonists were undisciplined and unscrupulous. Moreover, in addition to the colonists themselves, there were Indians who were at best heathen and at worst savage. The situation cried out for missionaries. The Wesleys had already responded. Frankly pleading with the young evangelist to come to America, John Wesley had written Whitefield from the wilderness, "Only Mr. Delamotte is with me." [41] This was the kind of appeal calculated to strike fire from the spirit-intoxicated youth. Eager to play disciple to Wesley's Paul, he soon passed to the point of playing the major role himself as he looked on a heathen world and set out to convert it. Meanwhile, he wrote to Charles Wesley—

lately returned to England—and offered himself to go to Georgia.

While Whitefield was waiting to sail to America, he continued to preach in Gloucester, in Bath, in Bristol, and in London. The rising tide of his popularity is best measured through his own eyes; for if there is possibility that he (understandably) exaggerated the number of his hearers or overestimated the intensity of their devotion, there is still the unquestioned index of what those days meant to him. His description of what happened in the months immediately before his departure for Georgia is vivid and memorable:

Here [London] I continued . . . reading prayers twice a week, catechising and preaching. . . . God was pleased to give me favour in the eyes of the inhabitants of the Tower. The Chapel was crowded on Lord's Days. Religious friends from divers parts of the town attended the Word. . . . I went to Gloucester. . . . here, I began to grow a little popular. . . . Congregations were very large, and the power of God attended the Word; . . . I made a little elopement to Bath, where . . . I preached at the Abbey Church twice. . . . application was made to me by several to print both my discourses. . . . the people of Bristol . . . having insisted upon my coming again . . . I paid them a second visit. Multitudes came on foot, and many in coaches a mile without the city, to meet me; and almost all saluted and blessed me as I went along the street. . . . I paid another visit to Bath. . . . People crowded, and were affected as at Bristol; . . . I took my last farewell at Bristol; but when I came to tell them, it might be, that they would *"see my face no more,"* high and low, young and old burst into such a flood of tears, as I had never seen before. Multitudes, after sermon, followed me home weeping; and, next day, I was employed from seven in the morning till midnight, in talking and giving spiritual advice to awakened souls. . . . The congregations [in London] increased, and generally on a Lord's Day, I used to preach four times to very large and very affected auditories. . . . About the middle of September, my name was first put into the public newspapers. . . . I now preached generally nine times a week. . . . On Sunday mornings, long before day, you might see streets filled with people going to church, with their lanthorns in their hands, and hear them conversing about the things of God. . . . The tide of popularity now began to run very high. In a short time, I could no longer walk on foot as usual, but was constrained to go in a coach, from place to place, to avoid the hosannas of the multitude. . . . Not that all spoke well of me. . . . A report was spread abroad, that the Bishop of London, upon the complaint of the clergy, intended to *silence* me. . . . Thousands and thousands came to hear. My sermons were everywhere called for. . . . Large offers were made me, if I would stay in England. . . . At the beginning of Christmas week, I took my leave; but, oh, what groans and sighs were to be heard, when I said, "Finally, brethren, farewell!" . . . I was nearly half-an-hour going out to the door. All ranks gave vent to their passions. Thousands and thousands of prayers were put up for me. They would run and stop me in the alleys, hug me in their arms, and follow me with wishful looks.[42]

This phenomenal popularity developed between the summer of 1736, when Whitefield preached his first London sermon, and Christmas week of the year following. No doubt some of the devotion to Whitefield was shallow. But it was real. One of his published sermons had already gone through three editions.[43] He *was* in demand as a preacher, and the grief of those who said good-by to him was genuine.

At long last he left. His leave-taking was protracted and melodramatic. It was watered by enough tears to launch the "Whitaker," the troopship on which he sailed. He went aboard on December 30, but it was not until early February that Whitefield saw the last of his native land.[44]

Chapter III

The Missionary to Georgia

WHITEFIELD'S decision to go to Georgia was not one lightly made or easily arrived at. Certainly it was not an evidence of eighteenth-century England's love of travel, so inordinate as to have become a joke with foreigners, especially the French, who dubbed it a "maladie du pays." [1] To Whitefield's countrymen *travel* meant the Grand Tour to Italy and France, not a visit to a wilderness of "pine-barren, oak-land, swamp, and marsh" [2] where the natives were, for the most part, "gluttons, drunkards, thieves, liars." [3] The Georgian prospect that called to Whitefield was one of urgent need. He understood it as a "matter of great importance that serious clergymen should be sent there," [4] and well he may have. It was with difficulty, if at all, that the Bishop of London maintained supervision over the clergy in the colonies. His commissaries, or personal representatives, had more prestige than authority. There were unfortunate instances in which they were not able effectively to discipline men without principle who wore the prophet's mantle loosely. This intelligence, coupled with Wesley's pointedly asking him, *"What if thou art the Man, Mr. Whitefield?"* [5] was enough to override his doubts and to strengthen his resolution in the face of importunate friends.

Great pressure had been exerted on Whitefield in the effort to keep him in England. Because he understood this and knew that the pressure would increase, he wrote to his family that he would come to bid them farewell only if they promised not to make his leave-taking difficult. Nevertheless, when he arrived at Gloucester, his relations joined in the chorus of others who "urged what pretty preferment" the young minister might find at home. Whitefield's mother "wept sore." [6] It was all to no avail; he had decided. There was no longer the possibility of choice, for he had received a "Call from Providence." [7]

At the last even John Wesley joined with those who asked Whitefield not to go to America, though for less obvious reason. The "Whitaker" lay at anchor in the harbor of Deal when Wesley, still smarting from an unhappy experience in Savannah, arrived at four-thirty in the morning. Hearing that his young friend and erstwhile disciple was leaving for America almost momentarily, Wesley did not interrupt his plans to proceed to London immediately, but left a letter for Whitefield containing a cryptic message which had been secured through sortilege: "Let him return to *London*." [8] Whitefield's answer to this advice was sensible and to the point. In the concluding part of a short letter to Wesley he wrote: "Your coming rather confirms . . . than disannuls my call. It is not fit the colony should be left without a shepherd." [9] And he proceeded to Georgia.

More surprising than Whitefield's resisting the requests of relatives and friends was his resolution in the face of a growing company of applauding followers. Popular acclaim is heady wine. The wonder was not that Whitefield (hailed on all sides) was guilty of any ill-concealed egoism. The wonder was that he showed no more self-centeredness than he did and that he ever came to the point of quitting the scene of such early and marked success. When Whitefield was first setting out for America, he did not have the perspective of maturity which enabled him eventually to speak objectively of the phenomenon of "first popularity (which is apt to make the strongest head run giddy) in the midst of which, persons very often do things, which after experience and riper judgment teach them to correct and amend." [10] But though he had no norm against which to measure his fabulous success, he did have a compelling conviction that he was doing what was right, doing what he must and ought in going to Georgia. It was for this reason that he could ignore the instruction of Wesley, even though it was Wesley who had first called the young missionary to the new world. The original challenge had been confirmed by the testimony within. When the counsel of a friend—even John Wesley—conflicted with the voice of his conscience, Whitefield had no choice.

Whitefield's eye was single. All that he saw or experienced was strained through the mesh of the gospel categories of his mind.

Thus rendered meaningful to him, the story of his first voyage to America was recorded with reference to his burning passion to awaken men to the new birth. None of his companions on the "Whitaker" were too far gone in sin for Whitefield to direct a word to them, and none were too young. He laid heaven's obligation on one child "not above four Years of Age":

Had a good Instance of the Benefit of breaking Children's Wills betimes. Last Night . . . I asked one of the Women to bid her little Boy that stood by her, say his Prayers, she answered . . . she could not make him. Upon this, I bid the Child kneel down before me, but he would not, till I took hold of its two feet, and forced it down. I then bid it say the *Lord's Prayer,* (being informed by his Mother he could say it if he would) but he obstinately refused, till at last after I had given it several Blows, it said its Prayers as well as could be expected, and I gave it some Figs for a Reward.[11]

A storm at sea was no more than the background against which he preached—a circumstance which had to be overcome to gain the attention of his hearers:

After this I went on Deck; but surely a more noble awful Sight my Eyes never yet beheld! for the Waves rose more than Mountain high; and sometimes came on the Quarter-Deck. I endeavoured all the while to magnify GOD, for thus making his Power to be known: And then creeping on my Knees (for I knew not how to go otherwise) I followed my Friend *H.* between Decks, and sung Psalms and comforted the poor wet People. After this, I read Prayers in the Great Cabin; but we were obliged to sit all the while. . . . tho' Things were tumbling, the Ship rocking, and Persons falling down unable to stand, and sick about me; yet I was never more cheerful in my Life, and was enabled, though in the midst of Company, to finish a sermon before I went to Bed, which I had begun a few Days before: So greatly was GOD's Strength magnified in my Weakness! [12]

Whitefield did not sail directly to America but went by way of Gibraltar, and his experience there was chronicled in the same spirit: The trappings of a Roman chapel and the "Images of the Virgin *Mary,* dressed up . . . in her Silks and Damasks" [13] moved him with pity for a bewitched populace who needed the gospel preached to them. A dinner party at Governor Sabine's was notable because there was *"some Fear of* GOD *. . . in that Place."* [14] At Gibraltar the traveler was most impressed by a group of pietists called "New Lights," whom he found worshiping regularly at early-morning service.[15]

Almost two months passed from the time he left Gibraltar until land was sighted in early May. How completely all that happened in the interim was interpreted by Whitefield in terms of his mission is apparent in the following observations which he made on March 20:

> To-day Colonel *C.* came to dine with us, and in the midst of our Meal we were entertained with a most agreeable Sight; it was a Shark about the Length of a Man, which followed our Ship, attended with five little Fishes called the Pilot-fish, much like a Mackerel, but larger. These I am told always keep the Shark company; and what is most surprising, though the Shark is so ravenous a creature, yet let it be never so hungry, it never touches one of them. Nor are they less faithful to him: For if at any Time the Shark is hooked, these little Creatures will not forsake him, but cleave close to his Fins, and are often taken up with him. *Go to the Pilot-fish, thou that forsakest a Friend in Adversity, consider his ways, and be abashed.* This simple Sight one would think sufficient to confute any Atheist (if there be such a Fool as a speculative Atheist) in the world.[16]

This testimony of Whitefield is offered as a sample not of his logic— of which it is far from atypical—but of his engrossing faith which he saw supported wherever he turned his eyes. In this faith he arrived in Georgia, but his happiness on reaching America did not obscure the knowledge that he would be "infinitely more joyful" when he should "arrive at the Haven of everlasting Rest." [17]

The man who came to Savannah on a May evening in 1738 was essentially the man as he continued for more than thirty years. Whatever appeared in him later was always present in germ—and often in actuality—in those first days in Georgia and on that first visit to America. The stamp of popularity was already upon him. He was destined to be as sought after in the colonies as he had been in England. Actually he was accepted in America even before he landed there. William Stephens, who had come to Georgia with the commission of secretary for the affairs of the trustees of the province, awaited Whitefield's arrival eagerly and promised himself "great Pleasure in his future Acquaintance." [18] This hope seemed well placed when he heard Whitefield deliver a sermon that was "very engaging, to the most thronged Congregation . . . ever seen" [19] in the colony. The young Englishman was liked immediately. He captivated even the "many loose Livers, who heard him gladly, and seemed to give due Attention." [20] This was no more than careful readers of the *Virginia Gazette* might have expected, for they knew already that Whitefield was "much followed" in England and his preaching "deservedly approved of." [21] They knew that in London hundreds of people, unable to gain entrance to the building where he preached, stood outside the "Church, which was incredibly full early in the Morning," while constables were stationed at the church doors to preserve the peace.[22]

When Whitefield left Georgia in late August, his departure was quite different from that of John Wesley eight months before. Wesley's sense of defeat was written between the following poignant lines, descriptive of his farewell to the colony: "Yet I had strength enough given to preach once more to this careless people; and a few 'believed. . . .' " [23] A sense of failure is explicit in his later confession: "I, who went to America to convert others, was never myself converted to God." [24] Whitefield, on the other hand, was eager to leave America only that he might return the sooner. His *Journal* testified to his success:

This being the Day of my Departure, it was mostly spent in taking Leave of my Flock, who expressed their Affection now more than ever. They came to me from the Morning to the Time I left them, with Tears in their Eyes, wishing me a prosperous Voyage and a safe return. They also brought me Wine, Ale, Cake, Coffee, Tea, and other Things proper for my Passage, and their Love seemed without Dissimulation. . . . I think I never parted from a Place with more Regret; for *America* in my Opinion is an excellent School to learn CHRIST in; . . . the longer I continued there, the larger the Congregations grew. And I scarce knew a Night . . . when the Church House has not been near full.[25]

The vast popularity which Whitefield achieved early and maintained for a lifetime was, essentially, the popularity of a preacher. And it was that of a roving itinerant whose activity was interrupted neither by wind nor weather, and whose sermons continued to the point at which he was almost literally out of breath. He was just such a man as this at the time of his death, and he appeared as such when he began his work in the Georgia colony on May 8, 1738. By daylight of the morning after Whitefield first set foot in Savannah, he was up "to read public Prayers, and expound the Second Lesson." [26] Plunging directly into the program of the parish, Whitefield suffered a return of fever that had attacked him in the last days of his voyage to America, but—nothing daunted—he was in the pulpit on May 14, even though he became ill in the midst of worship and had to retire before he began the "second service." [27] As soon as he was sufficiently recovered, he visited the villages of Thunderbolt, Highgate, and Hampton. In the meantime he had called on Thomas Causton, chief magistrate of the colony, and visited with Tomo Chichi, the famous Indian who had been presented at court in England. Communication between Whitefield and the old chief was difficult and hampered the evangelist's effort to declare the gospel. The young missionary managed, at least, to speak of hell to the old man—a hell which he described by "pointing to the Fire." [28] Wherever he went, Whitefield preached his message.

Usually (as was then the case in Savannah), Whitefield spoke to crowds of eager listeners. But he preached to individuals when he found himself with no more than one to listen. The point is that he was always at the business of witnessing. He was given to bursting into hymns as he rode or when he was at inns. "Others sing *Songs* in publick Houses," he wrote, "why should not we sing *Psalms?*" When he tipped servants, he was likely to present them with a tract and to preach a short sermon as well.[29] This, of course, was perfectly in keeping with the character of one who as a child "used frequently to imitate the ministers reading prayers, etc.," and who during the worst days of his adolescence "composed *two or three sermons.*" [30] Preaching was the breath of his nostrils. Often in the years that followed he found himself improved in health after delivering a sermon, and almost at the very moment of death he assured a friend, "I shall be better by and by; a good pulpit-sweat to-day may give me relief; I shall be better after preaching." [31] Whitefield's reputation as a popular preacher who had an unequaled attendance has endured. He was already that in the first ministry at Savannah. On June 4, 1738, William Stephens made an entry in his *Journal* regarding Whitefield's celebrity which might have been offered as objective comment on the evangelist's following, almost without exception, wherever he went, wherever he preached from that time: "Mr. Whitefield's auditors increase daily, and the place of worship is far too small to contain the people who seek his doctrine." [32]

Whitefield's doctrine was one of the new birth. The specific content of the message of the popular preacher and his method of presentation will be considered later. It may be observed now, however, that both his message and manner underlay the fact that Whitefield was a center of heated controversy, early and late. His career as incendiary was not so spectacular in the first days of his American sojourn as later. But even then one could sense the peculiar genius he had for lighting a fire and riding away while it raged in his absence.

Whitefield gave rather an irenic account of how he came to America to be minister at Frederica, Georgia, and "finding there was no minister at Savannah, and no place of worship at Frederica, by the advice of the magistrates and people . . . continued at Savannah." When he returned to England, the trustees of the colony at the "request of many" presented him the "living of Savannah." [33] Stephens, on the other hand, told a somewhat different story in which Whitefield assumed an episcopal attitude toward the parish of Savannah and gave directions about how affairs should be conducted there in his absence some time before he was invested with authority! Particularly Whitefield warned the colonists against one Mr. Dyson, a former minister "whose Character was grown infamous, by reason of a scandalous life, and frequent Debauchery." [34] At least in that case the assumption of prerogatives was mitigated, if not excused, by circumstance.

After Whitefield had departed for England, William Norris, duly constituted by the trustees, arrived in the colony in the erroneous supposition, most likely, that his position as rector of the Savannah church would be a pleasant one. He found the way thorny from the beginning. His first sermon was a mistake, for his emphasis on ethical morality and noble deeds was ill-received by the colonists, who had under Whitefield's preaching come to believe in salvation by faith alone—with an attendant belittling of the virtue of good works. "From whence the Propagation of such mysterious Doctrine at first sprung, is pretty well known," [35] wrote Stephens, who was by this time beginning to entertain grave doubts regarding Whitefield's infallibility. As the fall wore on, Norris was constantly needled by the comparisons of him with Whitefield, made at the suggestion of James Habersham, whom Whitefield had left as lay reader in his absence. More than once Norris complained of "false . . . Reports . . . endeavoring to ridicule him and make him contemptible." [36] Stephens confided to his *Journal* that

the whole Truth plainly . . . was this, that Mr. *Norris,* by the Trustees Appointment, was established Minister at *Savannah,* whilst Mr. *Whitefield* was gone for *England,* in Expectance of returning hither invested with that Appointment himself.[37]

Norris was apprehensive—advisedly so, as it developed—that Whitefield would take the living from him.[38] When Whitefield returned with the appointment, Norris resigned with dignity and without rancor.[39] Unfortunately that was not the last of the trouble. Whitefield subsequently invited Norris to tea and "flatly charged [him] with having preached false Doctrine." [40] The unhappy relations among Whitefield, Habersham, and Norris did not greatly affect the welfare of the colony or the future of Whitefield. But it is significant to note that Whitefield, who became so often in later years the friction that ignited the tinder, was on his first visit to America striking sparks that smoldered and burst into flame and smoldered again, but did not go out so long as he lived.

Yet the popular preacher was more than disputant; there is another role which he played that must be considered in order to see the potential man in the preliminary days: that is Whitefield the humanitarian. George Whitefield was ever a preacher to insist not only upon repentance, but also upon "fruits meet for repentance." [41] He was forever concerned with some charity, urging some humanitarian project. One of his aphorisms was that the *"Parsonage-House ought to be the Poor's Store-House."* [42] It does no injustice to the facts to say that he believed the parson, therefore, ought to take care of the poor. While he gave his energies to such varied humanitarian projects as building almshouses for widows[43] and raising funds for the library at Harvard which had been destroyed by fire,[44] he was particularly concerned with poor children—and most especially with their education.

Before he ever came to America, Whitefield said that he believed the "Blue Coat boys and girls [as children of charity schools were called] looked upon . . . [him] as their benefactor; and . . . frequently sent up their infant cries" [45] in his behalf. When he left London, he took with him about thirteen hundred pounds, contributed for the poor of Georgia and for charity schools.[46] He had been in the colony hardly a month before he had made arrangements for teaching the children in the villages of Highgate and Hampsted and had opened a school in Savannah.[47] The more he saw of conditions in the colony, the more he knew that the crying need was for a place provided for the "Maintenance and Education" of children—especially the orphan children. Envisioning an orphan house, he said that one "might be erected at *Savannah,* would some of those that are rich in this World's Goods contribute towards it." [48] From the first Whitefield had deliberately made it a "constant practice to improve . . . acquaintance with the rich for the benefit of the poor." [49] Here on his first visit to America his passion for befriending the homeless, his desire to educate those denied schooling, and his near genius for financing these tastes through the gifts and the efforts of others found their earliest expression.

Two steps were necessary for Whitefield to bring his plans for the colony to completion: he would have to be ordained as a priest in the Church of England, and he would need to secure money— a great deal of money, more, perhaps than he realized. Already he was assuming a possessive attitude toward Georgia and its colonists, to whom he referred as "my dear parishioners." [50] In the interest of the progress of the colony and, incidentally, of the Orphan House which he planned to erect, Whitefield was concerned with having certain governmental changes effected. Strangely, he was in favor of allowing rum and slavery in Georgia,[51] both of which had been forbidden by the conditions of the charter. (Of this position more shall be said in another connection.) His feeling on these matters was one of the factors which induced Whitefield to return to England where something might be done for the colonists in this regard. But his chief concern lay elsewhere. Shortly before leaving America he wrote:

What I have most at heart, is the building an orphan-house, which I trust will be effected at my return to *England*. In the mean while, I am settling little schools in and about *Savannah;* that the rising generation may be bred up in the nurture and admonition of the LORD.[52]

Prompted by such varied necessity, Whitefield left the colony with a burning desire to "hasten back as soon as possible."[53] Behind his urgency lay the hope of an orphan house in the new world.

By the time he was twenty-five, therefore, Whitefield was the man he ultimately acquired the reputation of being: an exceedingly, almost fabulously, popular preacher, who was often the center of controversy as he plied his way between two continents, preaching the new birth and collecting money for humanitarian projects— especially the orphan house in Georgia. His early days in America contained all the portents of the years to come, and he arrived in England in December of his twenty-fourth year,[54] well come to age. There he found himself alternately blasphemed and blessed by men who before either had not known or had ignored him.

Chapter IV

∭

The Preacher in the Fields

TRAVEL in the eighteenth century was both hazardous and disagreeble, and Whitefield's voyage from America to England in 1738 was particularly trying. He left Charleston on September 9 aboard the "Mary." [1] With the exception of a few days, there was a continual storm during the first month of the homeward passage. Early in November the ship's situation became serious. Whitefield's entry in his *Journal* for that day is pathetic in its simplicity. It contains as moving a profession of faith as he ever wrote:

> Our Allowance of Water now is but a Pint a Day, so that we dare not each much Beef. Our Sails are exceeding thin, some more of them were split last Night, and no one knows where we are; but GOD does, and that is sufficient. [2]

Two days later a "violent Wind" arose, and, shortly, passengers and crew began "to be weak, and look hollow Ey'd." By November 11 the plight was critical. Whitefield wrote:

> Our ship is much out of repair, and our Food by no Means enough to support Nature in an ordinary Way, and that of the most indifferent Kind too: An Ounce or two of Salt-Beef, a Pint of Water, and a Cake made of Flower and Skimmings of the Pot. [3]

Three days afterward the weary travelers were anchored off the coast of Ireland. Whitefield stopped there only briefly, but he remained long enough to observe that the natives seemed "to be very Ignorant," that he thought them well termed the *"Wild Irish."* [4] His arrival in London on December 8, 1738, was a happy one for Whitefield, who said of his homecoming:

42

In the Morning I set out for *London,* and was agreeably surprised with the Sight of some of my Christian Friends on the Road, who were coming to meet me, which put me in the Mind of St. *Paul's* Friends, meeting him at the three Taverns, and I like him, was not a little comforted.[5]

It was well that Whitefield found comfort in his friends. A kind of storm different from any he had experienced at sea was gathering thickly. During his absence from England his *Journal* of the voyages from London to Gibraltar and from Gibraltar to Savannah had been published and widely read. His followers had so eagerly awaited report of the Georgia mission that according to Whitefield manuscripts intended for private circulation had been published without his consent.[6] The public was sufficiently interested to warrant a pirated edition of the evangelist's personal history.[7] But many who read the *Journal* took exception to the excessive language and made their offense the occasion to placard as profane fraud what the faithful accepted as godly zeal. A year previously Whitefield's popularity had been enormous. Now he was derided. Two days after he reached London, he confided this to his *Journal* (if he can be said to have "confided" anything to those volumes) : "For five Churches have been already denied me; and some of the Clergy, if possible would oblige me to depart out of these Coasts." [8]

In its way hostile treatment from the established clergy was a compliment. The following unflattering portrait of the cloth was written by a contemporary observer:

In their Conduct, they curb not, but promote and encourage the trifling Manners of the Times: It is grown a fashionable thing, among these Gentlemen, to depise the Duties of their Parish; to wander about as the various Seasons invite, to every Scene of false Gaiety; to *frequent* and *shine* in all *public* Places, their own *Pulpits* excepted.[9]

But in spite of objection to Whitefield in ecclesiastical circles, he was ordained a priest by Bishop Benson on January 14 at Oxford. It was a "Day of fat Things" for him, starting early in the morning when he began the day singing psalms "lustily." Judging from the description in his *Journal* of happenings of that Sunday, the day was not climaxed for Whitefield with the "Imposition of Hands." For at that time (though he was "Before . . . a little dissipated"), his mind was "in a humble Frame." The high moment of the day for him came when he preached to a crowded, impressive congregation at St. Albans and felt such power that he was able to "lift up . . . [his] Voice like a Trumpet." [10]

The days that followed his ordination were by Whitefield's standards fatter days still. Sermons were more frequent, crowds were larger, loyalty was more dangerous, and hostility more common. Whitefield was overwhelmed with a sense of God's immanent presence, and he like the eye of a cyclone that ripped about him, moved calmly and quickly from place to place. He returned to London and, as the pages of his *Journal* record, busied himself with great activity: preaching to large and eager companies, taking collections for the poor (to which people contributed so gladly that on occasion they even tossed coins through the door of his departing coach), making a hurried call on the ailing hymn-writer Isaac Watts, and all the while meeting persecution "without any Emotion." [11]

By this time Lady Selina, Countess of Huntingdon, destined to become Whitefield's stanch patroness, was already looking with favor on the young celebrity. Eventually the list of guests assembled by her ladyship to hear the Methodist preachers whom she sponsored read like a roster of the peerage.[12] Among the many whom she lured or threatened into attending her chaplains were the Duchess of Marlborough, Lord Chesterfield, Lord Bolingbroke, Lady Suffolk (mistress of George II), Horace Walpole, and Lord Chatham.[13] It is uncertain when Whitefield was first brought to Lady Huntingdon's attention. That she was concerned about him by the time of his ordination is plainly seen in a letter written to Lord Huntingdon by Bishop Benson, describing the ceremony and expressing the hope that the act would give some "satisfaction" to Lady Selina and that she would not have further occasion to find fault with the bishop. The implication is that the countess had grown impatient with clerical disapproval of the evangelist. To this implicit apology the bishop added a specific endorsement: "Though mistaken on some points, I think him (Mr. Whitefield) a very pious, well-meaning young man, with good abilities and great zeal. I find his Grace of Canterbury thinks highly of him." [14] In any case the redoubtable Lady Huntingdon was increasingly interested in the young clergyman, and it was largely under her patronage that he descended on the "butterflies" of Bath "like a Shower of rain, and dampened them considerably." [15]

On the first Sunday in February, 1739, there was an incident in St. Margaret's, Westminster, which dramatized and publicized the growing difficulty Whitefield was experiencing in securing pulpits from which to preach. Thereafter few people felt "neuter" about the young man. Whitefield had arrived at St. Margaret's after the service was begun, because of "something breaking belonging to the Coach." As he was expecting to preach, he went directly to the minister's pew. It was locked. What happened next was variously reported. Whitefield wrote an account in his *Journal* in which he was the peaceful visitor, reluctantly consenting to preach for an insistent congregation:

[I] went through the People to the Minister's Pew, but finding it locked, I returned to the Vestry till the *Sexton* could be found. Being there informed that another Minister intended to preach, I desired several times that I might go Home. My Friends would by no means consent, telling me I was appointed . . . to preach, and that if I did not, the People would go out of the Church; at my Request, some went to the Trustees, Church-Wardens, and Minister; and whilst I was waiting for an Answer, . . . a Man came with a Wan [*sic*] in his Hand, whom I took for the proper Church-Officer, and told me I was to preach; I not doubting but the Minister was satisfied, followed him to the Pulpit.[16]

Whitefield rose the following Sunday "full of Love and Joy," but the day soon brought him distress of mind and body. He learned that "several Lies" had been told in the newspapers about his "Preaching at *St. Margaret's.*" Within the week a "somebody or other" wrote a "Letter in the *Weekly Miscellany* . . . with several Untruths" about the St. Margaret's affair.[17] That letter told of an unruly group who were as unscrupulous as they were eager in their zeal to have Whitefield preach, and finding the legally constituted preacher

as determined to do his duty as Mr. Whitefield was to do it for him, they at last effected that by *force* which they could not gain by *treaty.* So the preacher was safely confined in his *pew*, which was locked . . . and guarded by several lusty fellows; while another party conveyed the unlicensed intruder triumphantly up into the pulpit, and kept sentry on the stairs for fear he should be taken down in as forcible a manner as he got up.[18]

It makes relatively little difference which version of the St. Margaret's affair is correct. The disgraceful scene there became the real or pretended occasion for clerical opposition to Whitefield, who was now a doubly marked man.

When he left London, Whitefield set out for Bristol. On the way he preached at Basingstoke, where, he recorded characteristically, a mob did him the "Honour of throwing up Stones at the Windows," but that he "spoke so much the louder." [19] Before he reached Bristol, he had the questionable distinction of being refused the use of the Abbey church at Bath then or any time or on any occasion without a "positive Order from the King or Bishop." [20] In Bristol it was no better. Already taxed with having *"set the Town on Fire, and now . . . gone to kindle a Flame in the Country,"* [21] Whitefield found that an alleged earlier invitation to preach in the church of St. Mary Ratcliff had been withdrawn by the minister, Mr. Gibbs, who said he could not grant Whitefield's request without the chancellor's permission. Perhaps the invitation had been withdrawn because it was learned that Whitefield had said that he could produce two cobblers who knew "more of true Christianity than all the Clergy in the City" of Bristol.[22] Whatever the reason, Whitefield was received coolly by churchmen there, and he, of course, went at once to the chancellor and applied directly for permission to preach and take an offering for the proposed orphan house. The chancellor told the young itinerant that he would not "give any positive Leave, neither would he prohibit anyone that should lend" him a church. He advised Whitefield to go away until the bishop had ruled on the matter.[23] Such counsel was lost on the ardent preacher, who proceeded without qualm to the residence of the dean. The interview between the dean and the evangelist is recorded in Whitefield's *Journal:*

Soon after this, I took my Leave, and waited upon the Reverend the Dean, who received me with great Civility. When I had shewn him my Georgia Accounts, and answered him a question or two about the Colony, I asked him "Whether there could be any just Objection against my preaching in Churches for the Orphan House?" After a

Pause for a considerable Time, he answered he "could not tell." But, somebody knocking at the Door, he replied, "Mr. *Whitefield,* I will give you an Answer some other Time; now I expect Company." "Will you be pleased to fix any, Sir?" said I. "I will send to you," says the Dean.[24]

There is no gainsaying that Whitefield was maladroit in his dealings with the clergy. They for their part could have found little to commend him from the standpoint of scholarship. He had to his credit the distinction of having moved the people of Bristol and London (more than a year previously) and of having created, or at least precipitated, a disgraceful performance at St. Margaret's much more recently. It is not too surprising that a person in Whitefield's position should have been denied the indiscriminate use of parish churches.

It has been suggested that Whitefield was essentially a preacher who could no more keep from preaching than he could keep from breathing. Shut out from the churches, he cast about for a willing audience elsewhere and found one available, if not co-operative. The keeper of Newgate Prison was a Mr. Dagge, who had been one of Whitefield's first converts in 1737.[25] Evidently Dagge was one who translated creed into action, for he gained a reputation for humane and sensitive treatment of his prisoners. Dr. Samuel Johnson commended Dagge highly for his kindness to the poet Richard Savage, who had been arrested for debt.[26] It was Dagge who deserved credit for the great change in Newgate Prison from a "seat of woe on this side of Hell" unexceeded by "any region of horror," where the "filth, the stench, the misery and wickedness . . . shock'd all who had a spark of humanity," into a model prison in which "Every part of it" was made "as clean and sweet as any Gentleman's house." [27] Whitefield offered to preach at the jail. Dagge was obviously pleased to have Whitefield speak to the prisoners, and the minister began to expound and read prayers daily. This happy arrangement was short-lived. On March 12 Whitefield "Had the Pleasure of hearing that the Mayor and Sheriffs of Bristol had absolutely forbidden the Keeper of Newgate letting" him preach there again.[28]

Meanwhile Whitefield had made a most significant move, albeit he had done so almost by default. "About One in the Afternoon" on February 17, Whitefield had gone with William Seward and another friend to Kingswood, the mining district near Bristol. The newly ordained priest had "long yearned toward the poor colliers" because they were numerous and without a shepherd.[29] There were other reasons, too, for pitying the coal miners. Kingswood

was only three or four miles from Bristol, Bedworth [another mining center] about the same from Coventry, yet the miners had no part in the lives of these cities. To the traders and shopkeepers the colliers appeared in the same light as the barbarian tribes to the townsfolk of a Roman garrison on the outskirts of the Empire, and when the colliers came to town they bolted their doors and barricaded their windows.[30]

Here is Whitefield's account of his first preaching to them:

After Dinner, therefore, I went upon a Mount, and spake to as many People as came unto me. They were upwards of two Hundred. Blessed be God, *I have now broke the Ice; I believe I never was more acceptable to my Master than when I was standing to teach those Hearers in the open Fields.*[31]

Certainly he was acceptable to the miners, who were so affected that the preacher could see the "white gutters made by their tears, which plentifully fell down their black cheeks, as they came out of their coal pits." [32] One observer thought the colliers more willing to hear Whitefield than to do their work, and he made gloomy prediction of "prodigious Rise in the Price of Coals." [33] For the most part, however, little notice was taken of the Kingswood incident at the time.

Thus, almost casually, did the field preaching originate. Whitefield would have preferred churches. Three days later he came to Bristol and found that he had access to pulpits in the city. But this was a courtesy that he could not always depend upon as he learned in an interview with the chancellor the day following. The prelate who had professed neutrality to Whitefield on a former occasion now said to him plainly: "I am resolved, Sir, if you preach or expound any where in this Diocese, till you have a License, I will first suspend and then excommunicate you." [34] A man with less zeal might well have quit preaching. That was impossible for Whitefield. And so, inevitably, he took to the fields in preference now to churches and buildings where often many were turned away for "want of room." Less than a month after his first venture in the open air he wrote:

Being resolved not to give Place to any Adversaries, no, not for an Hour, I preached at *Baptist Mills,* a Place very near the City, to three or four thousand People. . . . I now preach to ten times more People than I should if I had been confined to the Churches. . . . *Every Day I am invited to fresh Places.* I will go to as many as I can.[35]

Once Whitefield made the break with convention, he liked the outdoor services. There were only "upwards of two Hundred" that first afternoon in Kingswood. Soon the crowds were being numbered by the thousands. On February 23 he "preached to near four or five thousand People, from a Mount in *Kingswood, . . .* The Sun shone very bright, and the People" stood in profound silence. Two days later there were "above ten thousand" to hear him.[36] In March he preached at Rose Green Common to "so great a multitude of coaches, foot and horsemen, that they covered three acres, and were computed at twenty thousand people." [37] Folk were beginning to ask why Whitefield should travel to Georgia to preach to Indian savages when the colliers were so close at hand.

When Whitefield returned to London, he found that he was barred from all the churches there save one, and it was soon closed to him.[38] In a letter to Howell Harris, a Welsh evangelist without ecclesiastical authority or sanction, who had come to admire him extravagantly, Whitefield wrote that he determined to "repeat that mad Trick" of preaching in the fields.[39] *Mad* it surely was, but the madness was no less popular in London than it had been in Bristol. The outdoor pulpits that Whitefield chose in London were Moorfields and Kennington Common. In the seventeenth century there were well-drained walks, lined with elms, laid out in Moorfields. It was the "city mall." By Whitefield's time taverns and gardens were opening, for it had become the "general recreation ground of the city." [40] Kennington Common was a "neglected waste," a place of execution most in use after Tyburn, and it was not uncommon to have there the sight of "men hanging in chains." [41] The response to Whitefield in these unlikely surroundings was immediate and lasting. The "prodigious Number of People" [42] who first came to hear him returned again and again. In time they built him a tabernacle. Years after the first messages by the startling outdoor preacher, John Newton recalled how he had risen on many a winter morning at four o'clock in order to hear Whitefield preach at five and had then seen "Moorfields as full of lanterns . . . as . . . the Haymarket is full of flambeaux on an Opera night." [43]

Of the success of Whitefield's sermons that spring, there is his general word that "many" came to him acquainting him with "what God had done for their Souls" through his "preaching in the Fields." [44] There are isolated instances of such converts as Joseph Humphreys, the first layman to assist Wesley in England,[45] or of Joseph Periam, who—converted by having read Whitefield's sermon on the new birth—was confined to Bethlehem Hospital because (among other offenses) he "prayed so as to be heard four Story high." [46] Periam was rescued from the madhouse only on condition of Whitefield's promising to take him to Georgia, although at one time during the negotiations to have him released the authorities speculated about the possibility of Whitefield's being insane as well as his follower.[47] But the record of the summer of 1739, however, tells of throngs of people who continued to attend Whitefield while he was detained in England, because the "Elizabeth," on which he had booked passage for America, had no crew. Her seamen had been forced into his majesty's service through the eighteenth-century practice of "the Press," and it was necessary to wait until other sailors could be secured.[48] In the meantime, as might have been expected, Whitefield preached often.

Opposition to Whitefield was growing daily. Church and state put barriers in his way. Unofficial critics heaped vituperative abuse upon him. A ribald attack on Whitefield and his followers was published anonymously.[49] Whitefield persisted. By August he was ready to sail to America. "My Master makes me more than a conqueror," he wrote from the departing "Elizabeth." [50] Such a sentiment was almost a prediction of his triumphal second visit to the colonies.

He arrived on October 30.[51] He went directly to Philadelphia, where his immediate and successful preaching program was reported by the *Pennsylvania Gazette*:

On Thursday last, the Rev. Mr. Whitefield began to preach from the Court-House-Gallery in this City, about six at Night, to near 6000 People before him in the Street, who stood in awful silence to hear him; and this continued every Night, till Sunday. . . . Before he returns to England he designs (God willing) to preach the Gospel in every Province in America, belonging to the English.[52]

In the same issue Benjamin Franklin announced his intention of publishing two volumes of Whitefield's sermons and two of his *Journals* if sufficient orders could be secured.

Whitefield did not tarry long in Philadelphia, but set out to New York. On the way he met the founder of the Log College, the Rev. William Tennent, whom he described as an "old grey-headed Disciple of Jesus Christ."[53] He was pleased to be received by the colonial celebrities, but Whitefield was a luminary himself. The crowds and the success were by now the usual accompaniment of his appearances. "The multitudes of all sects and denominations that attended his sermons were enormous,"[54] wrote Benjamin Franklin. And Whitefield was developing an ability to inspire generosity toward his charitable projects in the hearts of otherwise niggardly or disapproving listeners that was to become legendary. Through New Jersey on his way to New York, Whitefield worked with the tempestuous evangelical minister of dissent, that "Son of Thunder," Gilbert Tennent.[55] Others might consider Tennent "impudent and saucy" and accuse him of setting his listeners in the dead of winter to wallowing "in the snow night and day for the benefit of his beastly braying,"[56] but Whitefield found him a preacher who "went to the Bottom indeed, and did not daub with untempered Mortar."[57] The Presbyterian Tennent was a natural ally of a man like Whitefield. Winter was coming on, but Whitefield spoke often out of doors. In New York he preached in the fields, for Commissary Vessey had charged him with breaking canon law and refused him permission to speak in the church even before he asked for it.[58] Whitefield soon turned south again.

On Friday, November 23, he "parted with dear Mr. *Tennent.*" Moving slowly southward, he preached to great throngs of eager listeners, expressing surprise "how such Bodies of People so scattered abroad" could be "gathered at so short a Warning."[59] He had, of course, to stop at Philadelphia again. In England he had received many presents, the "Benefactions of Charitable People . . . towards Building an Orphan House in Georgia." These goods, which included such diverse but—from the colonial point of view— desirable items as "Snuffers and Snuff-Dishes, four, six, eight, ten and twenty penny Nails, Pidgeon, Duck and Goose Shot . . . colour'd Ginghams with Trimmings . . . Taffities . . . and sewing Silk," Whitefield had placed on sale in a house in Philadelphia.[60] But this was only a part of his collection for funds to begin the erection of the Orphan House. He cried his need, and people responded. They pressed money in his hands and gifts to his person as he traveled south. He made arrangements for a friend to receive gifts in his absence. And Whitefield noted with gratitude that they had given him "Butter, Sugar, Chocolate, Picles, Cheese and Flower" for his orphans. "Indeed," he wrote, "I could almost say they would pluck out their own Eyes and give me." [61]

With his voice lifted in testimony and his eye fastened on things of the spirit, Whitefield pressed on toward Georgia. Maryland gentility did not impress him. He pictured a society in which women were "as much enslaved to their *fashionable Diversions,* as Men . . . to their *Bottle* and their *Hounds.*" [62] He dined with the governor of Virginia[63] and paid his respects to Commissary Blair, the "most worthy Clergyman" he had met "in all America." [64] When Whitefield preached in Williamsburg, there was a "numerous Congregation, and 'tis thought there wou'd have been many more, if timely Notice had been given." [65] Although he did not find the religious situation in Virginia quite so bad as in Maryland, where it was "at a very low Ebb" and clergymen spoiled by too high salaries, Whitefield was far from finding religion vigorous in the Old Dominion. He wrote in his *Journal:* "But almost all are quite settled upon their Lees, and I could not hear of any true vital Piety subsisting in the Province." [66] But he was ever mindful of the things of the spirit. When in North Carolina he "observ'd a Variety of Birds, and in the Evening heard the Wolves on one Side . . . howling like a Kennel of Hounds," [67] it set him to musing about the enemies of God.

There was a dramatic consistency about Whitefield which is refreshing. He was coming ever closer to Georgia and to the site of the Orphan House for which he had been collecting money for some months. The trip along the eastern seaboard would have convinced Whitefield (had his already sturdy dogma wanted the buttress of observation) that he was striving toward a heavenly goal in seeking to establish the Orphan-House. It was to be an oasis of religion in a desert of paganism.

In his journey toward Georgia, Whitefield had found little encouraging religiously since he left Philadelphia. In South Carolina it was no better. On New Year's Day, 1740, about sunset he came to a tavern lying some five miles within the province. Whitefield was shocked but not intimidated when he entered to discover that the "Neighbours were met together, in order to divert themselves by dancing Country Dances." On the advice of his traveling companions he "went in amongst them whilst a Woman was dancing a Jigg" and endeavored to convince her "how well pleased the Devil was at every Step she took." The dancer at first tried to "out-brave" Whitefield; "neither the Fidler or she desisted; but at last she gave over, and the Musician laid aside his Instrument." The traveling preacher, however, was positive of the resentment he had sensed when, on retiring, he heard sounds of the music begun again. Early the next morning Whitefield "Rose . . . pray'd, sung a Hymn, and gave a sharp Reproof to the Dancers." [68] From such a world as this Whitefield hoped to save a few whom he would shelter at a site he proposed to call *Bethesda*—House of Mercy.[69] Meanwhile he judged South Carolina in damning understatement:

In *South Carolina* they have many Ministers, both of our own and other Persuasions; but I hear of no stirring among the dry Bones.—Mr. *Garden,* the present Commissary, is strict in the Outward Discipline of the Church. The Clergy have an annual Meeting, and most of them, I believe, are kept from open Immoralities.[70]

"And now," he added to the passage above, "I am come to Georgia." Whitefield reached Savannah on January 10.[71] He

lost no Time in setting forward the Work which he professed to have much at Heart, about an Orphan-House; and rode out to view the Land which Mr. Habersham had taken Care to provide against his coming, consisting in five hundred Acres, that he had taken Possession of in his own Name; where Mr. Whitefield gave such Orders and Directions as he thought proper.[72]

The first Sunday after his arrival he drew a large crowd for Savannah, because "Mr. Whitefield's *Name* . . . could not fail drawing all sorts of People to Church." [73] The inhabitants of the southern colony who welcomed him offered the same expansive adulation expressed in a poem printed the very week in the *Virginia Gazette:*

> See! See! He comes, the heav'nly Sound
> Flows from his charming Tongue;
> Rebellious Men are seiz'd with Fear,
> With deep Conviction stung.[74]

Before the year was out, there were many who had occasion to contemplate the true signifiance of the field preacher's arrival in America.

Chapter V

℧

The Awakener in the Colonies

MOST men in a lifetime experience less excitement and drama than did Whitefield in the single spring of 1740. Actual work on the orphanage was begun with such zeal and on such a scale that all who observed or participated in the furious building activity in the Savannah swamp were moved to commend or attack the enthusiasm of the undertaking's originator. The first entry of a *Journal* that Whitefield began on his return to Georgia in that year expressed his paramount interest in Bethesda:

January 11. Went this Morning with some Friends to view a tract of Land, consisting of five hundred Acres, which Mr. Habersham, whom I left School-Master of Savannah, was directed, I hope by Providence, to make a Choice of for the *Orphan-House.*[1]

The site was ten miles from Savannah, a good distance considering there was no road, and Whitefield approved. "I choose to have it so far off the Town," he said, "because the Children will be more free from bad Examples." [2]

Building a house of any size—much less one to accommodate "near forty little ones" [3]—required much material and many workmen. Whitefield impulsively cornered the market on manual labor. Stephens complained petulantly that there was

hardly one Sawyer of any Value in Town, but all hired, and engaged by him to go over and work where he meant to erect that Building: most . . . Carpenters, Bricklayers, &c. were likewise engaged by him, and a great quantity of Scantling Timber ready sawn was coming . . . from North-Carolina.[4]

This, of course, was counted extravagant by citizens of Savannah, where the "most substantial People" were the "most frugal" and

endeavored to "make the least Shew, and live at the least Ex-
pence." [5] Whitefield by contrast was as expansive in his plans as in
his preaching, and his description of the projected orphanage was
worked out in elaborate detail:

> It is to be sixty Feet long, and forty wide. A Yard and Garden be-
> fore and behind. . . . The House is to be two Story high, with an
> Hip-Roof: . . . In all, there will be near twenty commodious rooms.—
> Behind are to be two small Houses, the one for an Infirmary, the other
> for a Work-house. There is also to be a Still-House for the Apothecary;
> . . . it will be an expensive Work: But it is for the LORD CHRIST. He
> will take Care to defray all Charges.[6]

Not every one who watched the progress of Bethesda shared
Whitefield's faith in its future. Some were openly skeptical, especially regarding heaven's guarantee of the monies which the venture
required. "It would certainly be a fine Piece of Work, if finished,"
admitted Patrick Tailfer in his *Narrative of Georgia,* written during these days; "but if it were finished," he asked, "where is the
Fund for its Support: and what Service can an Orphan-House be
in a Desert and a forsaken Colony?" [7] Whitefield seemed to thrive
on the activity that was surely (and the confusion that was most
likely) attendant to the erection of so grand a building in so
modest a colony. He wrote in fine spirit: "I am building a large
house, have many servants, and a good stock of cattle." [8] But as the
work progressed, Stephens was less guarded in his comment and
wrote in his *Journal* that the building of the house "would have
turned to as good Account for the Publick, if a little less Haste had
been made in that work" which kept many people from the serious
business of planting.[9] A Mr. Jones, doubtless Thomas Jones, Advocate of the Regiment in the colony, pointed out more captiously
that Whitefield had paid "an *extravagant* Price for Stones . . .
without ever consulting, or advising, with any one but himself." [10]

Whitefield did not see his family (as he called those who were
to live in the Orphan-House) moved into Bethesda until the
following December. Meanwhile he rented a large place in Savannah, where he left the children already committed to him under
the care of friends who had sailed to America in his company on
the "Elizabeth"; and he continued the zealous work of gathering

the stray orphans of the colony for residence in his house of mercy.[11] It turned out to be not the idyllic task that he had envisioned, for not all the orphans were homeless; and there was a pronounced reluctance among some of the patrons of the fatherless to release their charges, especially when they were repaying in service the protection that was given them.

On February 4, when Whitefield met the magistrates of Savannah to hear the official reading of his land grant from the trustees of the colony, he claimed two orphan boys from Henry Parker, a responsible individual in the colony who was also present at the meeting. Parker argued that it was unfair to take the older boy (aged sixteen) from him, as the lad had "grown capable of doing him some Service." Whitefield replied that the "Boy would be so much the better for him and his Purpose, as he could be employed for the Benefit of the other Orphans," and he goaded Parker into losing his temper. Parker also lost the boys.[12] Possibly it was his success in that affair which prompted Whitefield to the foolhardy defiance of Oglethorpe—to say nothing of betraying a gross insensitivity—in the matter of the Mellidge orphans.

One of the first forty freeholders in the colony had been a man named John Mellidge, who died and left a family of small children in whom General Oglethorpe showed particular interest. Under the encouragement of the General the oldest boy, John, and the oldest girl were able to make a successful (and presumably happy) home for the orphans. Whitefield found them living peacefully together in the spring of 1740 and at once took possession of the younger Mellidges and placed them in his orphanage.[13] John appealed to Oglethorpe, who pointed out, sensibly, that the trustees had "granted the Care of the helpless Orphans to Mr. Whitefield . . . not . . . any Power to take by Force any Orphans who . . . [could] maintain themselves." [14] The governor's opinion, which John Mellidge now quoted to Whitefield in requesting the return of his brother and sister, had no effect. The founder of the orphanage "gave him for Answer, his Brother and Sister were at their proper Home already, and he knew no other Home they had to go to; desiring him to give his Service to the General, and tell him so." [15] This was not the kind of insult that Oglethorpe was disposed to indulge—especially when it came from a youthful preacher. Accordingly, Mr. Jones at the direction of the General (and as it happened, in Mr. Whitefield's absence) removed the children from the orphanage and gave them back to their brother, John. Whitefield was furious (although he glossed over the facts in his *Journal*) , but he could not secure the return of his erstwhile wards. The Mellidges remained together.[16]

It must not be imagined, however, that Whitefield was perpetrating pious fraud upon the colonists in his ardor to watch over the homeless. For the most part Bethesda was in fact what it claimed to be in name: a house of mercy. Before Whitefield's coming to the colony the "poor little ones were tabbed out here and there, and besides the hurt they received by bad examples, forgot at home what they learned at school." [17] Of those who first came to live in the Orphan-House, most "were in poor case; and three or four almost eaten up with lice." [18] There was one boy "that his Mistress tyrannized over . . . with great Cruelty, whilst her Master gave little Heed to Things of that Kind. He was . . . at least five foot high, and could hardly read his Primer." [19] Bethesda offered sanctuary for such as these, and people were quick to sense the asylum that the Orphan-House afforded. One case is recorded of a grown man who was so taken with the utopia at Savannah that he had "bid adieu to all worldly Care, . . . given himself up to Mr. *Whitefield*'s entire Disposal for his Service, . . . [and] left his Wife . . . [for] the *New Jerusalem*." [20] It was only through Whitefield's persuasion that a Negro woman (whose master had acceded to her wishes) was dissuaded from following the evangelist in similar fashion.[21]

The launching of Whitefield's Orphan-House venture, with all the comment and activity that accompanied it, was by no means for the evangelist the only exciting feature of the year. He was not too busy at Bethesda to ignore even minor fractions of the moral code, and when he realized the gravity of a particular situation in Savannah, he acted. Becoming outraged that "several Persons in . . . Town lived most scandalous Lives with their Whores, and went on *impure* in open Defiance of all Laws both divine and human," he made the circumstance the occasion of attending a session of the court in which he

rose and made an Oration, setting forth the Heinousness of such Crimes, in very pathetick Terms; shewing that . . . [the colony] must never expect a Blessing . . . unless the civil Power would give all possible Assistance, in rooting out this accursed Thing; concluding, that it was his firm Persuasion, the slow Progress that was made in the Advancement of the Colony, was owing to God's not permitting it to prosper whilst such barefaced Wickedness was, through Neglect, suffered to remain.[22]

Before the colonists had recovered from the shock of Whitefield's tactics, and while they were still uncertain as to the propriety of a parson's taking it upon himself to "harangue the Grand Jury with what would more properly have come from the Pulpit," [23] they had the unnerving experience of hearing him preach a sermon in which he paid his respects to the clergy of America "whom he inveighed against terribly, as slothful Shepherds, dumb Dogs &c." [24] Specifically, it was at this time that he asked the unhappy Mr. Norris, now minister at Frederica, to call on him and, after serving his guest tea, charged him with having preached heresy in Savannah.[25] During these days Whitefield also found time to write a long letter to the inhabitants of Maryland, Virginia, and the Carolinas, protesting the cruel and inhuman treatment of slaves.[26] He wrote a shorter one to John Wesley (as an unwitting omen of *the* letter that was to come) on the doctrine of election and final perseverance, concerning the truth of which Whitefield confessed himself "ten thousand times more convinced" than at their last meeting.[27]

All this happened in the spring before Whitefield had gone to Charleston (as he did about mid-March) and run afoul of Alexander Garden, the first man to exercise real commissarial functions in the American colonies for the bishop of London. The commissary did not suffer fools gladly. Whitefield he suffered least of all. The story of the altercation between Garden and the itinerant will be told in another connection. Meanwhile it is pertinent to observe that it was in the midst of an already tumultuous period of his life that Whitefield, when spring moved north that year, turned his face toward the east and rode to awaken the multitudes there with his trumpet voice.

On April 2 Whitefield and William Seward—a traveling companion of independent property who had come with the evangelist to America in August of 1739—set out in their own sloop, the

"Savannah," and reached Newcastle, Pennsylvania, ten days later.[28] The day was Sunday, and Whitefield preached in the absence of the parish minister, who was ill. Immediately thereafter Seward rode to Christian Bridge and Whiteclay Creek, announcing to Charles Tennent's Presbyterian congregation there, and to all he met on the way, that Whitefield would preach at Newcastle again in the afternoon. He returned with "Two or Three Hundred Horse, from Mr. Tennent's Meeting, to hear the Afternoon Sermon, which was on the Conversion of *Zaccheus.*" [29] Whitefield wrote of the occasion:

People were surprised, but much rejoiced at the News of my Arrival, which they expressed by flocking, as soon as they were apprized of my coming, to hear the Afternoon's Sermon. Mr. *Charles Tennent . . .* came with a great Part of his Congregation. People began to invite me several Ways to come and preach to them.[30]

Without question popularity such as Whitefield enjoyed is unusual in the annals of American preaching.

Seward soon returned to England and—as it happened—to his death.[31] But Whitefield continued a strenuous succession of preaching engagements. The eagerness with which men met him on that April afternoon was a portent of the heightened intensity which attended his ministry for some months.

In the vicinity of Philadelphia people had heard Whitefield before, and would recognize, even at the distance by which the pressing crowd might separate them from the speaker, the "Man of middle Stature . . . and of a comely Appearance" who moved "with great Agility and Life." [32] They knew him by his familiar gesture of holding the Bible aloft in an upraised hand.[33] But most of all they knew him by the magic voice, with its cadenced echo and its golden ring. "How awfully, with what thunder and sound did he discharge the artillery of Heaven. . . . And yet, how could he soften . . . even a soldier of Ulysses, with the love and mercy of God." [34] It was a voice that could make "attentive thousands tremble, or rejoice." [35] Here was no manuscript-bound preacher like Edwards, who took into the pulpit his tiny sermon booklets containing complete homily manuscripts in his spidery writing;[36] here was no conventional speaker like most colonial divines. The man spoke freely! In the closing days of 1737, when Whitefield had first ventured to preach a sermon (already written) without the notes at hand, he had been "fearful." [37] Yet he was able to speak without the "least Hesitation," and before long he found himself "constrained to" preach thus and only thus.[38] By the time he returned to the colonies on his second visit, his considered opinion was that "tho' all are not to be condemned that use Notes, yet it is a sad Symptom of the Decay of vital Religion, when reading Sermons becomes fashionable where *extempore* Preaching did once almost universally prevail." [39] Unhampered by notes or convention, he lifted up his "clear and musical Voice," [40] a voice equal to any occasion.

David Garrick, the actor, said that Whitefield could melt an audience simply by pronouncing the word "Mesopotamia" and vowed he would freely give a hundred guineas if he could pronounce "O!" like the great evangelist! [41]

With Whitefield there was not only the ready word to say; there was the well-chosen gesture to emphasize and the volume to project, even when there was "near 12,000 Hearers . . . Numbers melting. . . . and . . . Thousands cried out." [42] Cornelius Winter recalled that "he hardly ever knew him to go through a sermon without weeping, more or less." [43] It all Stemmed from the consummate ability of the child who used to entertain the magistrates at St. Mary's school in Gloucester. When Whitefield came, calling to the colonies to rouse themselves from the sleep of sin, that ability was long since developed and—which was more important—informed by a sense of divine mission.

The frantic immediacy of his message persuaded Whitefield that he could legitimately use unconventional methods to bring sinners to repentance. Surely an apathetic delivery would "constrain the hearers . . . to suspect, that the preacher [dealt] . . . only . . . in the false commerce of unfelt truths." [44] He pointed out that a certain prophet in the Bible was "commanded by the LORD GOD himself to smite with his hand, and stamp with his foot," and that the gospel minister was "Commanded to 'cry aloud, and spare not.' " [45] This was the rationale behind the dramatics which he employed. Interrupted "but every now and then [by] a Groan or Sob from his Hearers," Whitefield lost no opportunity to portray his truth in most vivid fashion:

He sometimes had occasion to speak of Peter's going out and weeping bitterly, and then he had a fold of his gown at command, which he put before his face with as much gracefulness as familiarity.[46]

Or again, in speaking to English audiences of the solemnity of damnation for sin, he pantomimed the mannerism and actions of a British judge placing the black cap on his head before sentencing a prisoner to death.[47] No imagination is required to know what Whitefield must have done with the following passage from his sermon on Abraham's offering up his son Isaac:

... but methinks I see the tears trickle down the Patriarch *Abraham*'s cheeks; and out of the abundance of the heart, he cries, Adieu, adieu, my son; the LORD gave thee to me, and the LORD calls thee away; blessed be the name of the LORD: adieu. . . . But sing, O heavens! and rejoice, O earth! Man's extremity is GOD's opportunity: for behold, just as the knife, in all probability, was near his throat, . . . "the angel of the LORD . . . called unto him." [48]

The hasty tendency to dismiss such histrionics as undignified and amateurish, appealing only to the unlettered in the backwoods of a colonial wilderness or the slums of London, must be revised in the light of tributes to Whitefield's acting ability by men like Garrick, already mentioned, who sometimes heard the same sermon as often as forty times, or Edward Shuter, who spoke of Whitefield "with great affection, and with admiration of his talents." [49] Whitefield's oratory was even complimented by so case-hardened a cynic as Lord Chesterfield, who heard the famed preacher at Lady Huntingdon's, where he so far forgot himself in listening to the preacher's description of a blind man tottering on the brink of a precipice that he bounded from his seat exclaiming, "By heavens, he's gone!" [50] Moreover, Whitefield was approved by Benjamin Franklin, an individual noted usually for his restrained and analytical evaluation of men and manners.[51] By any standard Whitefield was a unique speaker, and America flocked to hear him.

Accustomed though he was to the pronounced reaction with which the throngs of ardent listeners responded to his impassioned preaching, Whitefield was hardly prepared for the wave of awakening that engulfed colonial America, carrying him along on its crest. Wherever he went in that spring of 1740, the story was always the same.

In New Brunswick he preached to seven or eight thousand people and had hardly begun speaking when the "Groans of the Congregation" rose to great volume. "One Woman was struck down, and a general Cry went through the Assembly." [52] When he reached New York, he preached from a specially constructed scaffold.[53] And then, after exhorting on Long Island, he headed south again. On May 1 he confessed his "Spirits . . . exhausted," but when he reached Philadelphia on the tenth of the month, he found the faithful awaiting him with spirit enough and to spare. In their company the weary Whitefield was refreshed and quickly regained his old vigor. "Tho' GOD has shewn me great Things already in this Place," he wrote, "yet To-day I have seen greater." [54] That evening he went to a meeting of a society of young women and sensed the Spirit as soon as he entered the room. He has left a vivid description of what happened:

A wonderful Power was in the Room, and with one Accord they began to cry out and weep most bitterly for the Space of half an Hour. They seemed to be under the strongest Convictions, . . . Their Cries might be heard a great Way off. . . . five of them seemed affected as those that are in Fits. . . . and at midnight I was desired to come to one who was in strong Agonies.[55]

His vocabulary of superlatives was already taxed, and there were more amazing experiences to follow. Whitefield himself was overcome by the shattering intensity of the response at Fagg's Manor, as his account of it plainly shows:

Look where I would, most were drowned in Tears. The Word was sharper than a two-edged Sword, and their bitter Cries and Groans were enough to pierce the hardest Heart. Oh what different Visages were then to be seen? Some were struck pale as Death, others wringing their hands, others lying on the Ground, others sinking into the Arms of their Friends, and most lifting up their Eyes toward Heaven, and crying out to GOD. I could think of nothing, when I looked at them, so much as the Great Day.—They seemed like Persons awakened by the last Trump.[56]

Whitefield had always affected his listeners, but things had not gone quite so dramatically before. Until this time he had actually been rather disapproving of such outbursts and only the previous summer had written thus to John Wesley, whose preaching in London and Bristol was eliciting mass hysteria:

I cannot think it right in you to give so much encouragement to those convulsions which people have been thrown into, under your ministry. Was I to do so, how many would cry out every night? I think it is tempting God to require such signs. That there is something of God in it, I doubt not. But the devil, I believe, does interpose. I think it will encourage the French Prophets, take people from the written word, and make them depend on visions, convulsions, &c., more than on the promises and precepts of the Gospels. Honored Sir, how could you tell that some who came to you "were in a good measure sanctified." What fruits could be produced in one night's time? [57]

The spirit which he had censured in Wesley's hearers, however, appeared somewhat different to Whitefield when his own auditories reacted with uncontrolled emotion and sometimes with violence.

When he reached Savannah, the same spirit was abroad, and there was such a commotion at a service at which Whitefield preached that he had to admit that even he "never saw the like before." Not only did the adults bemoan their sinfulness, but the "little Lambs crying most bitterly" wailed over their lost state. After the service which marked Whitefield's return to Georgia the worshipers followed him back to his home, singing and praying as they went through the streets. They continued to stand without his door for some time, still praying aloud and crying. Inside there was praying "in every Corner of the House." About this time it began to "thunder and lighten, which added much to the Solemnity of the Night." It was all very grand and awful. Whitefield retired, but he slept little that evening.[58]

In brief summary, Whitefield had left Georgia the first part of April; he had gone to New York and returned by way of Philadelphia, preaching to large and enthusiastic congregations wherever he stopped. When he arrived in Savannah in the first week of June, he found there in the hearts of his parishioners the same deep concern for sin that he had observed in the middle colonies.

Whitefield passed the summer in the South. It could not have been pleasant for him, because the days were sultry, and he had always found hot weather oppressive. Also he was in trouble with the clergy: In July he was tried before a church court under circumstances and on charges that will be considered later. When fall came, he set out for Boston, where his stanchest supporters and his bitterest enemies were not of the Church of England, but of the Dissent, as he himself so often seemed to be. He arrived in the chief city of New England in late September. The story that grows weary in the telling with the constant repetition of identical details was exciting when it happened. There were the usual throngs of attentive listeners, the customary intensity of the speaker which was reflected in the attitudes and sometimes in the actions of the audience. Whitefield's *Journal* for the period is replete with references to his having preached at the meetinghouse of Dr. Joseph Sewall, distinguished pastor of Old South Church for fifty-six years, or having gone to hear Dr. Benjamin Colman at his Brattle Street Church, and then having preached himself on the common.[59] Pulpit and pew alike turned their eyes on Whitefield in Boston that fall. He scored both roundly for their sins. Timothy Cutler, haughty rector of Christ Church, said that the "fellow treated the most venerable with an air of superiority," [60] and certainly Whitefield did by his own confession open his "Mouth boldly, against the unconverted Ministers." [61] When Whitefield and one distinguished doctor of divinity who disapproved of each other met during these days on the streets of Boston, the native remarked pointedly, "I am sorry to see you here," to which the visitor replied: "And so is the devil." [62]

Whitefield criticized Boston for its manners as well as for its morals, thinking ill of the local funeral custom of "not speaking at the Grave." [63] His feeling was definite that "Ministers and People [there] . . . for the Generality, seem[ed] to be too much conformed to the World." [64] Yet he did remarkably approve of the external observation which proper Bostonians gave to the Lord's Day.[65] He himself kept Sunday much as the Jews had kept the Sabbath and after his acquaintance with New Englanders began its observance as they did at six o'clock on Saturday evening.[66]

Regardless of his censure Boston welcomed him and bade him such a warm, affectionate farewell, with thirty thousand people in attendance, that he was moved to declare that he had not seen such a sight before in America. Perhaps there was no single individual in Boston who admired Whitefield quite so much as Jonathan Belcher, who was at that time governor of New England and was later to be governor of the New Jerseys. When Whitefield left the vicinity, Belcher took him to the ferry in his own coach and kissed him good-by. Later in the same month the governor searched out Whitefield to take another farewell, and on that occasion the "Tears trickled down his aged Cheeks like Drops of Rain." [67] Here is a repetition of the same story that was told earlier. Whitefield's success in Boston—as in the Philadelphia area—was genuine and general.

While Whitefield was in Massachusetts, he visited briefly with Jonathan Edwards, arriving on October 17. It is to Whitefield's credit that he recognized greatness when he saw it. "I think, I may say," he wrote of Edwards, "I have not seen his Fellow in all *New England.*" This generous estimate of the titan of Northampton was not grudgingly given. Whitefield was often lavish in his compliments, but he was equally apt with a thorny word for those of whom he disapproved. He approved of Edwards, and even more he approved of his wife. Feeling "wonderful satisfaction in being in the House of Mr. Edwards," he said that he had not seen a "sweeter couple." At a time when Whitefield's mind was disturbingly drawn to the subject of matrimony, and he was fearful that he might not get a "daughter of *Abraham*" for his own, the sight of Mrs. Edwards, a "Woman adorn'd with a meek and quiet Spirit," who also talked "feelingly and solidly of the Things of God," caused Whitefield to "renew those Prayers, which for some Months" he had put up to God to help him in the selection of a proper wife. The visitor preached twice for Edwards, who according to Whitefield wept during the whole time of the second service. He also spoke briefly to the Edwards children. On Monday evening, October 20, he said good-by to Edwards, and there is no further record that they met again.[68]

Before he left New England, Whitefield visited both Harvard and Yale colleges.[69] How little he thought they measured up to the standards that should have characterized schools preparing ministers was evidenced in his subsequently published *Journal:*

As for the Universities, I believe, it may be said, their Light is become Darkness, Darkness that may be felt, and is complained of by the most godly Ministers.[70]

This, however, was a minor cavil, for the months of September and October had been good ones for Whitefield. His summary reaction was positive and favorable: "In short, I like *New England* exceeding well." [71]

When he started south again, Whitefield was covering familiar territory. In New Jersey he visited "dear Mr. *Gilbert Tennent*" once more. It impressed him to learn that although his friend had recently lost his wife who was "dear unto him," yet he was "enabled with great Calmness to preach her Funeral Sermon, whilst the Corps were lying before him." [72]

In the interim of Whitefield's activity in the East, his friends in Philadelphia had been busy with their own plans, and when he returned there on November 9, he discovered to his pleasure that they had built a tabernacle for him to preach in. True, it was not to be his exclusively; but it had been conceived at the inspiration of his supporters, for

it being found inconvenient to assemble in the open air, subject to its inclemencies, the building of a house to meet in was no sooner pros'd, and persons appointed to receive contributions, but sufficient sums were soon receiv'd to procure the ground and erect the building, which was one hundred feet long and seventy broad, about the size of Westminster Hall; and the work was carried on with such spirit as to be finished in a much shorter time than could have been expected. Both house and ground were vested in trustees, expressly for the use of any preacher of any religious persuasion who might desire to say something to the people at Philadelphia; the design in building not being to accomodate any particular sect, but the inhabitants in general; so that even if the Mufti of Constantinople were to send a missionary to preach Mohammedanism . . . he would find a pulpit at his service.[73]

The New Building, as it was called, stood near the corner of Fourth and Mulberry streets. Eventually it was to become the seat of the University of Pennsylvania, identified with the name of Whitefield and watched over by his statue.[74] But at the present the tabernacle still lacked a roof and a gallery. On the preacher's arrival the people "raised a convenient Pulpit, and boarded the

Bottom," and Whitefield spoke to several thousand. "The Joy of most of the Hearers, when they saw me," Whitefield wrote afterward, "was inexpressible." [75] Nevertheless, the popular preacher had other things to do than to bask in the admiration of the people at Philadelphia. He soon had it "much impressed" upon his mind that he should return to England. And Whitefield was not a man to go against these impressions of the Spirit. He determined to return to Georgia and then start for England.[76]

At Reedy Island on the way back he wrote the following résumé of his New England venture:

> I think it is now the 75th Day since I arrived. . . . My Body was then weak, but the Lord has much renewed its Strength. I have been enabled to preach, I think, 175 Times in Public, besides exhorting very frequently in private. I have travelled upwards of 800 Miles, and gotten upwards of 700 *l. Sterling* in Goods, Provisions and Money for my poor Orphans. Never did God vouchsafe me such Assistances. . . . All Things concur to convince me, that *America* is to be my chief Scene for Action.[77]

From another source comes an estimate of Whitefield's preaching in America and its awe-striking effect. The following testimony from one of Whitefield's common listeners bears the indelible hallmark of authenticity. It is the kind of evidence which makes it impossible to take lightly the immodest observations which Whitefield made about his own preaching. The document is remarkable from several points of view:

> Now it pleased god to send mr. whitfield into this land & my hearing of his preaching at philadelphia like one of the old aposels, & many thousands floocking after him to hear ye gospel and great numbers were converted to Christ, i felt the spirit of god drawing me by conviction i longed to see & hear him & wished he would come this way and i soon heard he was come to new york & ye jases [Jerseys] & great multitudes flocking after him under great concern for their Soule & many converted wich brought on my concern more & more hoping soon to see him but next i herd he was on long island & next at boston & next at northamton & then one morning all on a Suding about 8 or 9 oClock there came a messenger & said mr. whitfield preached at hartford & weathersfield yesterday & is to preach at middeltown this morning at

10 o clock i was in my field at work i dropt my tool that i had in my hand & run home & run throu my house & bad my wife get ready quick to goo and hear mr. whitefield preach at middeltown & run to my pasture for my hors with all my might fearing i should be too late to hear him i brought my hors home & soon mounted & took my wife up & went forward as fast as i thought ye hors could bear, & when my hors began to be out of breath i would get down & put my wife on ye Saddel & bid her ride as fast as she could & not Stop or Slak for me except i bad her & so i would run until i was almost out of breath & then mount my hors again & so i did several times to favour my hors we improved every moment to get along as if we was fleeing for our lives all this while fearing we should be too late to hear ye Sermon for we had twelve miles to ride dubble in littel more then an hour & we went round by the upper housen parish & when we came within about half a mile of ye road that comes down from hartford weathersfield & stepney to middeltown on high land i saw before me a Cloud or fog rising i first thought off from ye great river but as i came nearer ye road i heard a noise something like a low rumbling thunder & i presently found it was ye rumbling of horses feet coming down ye road & this Cloud was a Cloud of dust made by ye running of horses feet it arose some rods into ye air over the tops of ye hills & trees & when i came within about twenty rods of ye road i could see men & horses Sliping along in ye Cloud like shadows & when i came nearer it was like a stedy streem of horses & their riders scarcely a hors more than his length behind another all of a lather and fome with swet ther breath rooling out of their noistrels in ye cloud of dust every jump every hors semed to go with all his might to carry his rider to hear ye news from heaven for ye saving of their Souls it made me trembel to see ye Sight how ye world was in a strugle i found a vacance between two horses to Slip in my hors & my wife said law our cloaths will be all spoiled see how they look for they was so covered with dust that they looked allmost all of a coler coats & hats & shirts & horses We went down in ye Streem i herd no man speak a word all ye way three mile but evry one presing forward in great hast & when we gat down to ye old meating house thare was a great multitude it was said to be 3 or 4000 of people asembled together we gat of from our horses & shook off ye dust and ye ministers was then coming to the meating house i turned and looked toward ye great river & saw the fery boats running swift forward & backward bringing over loads of people ye ores roed nimble & quick every thing men horses & boats all seamed to be struglin for life ye land & ye banks over ye river lookt black with people & horses all along ye 12 miles i see no man at work in his field but all seamed

to be gone—when i see mr. whitfeld come up upon ye Scaffil he looked almost angellical a young slim slender youth before some thousands of people & with a bold undainted countenance & my hearing how god was with him every where as he came along it solumnized my mind & put me in a trembling fear before he began to preach for he looked as if he was Cloathed with authority from ye great god, & a sweet sollom Solemnity sat upon his brow & my hearing him preach gave me a heart wound by gods blessing my old foundation was broken up & i saw that my righteousness would not save me then I was convinced of ye doctrine of Election.[78]

Thus did the great awakener, like a trumpet from heaven, rouse the colonists from their apathy and sloth. After such stirring days Whitefield withdrew to Georgia and spent Christmas quietly at Bethesda before starting for England. It was just as well that he enjoyed a restful holiday. When he reached Charleston on January 4, 1741, he found a veritable hornet's nest. A Mr. Hugh Bryan had written a letter attacking the clergy in America. Whitefield had revised it for the press, and now Bryan had been jailed. On January 11 Whitefield was served with a warrant which charged him with having composed a *"false, malicious, scandalous,* and *infamous* LIBEL against the CLERGY" of the province "in Contempt of *His Majesty* and *His* Laws, against the *King's* Peace." Whitefield duly appeared before the magistrates, acknowledged that he had corrected the letter, and gave security to appear at the next general quarter sessions "under Penalty of £ 100 Proclamation Money." [79]

But if Whitfield was needled by the authorities at Charleston, he was beloved by the populace, who loaded him with sea stores in preparation for his voyage to England. He "Sailed over *Charlestown* Bar, January 24, and arrived at *Falmouth* on the 11th of *March."* With the exception of a four-hour storm it was a favorable passage with "uncommonly pleasant Weather and fair Winds" almost all the way.[80] The serenity of the journey was in marked contrast to the tempestuous atmosphere which he encountered in his native land.

The reasons for hostility toward Whitefield were varied, but the immediate occasion of it was his recent attacks on the late Archbishop Tillotson, whose works were widely read and approved in England, and upon John Wesley. Describing the situation Whitefield wrote:

70

The world was angry at me for the former, and numbers of my own spiritual children for the latter. One that got some hundreds of pounds by my Sermons . . . refused to print for me any more. And others wrote to me, that God would destroy me in a fortnight; and that my fall was as great as *Peter's*. Instead of having thousands to attend me, scarce one of my spiritual children came to see me from morning to night. . . . At the same time, I was much embarrassed in my outward circumstances. A thousand pounds I owed for the Orphan-House. Two hundred and fifty pound bills, drawn upon Mr. *Seward*, now dead, were returned upon me. I was also threatened to be arrested for two hundred pounds more.[81]

Whitefield's financial reverses and his loss of popularity, however, were temporary, and, unwittingly, he faced an eventful year.

Chapter VI

The Unwavering Witness

THREE things happened to Whitefield shortly after his return to England in 1741: He married a wife, he went to Scotland, and he broke with John Wesley. The first brought him no satisfaction, the second no novelty, and the third disturbed him profoundly when it occurred and until the breach was healed (which was not very long after).

Whitefield was not certain that he wanted to marry. He was certain only that he ought to marry, and that was quite a different thing. Whatever reasons he had for feeling as he did, one was plainly admitted—he needed a woman's help at Bethesda. The orphanage wanted a housekeeper's practiced eye and careful hand with provisions that were come by with great difficulty and at dear price. The near-undisciplined orphans and the ofttimes malcontent inmates of the establishment made one who could "be looked upon as a superior . . . absolutely necessary for the due management of affairs."[1] That was the practical side of the matter. As for the spiritual, Whitefield was careful to let not "lust or passion pervert or blind" his eyes.[2] He prayed that he might not have a wife until he could live as though he had none.[3] There is some room to believe that his prayer was answered, for no wife ever complicated her husband's professional life less. Whitefield's numerous letters filled with generous compliments for his sundry friends and acquaintances are scant of reference to his wife. He left her alone for long periods of time, and her death "set his mind much at liberty."[4]

Whitefield's first efforts to marry came to nothing. He wrote to the parents of a Miss E., later identified as Elizabeth Delamotte, the daughter of a Middlesex magistrate of Blendon, inquiring whether they would be pleased to give him "leave to propose marriage unto" their daughter, if they thought well of the matter.[5] On the same date

72

he wrote what surely must be one of the most curious letters of proposal ever to be received. He had already written her parents that they "need not be afraid of sending . . . a refusal," and now he addressed the young woman herself:

> I make no great profession to you, because I believe you think me sincere. The passionate expressions which carnal courtiers use, I think, ought to be avoided by those that would marry in the LORD. I can only promise, by the help of GOD, "to keep my matrimonial vow, and to do what I can towards helping you forward in the great work of your salvation." [6]

This was unusual restraint in one of Whitefield's chronic expansiveness, but such caution must not be unduly censured in him. His relationship with women and his observation of marriage had not predisposed him to an enthusiastic contemplation of any matrimonial arrangement for himself. He could remember little of his mother's first marriage or her life with his father, and what he had seen of her second marriage was none too happy. Certainly he retained an unpleasant memory of his brother's home at Gloucester, for there his termagant sister-in-law had driven young George from the house by her irascible disposition.[7] Outside his own home Whitefield probably observed marriage at closest range during his first voyage to America. On that trip he had occasion to insist that a soldier take back his discarded wife to whom he had been married scarcely a week.[8] When Whitefield preached his farewell sermon to his traveling companions at the end of his first Atlantic passage, he reprimanded the women who had crossed with him in the following manner:

> Your behaviour on shipboard, especially the first part of the voyage, I chuse to throw a cloak over; for to use the mildest terms, it was not such as became the gospel of our LORD JESUS CHRIST. However, of late, . . . you have taken more heed to your ways, . . . permit me to entreat you all in general, as you are all now married, to remember the solemn vow you made at your entrance into the marriage state, and see that you be subject to your own husbands, in every lawful thing: Beg of GOD to keep the door of your lips. . . . And live all of you so holy and unblameable, that you may not so much as be suspected to be un-

chaste; and as some of you have imitated *Mary Magdalen* in her sin, strive to imitate her also in her repentance.[9]

Clearly Whitefield's observations and experiences were not calculated to make him happy about the honorable estate of marriage.

Exactly what Miss E. responded to Whitefield is not recorded. They were not married, as it happened. In a letter to Seward, Whitefield confided his discovery that Miss E— D— was "in a seeking state only," and added: "Surely that will not do; I would have one that is full of faith." [10] In the end Whitefield settled on another, a widow. His description of her suggests that she was the type he had vainly hoped Miss E. might prove: "Once gay; but, for three years last past, a despised follower of the Lamb of God." [11] She was also wealthy according to the report of the wedding carried in the *Gentleman's Magazine,* which announced that she brought a dowry of ten thousand pounds.[12]

Shortly before he was married, Whitefield wrote to a friend that he was going "to retirement; being to enter into the marriage state" on the next day.[13] It was on November 14, 1741, that Whitefield wedded the widow, Elizabeth James, who at the time was between the age of thirty and forty years. The ceremony was performed at St. Martin's Chapel, near Caerphilly, in the parish of Eglws Illan.[14] Less than a fortnight later Whitefield was off on a preaching mission, having decided to leave his wife "in the country for some time." [15] There is no indication that enforced separation from his wife caused Whitefield undue concern then, or at any subsequent date. Indeed, he returned from America to England without his "yoke fellow" in the summer of 1748 and of her absence calmly said: "I left her abroad in the tent." [16]

Perhaps Whitefield's habit of leaving his wife so frequently alone while he responded to the gospel call accounts in part for his failure to achieve a "perfect" marriage. Whitefield plainly wanted a blessed union and believed it possible to effect one in Christian love. Precisely what happened is a matter of some speculation. In any case Cornelius Winter says flatly that Whitefield's was *not* a happy marriage:

He was not happy in his wife, but I fear some, who had not all the religion professed, contributed to his infelicity. He did not intentionally make his wife unhappy. He always preserved great decency and decorum in his conduct towards her. . . . She certainly did not behave in all respects as she ought. She could be under no temptation from his conduct towards the sex, for he was a very pure man, a strict example of the chastity he inculcated upon others.[17]

Whitefield is suspect of being something of a cross of iron as a husband, for Winter, who lived several years in the Whitefield household, tells how

his expectations generally went before the ability of his servants to perform his commands. He was very exact to the time appointed for his stated meals; a few minutes delay would be considered a great fault. He was irritable, but soon appeased. . . . Not a paper must have been out of place, or put up irregularly. Each part of the furniture must have been likewise in its place before [he retired at night].[18]

In the sparse records available about her Mrs. Whitefield does not seem unattractive. John Wesley wrote of being hospitably received by her and added that she was a "woman of candour and humanity."[19] Perhaps she would have preferred Howell Harris, the Welsh minister, for her husband [20] rather than Whitefield; but once married to the Englishman, she gave many evidenes of being both dutiful and devoted. If she objected to being left alone for days and weeks together, she left no complaint to attest to her unhappiness. When she was with her husband, she was often busy copying his letters;[21] and while he was ranging the countryside, she sent him mail when and as she could.[22] Whitefield's wife appears to have been somewhat more earthy than he, for on one occasion, when they were together on shipboard and there was threat of attack by an enemy vessel, she "set about making cartridges" while he was occupied at his prayer.[23] At another time in the face of a common danger she exhorted her husband, who admitted to a lack of natural courage, to "play the man," an incident to which Whitefield referred when he preached her funeral sermon.[24] Yet Mrs. Whitefield was far from holding the evangelist in contempt. Moreover she was always loyal to him, and when he was ill and seemed near death, she "stood weeping by."[25] The haughty Virginians, when she visited them in 1745, were agreeably impressed by Mrs. Whitefield; their published sentiment was complimentary, if restrained: "His lady is likewise an affable, well-bred Woman, and appears to be between thirty and forty Years of Age."[26]

The most serious evidence of Whitefield's unhappiness in his marriage with this woman, who surely brought many fine traits to their union, is found in the unwitting testimony that he gave in his references, not to his marriage, but to the very institution of matrimony. "Some people think it clever to have wives and children," he said while his wife was still alive, "but they want a thousand times more grace than they had when they were single." [27] This was a reflection quite in keeping with his warning to a friend almost fifteen years earlier that "marry when or whom" he would, a man might "expect trouble in the flesh." [28] Such apprehension more than balanced Whitefield's protestation of daily feeling the loss of his "right hand" after his wife's death.[29]

A graver indication of Whitefield's radical maladjustment to marriage was his wistful regret that he did not die in an accident that occurred shortly before the birth of his son. While he was taking Mrs. Whitefield for a drive, the chaise was overturned, and both he and his wife were thrown into a ditch. Writing of the near tragedy, Whitefield confessed, "I must own, to my shame, that I felt rather regret than thankfulness in escaping what I thought would be a kind of a translation, to our wished-for haven." [30]

The child was born soon thereafter but did not live. The *Caledonian Mercury* reported that George Whitefield's "Lady was safely delivered of a Son and Heir, at his House in Hoxton, to his great Joy and to that of the Faithful."[31] That was true. Whitefield publicly baptized his son and dedicated him to the ministry in a jubilant service for which a spirited hymn was specially composed.[32] The gladness was of short duration. The child born on October 5 of 1743 was buried the following February. At that time Whitefield wrote sadly to a friend: "Last night I was called to sacrifice my *Isaac;* I mean to bury my only child and son about four months old." [33] Twice thereafter Mrs. Whitefield expected a child, but the result was either miscarriage or stillbirth.[34] The Whitefields were survived only by their spiritual descendants.

Mrs. Whitefield, though an unsuccessful wife, was a constant one, and her husband, though oblique, was faithful. Their marriage lasted for almost twenty-seven years and was dissolved by Mrs. Whitefield's death following an attack of fever in the summer of 1768. After she died on August 9, the following epitaph was inscribed for her in the Tottenham Court Road Chapel:

To the Memory of Mrs. Whitefield, who after upwards of thirty years strong and frequent manifestations of [her] *Redeemer's* love, mixed with strong and frequent strugglings against the buffetings of Satan, many sicknesses, and indwelling of sin, was joyfully released August the —— 1768.[35]

Whitefield's first trip to Scotland in 1741 was more significant to him—though not necessarily for him—than his marriage in the same year. In March of 1739 he had been briefly in Wales.[36] There, before either he or Wesley had visited in that part of Britain, Whitefield had recognized a work to his liking, progressing largely through the efforts of Howell Harris, a man of whom Whitefield highly approved. Harris' character and worth had been attested by the persecution he had endured, persecution described by Whitefield in a *Journal* of an earlier period:

Many Alehouse People, Fiddlers, Harpers, &c (*Demetrius* like) sadly cry out against him for spoiling their Business. He has been made the Subject of Numbers of Sermons, has been threatened with publick Prosecutions, and had Constables sent to apprehend him.[37]

Save for this short Welsh interlude Whitefield's labors had been in England and America—or en route between the two. Now he turned his face toward Scotland.

Originally Whitefield was invited to come to Scotland by Ralph Erskine, who with his brother Ebenezer had been a moving spirit in the formation of the Associate Presbytery,[38] a reactionary body that had seceded from the Church of Scotland in 1739. The Erskines, who were ardent evangelical reformers, liked what they heard of Whitefield and urged him to come and work with them. For two years before their meeting with the field-preacher the Presbyterian brothers had been praying for him "in the most public, explicit . . . almost . . . extravagant manner." [39] Whitefield accepted their invitation but soon became *persona non grata* with his hosts. His catholic spirit was too much for the exclusive zealots of the Associate Presbytery. Before his arrival in Scotland, Whitefield had written Ralph Erskine that he felt the schismatic group a "little too hard" on him.[40] Almost immediately on his arrival he found himself completely rejected by the members of the new presbytery; they would not even hear the famous evangelist preach after he proved himself unwilling to be allied with their partisan interests.[41] It was no more than might have been expected of the man who said that "if the Pope himself would lend" him a pulpit, he "would gladly proclaim . . . therein." [42] The people, on the other hand, "were ready to shout for joy" at the coming of the renowned English preacher.[43] When he left their chief city after preaching to multitudes of rapt listeners, he exclaimed, "O Edinburgh, Edinburgh, surely thou wilt never be forgotten by me!" [44] The city was no less inclined to forget Whitefield, for when he returned some time later, he was in "danger of being hugged to death by the enthusiastic reception of its citizens." [45]

Whitefield never spoke to the Scots in such throngs, nor felt himself so elevated as during the season when he first visited Cambuslang on his second trip to Scotland. It was in July of 1742 that he wrote the letter from which the following is taken:

> On *Friday* night I came to *Cambuslang,* to assist at the blessed sacrament. On *Saturday* I preached to above twenty thousand people. In my prayer the power of GOD came down and was greatly felt. In my two sermons, there was yet more power. On sabbath day, scarce ever was such a sight seen in *Scotland.* There were undoubtedly upwards of twenty thousand people. Two tents were set up, and the holy sacrament was administered in the fields. . . . On *Monday* morning, I preached again to near as many; but such an universal stir I never saw before. The motion fled as swift as lightning from one end of the auditory to another. You might have seen thousands bathed in tears. Some at the same time wringing their hands, others almost swooning, and others crying out, and mourning over a pierced Saviour. . . . All night in different companies, you might have heard persons praying to, and praising God. . . . It was like the passover in *Josiah*'s time.[46]

In Edinburgh that summer the managers of Heriot's Hospital erected a tent in which Whitefield might preach with adequate "defence against the weather." There were two thousand seats in semicircular tiers which an eager public quickly rented for the season, paying more for those in the shade. A few free places—those without rails—were available, and there were free accommodations for soldiers. But most of the seats by far were rented, and easily. The hospital received the income from this venture.[47]

Whitefield continued to return to Scotland at frequent intervals as long as he lived. He always found it a joy to speak to the Scots and was continually impressed by the "rustling made by opening the bibles" as soon as he had "named" his text.[48] The members of the Associate Presbytery eventually made public announcement of their penitence for having had any part in the sinful reception "given to Mr. George Whitefield, a professed Member and Priest of the superstitious Church of England," [49] but his popularity with the Scots at large remained firm. In all he went on fourteen preaching tours of Scotland, the last in 1768, scarcely two years before his death. He was welcomed then as warmly as he had been when he had first come there. Friends of twenty-seven-years' standing sought him out.[50] Of that final visit Whitefield wrote: "Could I preach ten times a day, thousands and thousands would attend." [51] It was true. From their first meeting Whitefield loved Scotland, and Scotland loved him.

Whitefield's feeling for Wesley was quite as warm as his affection for Scotland, but the relationship was not so continuously cordial nor always so mutually commendatory. George Whitefield and John Wesley were fast friends from the first days of Methodism. The sermon Wesley preached on the death of Whitefield was one of deep esteem for his late companion. Nevertheless, in 1741 there was a temporary rift between these two that was precipitated by Wesley's sermon on "Free Grace," which affirmed an antipredestination theology that Whitefield could not accept or permit to go unchallenged.

Wesley had preached the sermon in Bristol, where he had gone at Whitefield's invitation to continue in the field-preacher's absence the work that had been begun with the miners. Shortly after Whitefield's departure for his second visit to America the sermon was published, and Whitefield, who saw it first during the latter part of 1739 while he was still in the colonies, promptly wrote Wesley remonstrating with him.[52] It was a private letter, of course, but some busybodies surreptitiously printed copies of it and then distributed them openly to worshipers entering the door of the Foundry, where Wesley was conducting service. On that occasion Wesley announced that he would follow a course that would have been acceptable to Whitefield, had he been there, and publicly tore one of the copies to shreds.[53] The people followed his example. Estrangement seemed inevitable. The attack that Wesley had made on election—a doctrine that Whitefield firmly held—apparently rankled him from the time he first read of it. Almost immediately on returning to England in 1741 he published a pamphlet entitled *A Letter to the Reverend Mr. John Wesley: In Answer to his Sermon, entituled FREE GRACE.*[54] The break was thus frankly acknowledged. Partisans endeavored to intensify the feeling and enlarged the dispute. Yet even so, the coolness between these two men did not last long. At the time of the disagreement Wesley said that it was "not merely the difference of doctrine that caused the division. It was rather Mr. Whitefield's *manner.*" [55] But amends were soon made. The bonds of common interests were stronger than the factions of divisive doctrines. Within eighteen months Whitefield wrote his old friend in becoming fashion: "Let . . . controversy die," he begged. "It has died with me long ago." [56]

Far from creating any unbridgeable breach in Methodism, Whitefield aided in preserving a basic unity as long as he lived. Charles Wesley hymned the reconciliation of his brother and Whitefield in a poem which spoke of finished strife and "friends at first . . . friends again at last." [57] The warm association of the reunited companions was resumed as in former days and continued until interrupted by death. Whitefield's attitude toward Wesley after harmony was restored is suggested in his reply to the question of a censorious Calvinist who asked him whether he thought they might see John Wesley in heaven: "I fear not," said Whitefield; "he will be so near the throne, and we shall be at such distance, that we shall hardly get a sight of him." [58]

After his return to England in the spring of 1741 Whitefield did not leave the British Isles again until midsummer of 1744, at which time he and his wife sailed for America from Plymouth in the month of August.[59] When they arrived, Whitefield was desperately sick and continued so ill for a while that he could not "bear the sound of a tread of the foot, or the voice of friends who came to see and pray" with him.[60] He recovered in time and went about his usual business of itinerant preaching. The facts speak for themselves in a letter written from Philadelphia on September 11, 1747:

I have good news from *Georgia,* and from my new plantation in *South Carolina.* Many negroes are brought under conviction. We saw great things in *New-England.* The flocking and power that attended the word, was like unto that seven years ago. Weak as I was, and have been, I was enabled to travel eleven hundred miles and preach daily. I am now once more going to *Georgia* to settle all my affairs, and shall get ready to embark.[61]

Although he had written of his continued popularity and that the Orphan-House "like the burning bush . . . flourished unconsumed," [62] all was not well with Whitefield. His arrival in America had been shortly after Charles Chauncy, the celebrated New England divine, published *Seasonable Thoughts on the State of Religion in New England,* in which Whitefield was represented in a most unflattering light. Chauncy was a man of reputation and character, and it was a matter of reproach to have him ask Bethesda's founder pointedly "what became of his little Flock" while he ranged over the country.[63] Chauncy had "collected the most exaggerated accounts" of Whitefield's activities from those who were his "most zealous opposers" and published them in such a way that they threw the "greatest odium and reproach upon" his work.[64] He accused the roving evangelist of judging his fellow ministers as unconverted in "open Violation of the Christian Law of *Charity*." [65] The charge of spiritual pride was also brought against Whitefield, whom Chauncy taxed with reveling in the adulation of the multitude in an attitude that was "downright gross Idolatry." [66]

Chauncy's attack was a galling one. No doubt it had something to do with the choice of task that occupied Whitefield during his return voyage to England in 1748. In the four-year period of his third visit to America, Whitefield had, as usual, ranged from Georgia to New England, preaching frequently, often three times a day, to attentive throngs. But he had surely seen evidence that other eyes than his had read Chauncy's book and possibly with some approval. Yet however he might have wished to recall his *Journals* or however seriously he might have intended to revise those products of his own pen which had become the instruments of his undoing, he had no leisure in which to do so until he was at sea. Once he was on board the "Betsy," bound for his native land, he set himself to the business of deleting from his published writings those passages that had proved offensive to some and made him the target for embarrassing questions like those of Chauncy. It was with a feeling of satisfaction and accomplishment that, before he had docked in England, he wrote:

Yesterday I likewise made an end of revising all my journals. Blessed be GOD, for letting me have leisure to do it. I purpose to have a new edition before I see *America.* Alas! alas! In how many things have I judged and acted wrong.—I have been too rash and hasty in giving characters, both of places and persons. Being fond of scripture language, I have often used a style too apostolical, and at the same time I have been too bitter in my zeal. Wild-fire has been mixed with it, and I find that I frequently wrote and spoke in my own spirit, when I thought I was writing and speaking by the assistance of the spirit of GOD. I have likewise too much made inward impressions my rule of acting, and too soon and too explicitly published what had been better kept in longer, or told after my death. By these things I have given some wrong touches to GOD's ark, and hurt the blessed cause I would defend, and also stirred up needless opposition. This has humbled me much since I have been on board, and made me think of a saying of Mr. *Henry's, "Joseph* had more *honesty* than he had *policy,* or he never would have told his dreams."[67]

It is apparent that Whitefield was returning to London, not a completely changed man, but one who would endeavor to be more circumspect. The amended edition of his *Journals* was published, and it became difficult to come by the originals almost within Whitefield's lifetime.[68] But their author persisted in writing in his letters and saying from the pulpit the kind of thing which had been regarded as obnoxious in his *Journals.* It was only natural, therefore, that objection to Whitefield should have continued.

In America, Whitefield's opposition was generally the attack of pulpit and pamphlet. In England it was sometimes physical. During his life he suffered persecution that was never worse, often lighter, and usually less frequent than that to which other Methodists were subjected. He was pelted with his share of dirt and rotten eggs, but this was common treatment for Methodists.[69] Indeed, there was nothing unique in the abuse he received, even when it was more dangerous. Once a man tried to stab him.[70] Another time a foolhardy individual (not reckoning with the volume of Whitefield's voice or the readiness of his wit) attempted to best him with a drum. Whitefield was preaching in the fields when a recruiting drummer appeared and did his utmost to drown out the preacher; but the man left in "great good humour" when Whitefield appealed to him saying, "Friend . . . you may beat up volunteers for King George, I for the Lord Jesus Christ. In God's name then don't let us interrupt each other, the world is wide enough for us both." [71] Whitefield also received anonymous letters,[72] and he had on one instance to contend with the antics of some merry-andrew who tried to divert the attention of the congregation and distract Whitefield by flicking him "with a long heavy whip." [73] There were three occasions, however, any one of which might have ended fatally for Whitefield.

Once as he was preaching at Exeter, a man maliciously threw a stone at him and wounded him seriously.[74] Again, he was attacked in his rooms by some rowdies and would have been killed had it not been for the intervention of his resourceful and fearless landlady. Set upon by one of the ruffians, Whitefield screamed, "Murder," and brought the mistress of the house rushing into the preacher's quarters. She routed the first attacker but was herself seized by his cohort and thrown down the stairs so that her "back was almost broken." Yet she managed along with her daughter so to alarm the neighborhood that the scoundrel fled, while Whitefield retired in safety, though "not without reflecting, how indispensably necessary it was for christians and christian ministers to be always upon their guard." [75]

Whitefield's narrowest escape came as he preached in Dublin in the summer of 1757. He was speaking on "Oxminton-Green, a large place like *Moorfields,* situated very near the barracks." Having gone through the barracks and having pitched his tent, he delivered a sermon which was generously interlarded with patriotic exhortation to which the Irish took easy exception. Whitefield noticed little molestation as he spoke, "only now and then a few stones and clods of dirt." Then, suddenly, violence broke out, and the preacher (deserted by the four Methodists and the soldier who had come with him) was left to the mercy of the mob. "But their mercy," said Whitefield, "was perfect cruelty." He took refuge in the house of a reluctant protector and was saved from further disgrace and injury by the arrival of a "methodist preacher, with two friends, . . . [and] a coach." Leaping into it, the victim of dirt and stone bruises "rid in gospel triumph through the oaths, curses, and imprecation of whole streets of papists unhurt." [76] In spite of such episodes as this, however, Whitefield was relatively free from physical abuse. And the humiliation that he endured from attacks—of whatever kind—was in a measure offset by the patronage he enjoyed from Selina, Countess of Huntingdon. That remarkable individual sponsored and assisted Whitefield in marked degree from the time of his return to England following his third visit to America until the end of his life.

The Countess of Huntingdon was a woman of rank, "daughter of Washington Earl of Ferrars, and widow of Theophilus Earl of Huntingdon." [77] It has been said, but not substantiated, that "there was a decided insanity in her family." [78] In any case, she was a figure of English society and an institution at Bath, where her baroque costumes impressed gatherings accustomed to outlandish dress.[79]

Her prestige, however, was not due solely or primarily to her striking appearance. It was society's logical award for her executive ability and natural resourcefulness. "One day when Lady Hunting-don was present in the Pump Room," wrote Barbeau,

a Quakeress suddenly saw fit to lift up her voice against the follies and vanities of this world; the assembled company gave noisy expression to their impatience, whereupon Lady Huntingdon, rising from her seat, went to the preacher, praised aloud her courage and zeal (although she differed widely from her in her own religious opinions), then, taking her by the hand, accompanied her to the door, and quietly returned to her seat.[80]

This commanding and capable woman of title had shown a pronounced bent toward religion since her childhood. Part church-woman and part dissenter, she had championed Methodism without regard for the sneers or the ridicule her unconventional behavior had occasioned. Lady Huntingdon began to take special interest in Whitefield about the year 1747, although she had previously shown her approval and concern for his person and career.[81] White-field's response to the attention she paid him borders on the servile. In August of 1748 he wrote to her:

Ever since the reading your Ladyship's condescending letter, my soul . . . has been overpowered with his presence who is All in All. When your ladyship stiled me "your friend," I was amazed at your condescension. . . . Quite astonished at your Ladyship's condescension, and the unmerited superabounding grace and goodness of Him who has loved me and given himself for me, I subscribe myself, honoured madam,

>Your Ladyship's most obliged, obedient,
>humble and willing servant,
>G. W.[82]

Subsequently, Whitefield was made one of her ladyship's chaplains. He was deeply grateful for that evidence of her regard. Until the end of his life he was her frequent guest, and he preached to many "noble" visitors at her various residences.

On one occasion Lady Huntingdon persuaded Beau Nash himself to hear Whitefield; but the King of Bath was so outraged by the reaction of the wags of the town (who wrote mocking "Verses . . . on her Ladyship and Mr. Nash, which were fastened to the walls of the pump-room and assembly-room") that he refused ever to set foot in the countess' house again.[83] On the other hand Lady Chesterfield met Whitefield at the Lady Selina's and was by her own admission so influenced by him that she was twitted by George II for appearing at court in a dress of such somber color that his majesty thought it must have been chosen for her by the evangelist, on whom she had been in attendance for a "year and a half." For when the king saw Lady Chesterfield in a sober dress with a "brown ground," he "first smiled and then laughed quite out," and said, "I know who chose that gown for you:—Mr. *Whitefield*." [84] And even Chesterfield himself, though he was never converted to Methodism, was no enemy of the movement and said of Lady Huntingdon's enthusiasm for the sect that her zeal "raised it with many people and lowered it with none." [85] Particularly Lady Huntingdon dignified Methodism in the eyes of the aristocracy, who listened willingly to her testimony when they might have spurned that of less distinguished persons and attended services in her lodgings when they would have refused to worship at a foundry or in the fields.

In her lifetime the countess built four chapels, all of them in places of fashionable resort, to accommodate the polite world. When her chapel at Bath was dedicated in 1765, Whitefield was one of six clergymen who were summoned to the ceremony. The chapel itself was "very neat, with *true* Gothic windows, . . . mahogany stands for branches, . . . two eagles with red cushions for the parson and clerk, . . . a third eagle for a pulpit. Scarlet arm chairs to all three.

On either hand a balcony for elect ladies." [86] An immense crowd attended, and there were "great numbers of the nobility who had been specially invited by Lady Huntingdon." [87] Whitefield found the chapel "extremely plain, and yet equally grand." [88] The countess' chaplain moved with easy grace in the world to which Lady Huntingdon gave him entree. The drawing rooms at Bath housed a different world from that of the street corner and the field. And in a measure Whitefield's acceptance by certain people of fashion was compensation for the abuse he received at the hands of the mob. But he did not forget, nor did he lose, his popularity with the masses of England.

The affection which his own countrymen felt for Whitefield was variously expressed, perhaps never more positively than in the erection of buildings in London specifically designed for his use in religious services. When Whitefield returned from his second trip to America, some friends erected a large wooden shed on the edge of Moorfields to protect congregations in cold and rainy weather. The tabernacle was in use by June of 1741, when Whitefield mentioned in a letter that it had been completed.[89] Originally the plan had been to use the building only temporarily, but ten years later it was still the scene of regular services. The suggestion to replace the wooden structure with a permanent one came out of a discussion among Methodist friends gathered at Lady Huntingdon's Ashby residence. An ingenious plan was worked out, and a new tabernacle was constructed around the old one in order that worship services might go on uninterrupted.[90] The "first brick . . . was laid with awful solemnity" in March of 1753,[91] and the congregation was in the finished meetinghouse by summer.[92]

Three years after this, in 1756, in another part of the city in the midst of fields and gardens there was laid the foundation for the historic Tottenham Court Road Chapel. Whitefield had secured "near six hundred pounds" as soon as he announced his intention to build a "place for the gospel at the other end of town." [93] The completed sanctuary was being used in November of the same year in which it was begun.[94] The "beautiful spot of ground" which surrounded the chapel became the location for twelve "alms-houses . . . for some godly widows." [95] It was of these women, who received half a crown a week from the sacrament money, that Whitefield once said to a visitor: "There are my life guards. In those Houses

I maintain twelve poor widows and their prayers help to keep me alive." [96]

The unprecedented popularity of these two centers of religious activity and the vigorous following which attended services there long after Whitefield's death are attested by a comment of a student of Methodism made in 1877 regarding the Moorfields' second tabernacle, of which he said: ". . . there are thousands still living who have often gazed with reverence at the low unpretentious edifice where Whitefield so often mounted his pulpit throne, and not a few who found salvation within its walls." [97]

Whitefield had returned from his third visit to America well accustomed to invective and insult. England was by no means ready to accept him without reservation. Indeed, some years of persecution were still before him. Yet he found a growing tolerance for himself and Methodists among men of high places, and he enjoyed an increasingly numerous following among the masses, who warmed his heart by their faithfulness and their zeal.

Whitefield's fourth and fifth visits to America were so brief that the colonies hardly realized he had arrived before he had departed. In October, 1751, a few hundred miles off the shore of North America for the fourth time, the impatient evangelist exhorted with himself as he contemplated another rich season in the new world: "Stir up then, my sluggish soul, and begin to exert thyself for Him." [98] Happily on his arrival he found the Orphan-House "in a flourishing way" and began at once to make plans for his spring campaign.[99] But when warm weather came, he was not preaching in the New England fields; he was back in London, having made sudden resolution to embark for England in an effort to put the Orphan-House on a "proper footing" before the charter of the trustees expired.[100] Characteristically, he took time off from pressing business in London to write the following to Benjamin Franklin, who was currently enjoying celebrity for having satisfactorily explained the phenomenon of the Leyden jar:

I find that you grow more and more famous in the learned world. As you have made a pretty considerable progress in the mysteries of electricity, I would now humbly recommend to your diligent unprejudiced pursuit and study the mystery of the new-birth. . . . You will excuse this freedom. I must have *aliquid Christi* in all my letters.[101]

Whitefield satisfied himself as to the future of the Orphan-House and was able in the latter part of 1752 to say confidently that he feared only that Bethesda might grow too great in a worldly way. Certainly he was unconcerned over the "few evil reports" of its detractors.[102]

Worldiness, of course, was the gravest danger that could threaten Bethesda. It was more terrible than the Spanish invaders who had once robbed the Orphan-House of a "schooner loaded with bricks," [103] more frightful than the former want that had driven the orphans to rely on the hospitality of the Indians for food when the usual sources failed.[104] Whitefield was constantly on guard against Satan's invading the stronghold of faith by insidious wiles. It followed naturally that in his absence from the orphanage he admonished the children continually by letter.

"You may well wonder," he wrote Rebekah B., "that GOD has not sent you to hell long ago." He told "Dear Betty" that he was glad she had begun to feel a hardness of heart and an inability to pray, for it meant that the child was coming under conviction and leaving conventional Christianity behind. His advice to Mary A. was stern and pointed: "You may now see what a poor wretch you are, how proud, how earthly, how sensual, how devilish." [105] Far from being ill-received, these letters were answered in kind. The lambs at Bethesda were keenly aware that the "Devil goes about like a rorring Lion seeking whome he may devour." They were, consequently, very grateful when there had "been a Stirring amongst the dry Bones." [106]

Whitefield believed that one should "bear with young Christians, and not knock a young child's brains out, because he cannot speak in blank verse." [107] But he did not doubt that the child—even the young child—was capable of religious experience understood and expressed in terms that were Whitefield's own. As a description of the heights of religious enthusiasm which the children reached in the house of mercy where there was constant warfare against worldliness, "stirring" was something of an understatement. Once Joseph Periam

had left them in the School picking Cotton; and, while they were working, one of them said to another, *If we do not believe in the Lord Jesus Christ, We shall all go to Hell; . . .* Immediately, the Boy to whom he spake, fell down upon his Knees, and began to pray; and then another, till they were all on their Knees. . . . 'twas not long before the whole Family was gathered round about them. . . . The dear little Lambs continued crying out . . . an Hour or two.[108]

Another time Mr. Habersham "wept over 25 or 30 dear Lambs upon their Knees before God, some pleading the Promises, and others calling on Jesus." [109]

Such expression of religious concern must not be regarded unusual in an establishment where but half an hour's free time was allowed in twenty-four: "The oeconomy observed here is as follows," wrote Whitefield:

The bell rings in the morning at sun-rise, to wake the family. When the children arise, they sing a short hymn, and pray by themselves: then they go down and wash; and by the time they have done that, the bell calls to public worship, when a portion of scripture is read and expounded, a psalm sung, and the exercise begun and ended with a prayer. Then they breakfast, and afterwards go some to their trades, and the rest to their prayers and schools. At noon, they all dine in the same room, and have comfortable and wholesome diet provided. A hymn is sung before and after dinner: then, in about half an hour, to school again; and between whiles find time enough for recreation. A little after sun-set the bell calls to public duty again, which is performed in the same manner as in the morning. After that they sup, and are attended to bed by one of their masters, who then pray with them, as they often do privately. On the sabbath-day they all dine on cold meat provided the day before, that none may be kept from public worship, which is attended four times a day in summer, and three in winter.[110]

The letters written and received by the children of such an orphanage as this were quite in keeping with their life under Whitefield's direction. It was typical of the whole situation that they greeted each new arrival at Bethesda with a specially composed hymn:

> What tho' our Parents dear are dead,
> Yet our great God provides:
> Our Bodies here are cloth'd and fed;
> Our Souls have Christian Guides.[111]

Perhaps it was having supper with Gilbert Tennent and Samuel Davies in Christmas week of 1753 that turned Whitefield's attention toward America, for it was shortly after his visit with them that he began to make arangements for sailing again to the colonies.[112] The two clergymen had come to England to raise money for New Jersey College. They secured contributions that "amply enabled them to erect a convenient edifice for the accomodation of the students, and to lay a foundation for a fund for the support of the necessary instructors."[113] From whatever immediate stimulus, Whitefield embarked from Gravesend on the seventh of March, 1754, bound for Georgia for the fifth time. He took with him twenty-two destitute children whom he planned to settle at Bethesda.[114]

Whitefield went to America by way of Lisbon, where the "Success," on which he sailed, lay at anchor for at least a month during the Lenten season. A reputable merchant invited the evangelist to be his guest and showed him the "ecclesiastical curiosities of the country."[115] The processions and ceremonies of an unashamedly Roman city scandalized Whitefield with a horrible fascination. His letters telling of the sojourn in Portugal fill twenty-six closely printed pages and are by far the most detailed and colorful he ever wrote. The man who visited the lush wilderness around Savannah and made no comment on the fragrance of the "Laurel Tulip" and took no notice of the native "Turtle-Doves . . . *Virginia* Nightengale, [or] the mocking Bird," which had delighted more sophisticated travelers than he,[116] was at great pains to catalogue every detail of the Lenten spectacle. Whitefield's religious sensitivity was shocked, but his instinct for theater appreciated the devices to which his aesthetic sense succumbed. Of a tableau he remarked that the "music on this occasion was extremely soft, and the church . . . illuminated in a very striking manner." He observed that the people responded to the priest's exhortation "by beating their breasts, and clapping their cheeks, and weeping heartily."[117] He pointed out objectively that one celebrant "gradually lifted up his voice 'till it was extended to a pretty high pitch, though . . . scarce high enough for so large an auditory."[118] No part of the setting was omitted, as the following excerpt from a description of an altar illustrates:

Its basis was studded with many precious stones, and near the top were placed silver images, in representation of angels. Each step was filled with large silver candlesticks, with wax-tapers in them, which going up by a regular ascent, 'till they formed themselves into a pyramid, made a most glittering and splendid blaze.[119]

His narration of the Franciscan procession and of the Good Friday service could almost serve in lieu of rubrics.

Whitefield concluded that "oratory . . . that stands in need of such a train of superstitious pageantry" was completely destitute of divine power.[120] Oddly, he did not preach in Lisbon himself, nor try to. But he left the city praising "protestant liberty and simplicity more than ever." In this renewed faith he reached America on May 26 after a six-weeks passage.[121]

The colonies received him as before, many coming "forty or fifty miles" to hear him preach. He did not tarry long, however; with regret at leaving America, especially Bethesda, to which he "often would . . . have fled" had he "wings like a dove," Whitefield sailed for England about the end of March, because he felt it was the will of God for him to return.[122] It was eight years before the colonies saw him again. When he did come back to America on his sixth visit, his absorbing interest was a plan for turning Bethesda into a college. "But it was a call to a disappointed hope," as a sympathetic historian of the orphanage observed.[123]

After an absence of so long a time Whitefield was welcomed more warmly than usual. When he proposed going southward, after spending only a short time in Boston, the people sent a "gospel hue and cry after" him.[124] It was more than an eagerness to hear the magic voice that caused them to greet him so cordially. In 1761 Whitefield had collected from London congregations "near six hundred pounds . . . for the *German* and *Boston* sufferers." [125] New Englanders did not ignore or forget this thoughtful courtesy. Even the frostiest Bostonians were melted by Whitefield's attention, and they thanked him publicly:

At a Meeting of the Freeholders, and other Inhabitants of the Town of Boston . . . it was voted unanimously, That the Thanks of the Town be given the Rev. Mr. George Whitefield, for his charitable Care and Pains in collecting a considerable Sum of Money in Great-Britain, for the distressed Sufferers by the great Fire in Boston, 1760; and a respectable Committee was appointed to wait on Mr. Whitefield, to inform him of the Vote.[126]

Whitefield wrote in warmth of the eager reception in New England on this latest preaching venture: "Invitations come so thick and fast from every quarter, that I know not what to do." [127]

The threat of an epidemic of smallpox at this time somewhat curtailed Whitefield's congregations, for Boston was quarantined. Road blocks were set up across the routes leading into the city, and travelers were thoroughly smoked before certificates for admission into Boston were issued.[128] This circumstance, along with the fear which men naturally entertained regarding the dread disease, was a barrier for many who otherwise would have crowded to hear Whitefield. Even so Whitefield preached often while he was in Boston, and the city delighted to honor him.

Whitefield now laid the citizens of Massachusetts colony under further obligation by rising to the occasion of their need and by soliciting aid for the library of Harvard College (which had been destroyed by fire) and for Mr. Wheelock's school for Indians, which was "such a promising nursery of future missionaries." [129] So completely did he charm Boston and environs on this sixth visit to America that even the students at Yale responded and voluntarily crowded into the chapel while they sent word to the preacher by their president entreating him "to give them one more quarter of an hour exhortation." [130]

Struggling against the stream of such popularity (which was not unique to the Boston area), Whitefield did not reach Georgia until well into December of 1764, more than a year and a half after his embarkation for America.[131] Once arrived, however, he lost no time in endeavoring to achieve the goal he had set for himself. He asked James Wright, Captain-General and Governor-in-Chief of His Majesty's Province of Georgia, for a grant of two thousand acres of land to enable him to convert Bethesda into a college "for the education of persons of superior rank; who thereby might be qualified to serve their king, their country and their GOD, either in church or state." Two days later both houses of the assembly presented an address to Governor Wright requesting him to use his utmost endeavors in behalf of the plan Whitefield had suggested.[132]

Confident that the dream of a college would be realized, Whitefield left for England, having already written excitedly, "All things, in respect to Bethesda went on successfully. . . . His Excellency . . . expressed his satisfaction in the warmest terms." [133] The frustration of Whitefield's hope was largely due to his unwillingness to have the institution become a college of the Church of England, with the provost one of her priests and her liturgy exclusively mandatory in the religious life of the school. The involved correspondence which Whitefield had with the Archbishop of Canterbury over the affair he reported to Governor Wright and, in concluding, informed the executive of a new plan for education at Bethesda:

I now propose to add a public academy, to the Orphan-House as the college of *Philadelphia* was constituted a public academy, as well as charitable school, for some time before its present college charter was granted by the honourable proprietors of *Pennsylvania* in the year 1755.[134]

Bethesda never attained status or recognition as a school. Later the Orphan-House was called an "academy" in the *Georgia Gazette*'s account of Whitefield's entertaining the governor and council "politely . . . with a handsom and plentiful dinner," but it remained an Orphan-House. Moreover, a current report held to it that there were "but few Orphans in the house, and no symptoms of grace in any." [135] The great preacher seemed powerless to realize the vision that he had entertained for his house of mercy. The signs were plain that George Whitefield, who never grew weary of the work of God, was beginning to grow weary in it. Whitefield's sun was setting. It was not being eclipsed—it was simply setting. And the sunset was to be a blaze of glory.

After returning from his sixth journey to America the great trumpeter remained in England till the fall of 1769. His latter years were relatively peaceful. Methodism was no longer the novelty or the danger that it had been in the exciting days of Whitefield's youth. He lived in rooms by the Tottenham Court Road Chapel in such a gospel atmosphere that even the teacups were inscribed with quotations from scripture, "all of which were expressive of the resemblances of water or food to the blessings of the Gospel."[136] Long since grown quite fat,[137] Whitefield remained active, and he still preached with frequency and fire. "Have been enabled to preach five times this week," he wrote in May of 1769, and added, "Field-preaching, field-preaching for ever!" [138] But Whitefield was sensitive to the changed and changing times; earlier than most he saw the insolent light of a new day that was breaking: "O London! London!

highly favoured London! . . . There are few that like to go out into the fields; broken heads and dead cats are no more the orna-- ments of a Methodist, but silk scarves." [139]

One of his last public services in England had been the opening of the Countess of Huntingdon's Tunbridge Wells Chapel. The occasion of its dedication was a gala day. Early in the morning, Sunday, July 23, 1769, the people who had flocked into Tunbridge gathered before the countess' residence and sang and prayed until time for public worship to begin. "It is impossible," wrote Lady Huntingdon, "to express the delight . . . I experienced on being awoke at an early hour of the morning by voices of praise." [140] The chapel could not accommodate the visitors, and Whitefield preached on a mound raised before the door for that purpose. The sermon was a "perfect piece of oratory," and he cried out—as often before: "Look yonder! what is that I see! it is my agonizing Lord! hark! hark! do not you hear? O earth, earth, earth, hear the word of the Lord!" [141]

Hardly had the echoes of these words died when Whitefield departed from England. On the thirtieth of November after a long and trying passage he was once more in America.[142] As always, he was received by crowds, who gave him "scarce the least leisure." [143] Whitefield remained in the South during the winter and in the spring turned north and left his beloved Bethesda forever. His last letters were genuinely happy ones, telling of "many new, as well as old doors . . . open, and . . . many invitations." Through a full summer he preached daily except when he was "so ill . . . that . . . [he] could not . . . though thousands were waiting to hear." [144]

In the midst of this characteristic activity and popularity

the Reverend Mr. George Whitefield . . . well known all over the British Empire as a faithful, laborious, and successful Minister of the Gospel of Christ . . . was seized with a violent fit of asthma, which . . . put a period to his labours in this life.[145]

PART II

The Message and How It Was Received

Chapter VII

The Theology of George Whitefield

An admirer of Whitefield described him early in his career as being "thoroughly Calvinist." [1] This—coming as it did from a Presbyterian minister in Dundee and published in the *Glasgow Weekly History* —can hardly be taken as a cavalier judgment. Rather it was the considered opinion of one to whom conformity to the standards of Calvin was a matter of grave concern. It is incorrect, however, if for no other reason, because the field-preacher forfeited the legitimate right to be bracketed with the Genevan by the highly unsystematic presentation of his thought. For that matter, Whitefield himself denied that he was a Calvinist except by happenstance. The "Calvinistical scheme" he embraced because he felt himself taught it of Christ.[2] "Alas," he confessed to Wesley, "I never read any thing that *Calvin* wrote"; and he added with a self-assurance of being individually called by God, "my doctrines I had from CHRIST and his apostles: I was taught them of GOD." [3]

Strictly speaking, Whitefield was not even a theologian, not so much because he did not produce a theology—as he did not—but because he did not address himself formally to the problems of speculative thought, nor attempt to systematize his dogma in any organized form. Actually, there was an unbecoming pride of ignorance which was a recurrent, though not dominant, note in Whitefield's thought. Having little sympathy for the "letter learned," [4] especially among the clergy, whom he sometimes thought as unknowing of the new birth as a "blind man . . . of colours," [5] he was deeply distrustful of "Ministers that . . . declaim of CHRIST, and prove from books that he is the Son of GOD." [6] Such classics as Caesar and Homer he considered trifling things,[7] and it was atypical that he occasionally made use of such allusions as Socrates' monitor or the Lyrnean head.[8] Cornelius Winter, who became a member of Whitefield's household rather late in the evangelist's life, soon found that his patron "did not intend to promote . . . [his] literary improvement. Indeed, he said, Latin was of little or no use." [9] However strange this sometimes arrogant hostility to learning and disciplined thought appears in the individual whose publications always noted on the title page that he was "Late of Pembroke College," it sheds at least this light on the man and his work: Whitefield was not an intellectual, and his theology, therefore, was incidental.

Whitefield saw himself in a prophetic role which set him above the demands of organized study, though whether this was from a sense of destiny or from the sort of implied spiritual pride that has made him repulsive to some is a question that must be temporarily deferred.[10] He felt himself called to preach—not to teach, but to declare the gospel, a challenge he did not accept before he had "prayed a thousand times till the sweat . . . dropped from [his] face like rain." After once responding to heaven's call Whitefield never returned to Gloucester without walking by the house and looking up at the window that opened from the room in which he had wrestled thus with the angel of vocation.[11]

What speculative theology there is in Whitefield's work is sparse and scattered, hidden in the pages of his books like fruit lost in the leaves of barren trees. Nor is it rare, exotic fruit, even when it is found. He looks at marine life and sees a confutation of atheism.[12] He reads the obituaries in a newspaper and observes: "The question is, whether there will be a resurrection, or what will be the consequence? Whatever it be, this is our consolation, 'The LORD reigneth.' "[13] He states conventionally that the "Father creates, the Son redeems, and the Holy Ghost sanctifies all the elect people of GOD."[14] Or he expends his energy on some such relatively trivial aspect of theological thought as the following:

How soon man fell after he was created, is not told us; and therefore, to fix any time, is to be wise above what is written. And, I think, they who suppose that man fell the same day in which he was made, have no sufficient ground for their opinion. The many things which are crouded together in the former chapter, such as the formation of *Adam's* wife, his giving names to the beasts, and his being put into the garden which GOD had planted, I think require a longer space of time than a day to be transacted in. However, all agree in this, "man stood not long." How long, or how short a while, I will not take upon me to determine.[15]

Almost any single sermon states the whole of his formal theology. His ideas are few; they are bluntly put and endlessly repeated. A consideration of this theology is not the examination of a system; rather it is the enumeration of points of view which possibly do and possibly do not fit together into a scheme.

The final and unquestioned authority for Whitefield was the Bible. He regarded it with the typical evangelical and Methodist attitude as a single volume of one texture and of equal value throughout. It is still possible to feel the passion in his address to a hypothetical agnostic to whom Whitefield appealed in a sermon on the Holy Ghost, preached in Kent when he was twenty-five years old:

If thou canst prove, thou Unbeliever, that the Book, which we call *the Bible,* does not contain the lively Oracles of *God;* if thou canst shew, that holy Men of old did not write this Book, as they were inwardly moved by the Holy Ghost, then we will give up the Doctrine . . . ; but unless thou canst do this, we must insist upon it . . . if for no other, yet for this one Reason, because that *God,* who cannot lie, has told us so.[16]

This biblicistic zeal did not abate. On the eve of his last departure for America, because of the very real possibility that he might "die in the way . . . in the ship," [17] Whitefield spoke with the utmost sincerity and with an urgent sense of a necessity for insisting upon those things he might never have another chance to tell his hearers. On that occasion he was still pleading for men to give "this book of God, the grand charter of salvation, one fair reading through." [18] It remained always for Whitefield "sufficient to affirm, that GOD himself, in his Holy Word, hath told us so." [19]

Whitefield knew his Bible. That, however, is not quite the same thing as saying that he understood it. His fondness for the canon was obvious in a penchant for using its idiom with a diligence that often outstripped the aptness of his metaphor. Correctly discerning the gathering storm of controversy over ownership of slaves in South Carolina, he remarked that the "opposition, as yet," seemed "to be only like a cloud rising out of the sea, no bigger than a man's hand." [20] He wrote to a titled English woman: "My heart's desire . . . is that your Ladyship, having put your hand to the plough, may be kept from looking back!" [21] When friends did not arrive on schedule for a visit, he inquired, "Why then tarry their horses? Why are they so long in coming?" [22] Somewhat cryptically, in the days before his marriage he said that he expected "shortly to cry out with the spouse, 'Look not upon me because I am black.' " [23] On at least one occasion he showed inexcusable ignorance and described the veil of the temple as a "curtain that parted the two places, where the Jews and Gentiles worshipped." [24]

It must be remembered, then, that although the Bible was Whitefield's theological authority and norm, it was not necessarily the source of his dogma. His approach to Holy Writ was noncritical and highly subjective. The doctrines that he preached were biblical to the extent that he buttressed them with quotations from scripture, not in the sense that they originated from the Bible. For Whitefield was more likely to begin with the thirty-nine articles and most likely to begin with his own conversion experience.

Whitefield's theology pivoted on a grim conception of the human situation. "Grim" is almost an understatement of his estimate of man's condition. He considered man's will "as directly contrary to the will of GOD, as light is contrary to darkness" and his body "vile indeed! . . . subject to such vile diseases, put to such vile, yea very vile uses, and . . . to come to so vile an end." [25] Preaching on the resurrection of Lazarus, he described the lifeless body of Jesus' friend in too clinical detail and then said to his hearers: "Stop there now, pause a while; . . . this dead, bound, entombed, stinking carcase, is but a faint representation of thy poor soul in its natural state." [26] Throughout his ministry he maintained, even as he had said early in his career, that "Man was half a Devil and half a Beast." [27]

In a preface to the publication of a volume of Whitefield's sermons, Joseph Smith, independent minister of Charleston, South Carolina, pointed out the basic and consistent emphasis which the revivalist laid on man's depravity:

One of the doctrines, which he has hardly passed over in silence in any single discourse, is that of original sin. . . .

By original sin I mean nothing less than the imputation of Adam's first sin to all his posterity by ordinary generation; which imputation is the resultance of his being constituted to act for them in the extensive capacity of a legal representative; the consequence of which is, that inherent corruption of nature, and those sinful propensities, we are now born with into the world.[28]

Whitefield's entry in his *Journal* for July 31, 1739, noted that he preached at Newington from Gen. 3:15, a verse in which the serpent is cursed after Adam and Eve have eaten the forbidden fruit. Whitefield's comment was: "I hope the Seed of the Woman is now bruising the Serpent's Head." [29] Interestingly enough, the sermon on this text was placed first in Whitefield's collected works. In it he expounded at great length on a fall, historic enough to be indicated on the pages of a calendar or the face of a clock, which came as a consequence of man's willful disobedience.

Created by God and placed in a garden of delights, man, according to Whitefield, fell and had no one to blame except himself. Verse by verse the preacher went through the Genesis story of Adam and Eve and exhibited them in an estrangement from God which they had deliberately brought upon themselves:

And what are the consequences of their disobedience? . . . Their eyes are opened; but, alas! it is only to see their own nakedness. . . . Naked of GOD, naked of every thing that was holy and good, and destitute of the divine image.[30]

Not only did man fall, but all nature fell with him:

An unhappy mutiny and disorder then fell upon this world; those briars and thorns which now spring up and overspread the earth, were but poor emblems, lifeless representations of that confusion and rebellion which sprung up in, and overwhelmed, the soul of man, immediately after the fall. He now sunk into the temper of a beast and devil.[31]

Whitefield saw evidence of human depravity wherever he looked. He found the people of his times obsessed with personal and wicked pleasure. "Do *play-houses, horse-racing, balls* and *assemblies,* tend to promote the glory of GOD?" he asked. He wailed bitterly that these frivolities, which were "exceeding sinful," were supported by a public fund.[32] Yet he expected no more of an unregenerate society and told without surprise the story of a dying woman

so fond of gaming, that tho' she had the pangs of death upon her, yet when in the midst of her fits, or just coming out of one, instead of asking after Jesus, where he was to be found, she asked, what is trumps? [33]

Whitefield, however, did not need the corroborating evidence of what he saw in secular society to convince him of the gravity of man's plight. The tragic pattern of sin was woven into the fabric of life itself. He often thought original sin the "reason why little children are seized with such terrible disorders as often carry them out of the world, with ten times more agony than parents feel." It was plain to him that parents could discern corruption in a child as soon as he comes into the world. "Is not this a strong proof that man is fallen from God?" [34] he demanded; there could be no stronger proof of the imputation of Adam's guilt" [35] in Whitefield's opinion. These supporting observations in reality did no more than echo the truth that was written already in the heart of man. Whitefield challenged men to look honestly at themselves and then deny the condemnation of original sin:

I appeal to the experience of the most learned disputer against divine revelation, whether he does not find in himself, that he is naturally proud, angry, revengeful, and full of other passions contrary to the purity . . . of GOD. And is not this a demonstration that some way or other he is fallen from GOD? [36]

It was demonstration enough for Whitefield and reason enough for him to refer to himself over and over again as "hell-deserving." [37]

He looked upon Adam's representation of humanity not only as a fact but as a proper and understandable one. Adam was a real person for Whitefield, whose logic was not the best, but whose position was clear:

Adam fell, and being our federal head, we fell in him. Why, says a Deist, and too many professors also, pray what business had God Almighty to make our fall or our standing depend on another? you will not object to this you church of England men, will you? then why have you god-fathers and god-mothers to promise for you? why have we members of parliament to be the heads of the people, and what the parliament does, the people do, you have constituted them your heads and representatives. . . . O there is not a single man but would have chosen Adam to be their representative . . . ; now pray why should we quarrel with him for acting in the manner we ourselves should have done . . . ? [38]

The doctrine of original sin which Whitefield found so positively attested by his own experience was articulated for him in the articles of the Church of England. Whatever ambiguity others might have found in its articles, Whitefield found none. He said that "was it possible for the compilers . . . to rise again from the Dead . . . they would insist on their being taken in the Grammatical Sense. They cannot . . . admit of a two-fold Interpretation." [39] Their sense was crystal-clear to him. He, accordingly, found it possible to proclaim a radical statement of the doctrine of original sin as the only possible meaning of the statement in Article IX of the Church of England that man after the fall of Adam was "far gone" from original righteousness:

I affirm that we all stand in need of being justified, on account of the sin of our natures: for we are all chargeable with original sin, or the sin of our first parents. Which, though . . . denied by a self-justifying infidel, . . . can never be denied by any one who believes that St. *Paul's* epistles were written by divine inspiration; where we are told, that "in *Adam* all died;" that is, *Adam's* sin was imputed to all: . . . "That we are all . . . by nature the children of wrath." And . . . that "Death came upon all . . . , even upon those, (that is, little children) who had not sinned after the similitude of *Adam's* transgression." . . . So that what has been said in this point seems to be excellently summed up in that article of our church, where she declares, "Original sin . . . is the fault and corruption of every man." [40]

In Whitefield's theology the practical consequence of the fall was man's complete and utter inability to save himself. Man's utmost efforts which he was bound in duty to exert were of nothing worth.[41] "Man is nothing," he wrote: "he hath a free will to go to hell, but none to go to heaven, till GOD worketh in him to will and to do." [42] That was what the young field-preacher was saying in the summer of 1739 when he cried to the multitude: "Every minister should be a *Boanerges,* a son of thunder, as well as a *Barnabas,* a son of consolation. . . . We must first shew people they are condemned, and then shew them how they must be saved." [43] The choice of words was exact, theologically, for it was of prime importance in Whitefield's professed creed that man must "be saved," that he could do nothing to save himself and could no more effect his own salvation than he could "turn the world upside down" or "measure the moon for a suit of clothes." [44] The hopeless inability of man to save himself demanded that he be elected for salvation. Whitefield was prepared to yield to this demand intellectually. Early and late he preached election. In the 1739 sermon on the fall already referred to, Whitefield spoke of the "LORD JESUS . . . in heaven, ruling over all, and causing all things to work for his childrens good." [45] Later, in the autumn of the same year in which he preached on Adam's sin, he wrote that the doctrines of "election, and free justification in CHRIST JESUS," were daily more and more pressed upon his heart.[46]

It was about this time, wrote John Whitehead, in his biography of John Wesley, that

Mr. Wesley printed a sermon against the Calvinistic notion of predestination, and sent a copy to Commissary Garden, at Charlestown, where Mr. Whitefield met with it . . . . though the subject was treated in that sermon, in a general way, without naming or pointing at any individual, yet he found himself hurt, that Mr. Wesley should bring forward the controversy.[47]

During his next passage to England, Whitefield wrote to Charles Wesley, much aggrieved that his brother John's sermon had been published. Whitefield protested his friendship for the Wesley brothers and added: "But I must preach the gospel of Christ, and that I cannot *now* do, without speaking of Election." [48] He never stated his belief in election more positively than in his subsequently published answer to his good friend's sermon on "Free Grace."

Wesley had put his position very succinctly:

Call it by whatever name you please, "election, preterition, predestination, or reprobation," it comes in the end to the same thing. The sense of all is plainly this,—by virtue of an eternal, unchangeable, irresistible decree of God, one part of mankind are infallibly saved, and the rest infallibly damned; it being impossible that any of the former should be damned, or that any of the latter should be saved.[49]

Whitefield's reply was no less unequivocal:

But who ever asserted, that thousands and millions of men, without any preceding offence or fault of theirs, were unchangeably doomed to everlasting burnings? Do not they who believe GOD's dooming men to everlasting burnings, also believe, that GOD looked upon them as men fallen in *Adam?* And that the decree which ordained the punishment, first regarded the crime by which it was deserved? How then are they doomed without any preceding fault? Surely Mr. *Wesley* will own GOD's justice, in imputing *Adam's* sin to his posterity; and also, that after *Adam* fell, and his posterity in him, GOD might justly have passed them ALL by, without sending his own Son to be a saviour for any one. Unless you heartily agree to both these points, you do not believe original sin aright. If you do own them, then you must acknowledge the doctrine of election and reprobation to be highly just and reasonable. For if GOD might justly impute *Adam's* sin to all, and afterwards have passed by all, then he might justly pass by SOME.[50]

Again:

For, without doubt, the doctrine of election and reprobation must stand or fall together.

But passing by this . . . I frankly acknowledge, I believe the doctrine of reprobation, in this view, that GOD intends to give saving grace, through JESUS CHRIST, only to a certain number, and that the rest of mankind, after the fall of *Adam,* being justly left of GOD to continue in sin, will at last suffer that eternal death, which is its proper wages.

This is the established doctrine of scripture, and acknowledged as such in the 17th article of the Church of *England.*[51]

The situation between the two men has been summed up with some wit, and not unfairly, in an imaginary correspondence between them with the following exchange of letters:

Dear George—

I have read what you have written on the subject of predestination, and God has taught me to see that you are wrong and that I am right.

—Yours affectionately,

J. Wesley

Dear John—

I have read what you have written on the subject of predestination, and God has taught me that I am right and you are wrong.

—Yours affectionately,

G. Whitefield [52]

To the end of his days Whitefield did not change his belief concerning predestination. He might regard the death of Governor Belcher and Aaron Burr, president of The College of New Jersey, as dark providences, but they were the providences of God, nonetheless, for Whitefield was committed to a belief that "JESUS lives and reigns." [53]

In the last series of sermons that he preached before leaving England, never to return, George Whitefield was still trumpeting the doctrine of election:

For my own part I know no other doctrine that can truly humble the man; for either God must chuse us, or we must chuse God; either God must be the first mover, or man must be the first mover; either God must chuse them on account of some goodness, on account of some purity, or acts of piety, or God must chuse them merely of his grace, for his own name's sake, and to let us know that we have not chosen him, but he has chosen us. I verily believe, that the grand reason why such doctrine is so spurned at, and hated by carnal people, is, that it strikes at the very root of human pride, cuts the sinews of free-will all to pieces, and brings the poor sinner to lie down at the foot of sovereign grace; and, let his attainments in the school of Christ be ever so great, it constrains him to cry out, Lord, why me! why me! [54]

This was the precise point at which Whitefield's theology was explained—at least in part—by his life. It was not logical that the tavern-keeper's son should have come to Whitefield's pre-eminence. The servitor became "intimate with . . . noblemen, and . . . ladies of quality." [55] The student who was shunned by his fellows at Pembroke saw vast throngs hanging eagerly upon his words, flying to him as *"Doves to the Windows."* Whitefield could only ask himself: "And has not GOD set his seal to our Ministry in an extraordinary Manner?" [56] It was impossible to ignore the obvious implications in this question. Even less could he deny the definitive character of the divine power in his conversion. Of his experience of regeneration he said: "I know the place; . . . whenever I go to Oxford, I cannot help running to that place where Jesus Christ first revealed himself to me, and gave me the new birth." [57] Assurance had come to him after his own best efforts had proved incapable of securing his redemption. In the contemplation of his life Whitefield could not escape the belief in the doctrine of election. Yet Whitefield maintained his position in the knowledge that it was an unpopular one and that men were "afraid to suck it in." [58]

The foundation on which man's salvation rested according to the field-preacher was the imputed righteousness of Christ, who "as GOD . . . satisfied, at the same time that he obeyed and suffered as man." [59] Whitefield's Chalcedonian Christology was self-consciously set forth as central to his preaching in the sermon, "What Think Ye of CHRIST?" in which he said: "If JESUS CHRIST be not very GOD of very GOD, I would never preach the gospel of CHRIST again. . . . It is the divinity of our LORD that gives a sanction to his death." [60] This was the same Christology that he presented in a sermon on "Jacob's Ladder," in which he affirmed that Jesus Christ was "very God, and very man, begotten (and not made) of the Father." [61] Father and Son were for Whitefield "coequal, coessential, coeternal, and consubstantial." [62] It was not difficult to identify Whitefield's position with reference to the person of Christ: he was man and God. This point of view was constant in all that the evangelist said and wrote.

His zeal for the deity of Christ did not sap the vigor with which he maintained the perfect humanity of Jesus. He wrote into the "Observations on Select Passages of Scripture, Turned into Catechetical Questions," his belief that the information of Christ's growing weary was included in Holy Writ for the sake of teaching that Christ was "truly man." [63]

The humanity of Jesus made him for Whitefield a "lamb of GOD's providing indeed . . . to satisfy his own justice, and to render him just in justifying the ungodly." [64] Whitefield found it impossible that any save God himself should satisfy God by his sacrifice, and yet it was mandatory that man should suffer for his own guilt. The ghost of Anselm stood close beside Whitefield as he wrote:

Man is permitted to fall, and become subject to death; but JESUS, the only begotten Son of GOD, begotten of the Father before all worlds, Light of light, very GOD of very GOD, offers to die to make an atonement for his transgression, and to fulfil all righteousness in his stead. And because it was impossible for him to do this as he was GOD, and yet since man had offended, it was necessary it should be done in the person of man; rather than we should perish, this everlasting GOD, this Prince of Peace, this Antient of Days, in the fulness of time, had a body prepared for him by the Holy Ghost, and became an infant. In this body he performed a compleat obedience to the law of GOD; whereby he, in our stead, fulfilled the covenant of works, and at last became subject to death, even death upon the cross; that as GOD he might satisfy, as man he might obey and suffer; and being GOD and man in one person, might once more procure a union between GOD and our souls. [65]

Only in this supreme work of Christ was there any merit, any righteousness which could effect the redemption of man's soul. And Christ's perfect obedience "excluded works, indeed, from being any cause of our justification in the sight of GOD." [66]

Man's effort to "patch up a righteousness" of his own good works was manifestly foolish. "Do you think you are christians," warned Whitefield,

because you lead moral decent lives, do no one any harm, go to church, and attend upon the outward means of grace; no, my brethren, you may do this, and a great deal more, and yet be very far from having a saving, experimental knowledge of JESUS CHRIST. [67]

Man's own righteousness was calculated in Whitefield's opinion to do him no more good than the "fig-leaves did *Adam* and *Eve,* that is, none at all." [68]

Such stringent dogma as this was not always accepted, even from Whitefield. Once in Philadelphia after the distinguished visitor had finished his sermon, a "young Gentleman, once a Minister of the Church of England," stood up and "with a loud Voice, warned the People against the Doctrine," urging in opposition to Whitefield that there "was no such Term as *Imputed Righteousness* in the Holy Scripture." [69] Another man in Virginia confessed that he was shocked to hear Whitefield say that "the best Prayer we ever made in our Lives deserv'd Damnation." [70] Whitefield simply could not suffer heretics on the score of predestination to go unchallenged.

Indeed, it was the basis of Whitefield's quarrel with the established clergy that they fostered the belief that man could by his own good works help to effect his own salvation. Too often, thought Whitefield, clergymen were "blind unregenerate, carnal, luke warm, and unskillful guides," who encouraged men in the delusion that they could lift themselves by their own boot straps.[71] Writing to the religious societies of England, he expressed profound grief that "one of most reputed orthodox prelates in the kingdom, in a late pastoral letter advises his clergy, 'So to explain the doctrine of justification in the sight of GOD by faith only, as to make good works a necessary condition.' " [72]

So passionately did Whitefield disbelieve in the efficacy of man's righteousness that he openly denounced Archbishop Tillotson (who did not see man's role in the drama of salvation as "merely passive") [73] and said that his grace "knew no more of Christianity than Mohamet." [74] This was an estimate that an admiring and respectful public was not prepared to accept regarding a well-loved figure. The populace was unmoved by Whitefield's protestation that his objection was not to Tillotson's personal character but to his books, which —the critic pointed out—Increase Mather had also considered unsound.[75] Whitefield, however, undisturbed by the outraged reaction to his censure of Tillotson, offered the same judgment of the Bishop of London.[76] And his abhorrence of the *Whole Duty of Man* was so great that he "constrained Multitudes of the ignorant unthinking Populace to commit . . . [it] to the Flames, particularly in the city of Philadelphia." [77] The author of this work (supposedly

Richard Allestree) had written in the seventeenth paragraph of the preface that the "SECOND COVENANT was made with Adam and us in him" and that it was composed "of some mercies to be afforded by God, and some duties to be performed by us." [78] This according to Whitefield was "exceeding false divinity," [79] for in his understanding it was only after men had been "brought out of Conceit" about their own righteousness and betaken themselves to the righteousness of Christ that they were saved.[80]

This saving righteousness of Christ was appropriated in an act of faith. But the faith itself according to Whitefield was a gift of God; and it was impossible to come to God, he said, until "God . . . put his faith in us." [81] Before the fall "man had no other will but his Maker's," [82] but since that disaster, depraved humanity could never get near to God in its "own Strength." [83] Not only was the divine choice of man for salvation beyond the capacity of mortals to effect, but salvation itself was the work of God, achieved by a will that could know neither let nor hindrance. Whitefield said it very plainly:

Our Salvation is all of GOD, from the beginning to the end; it is not of works, lest any man should boast: man has no hand in it: it is CHRIST who is to be made to us of GOD the Father, wisdom, righteousness, sanctification, and eternal redemption.[84]

Once chosen of God, however, man was given faith to turn to Christ, and in that faith he was justified.[85]

Whitefield explained lucidly what he meant by justification. It is, he told his hearers,

as though . . . you have your sins forgiven, and are looked upon by GOD as though you never had offended him at all: for that is the meaning of the word justified, in almost all the passages of holy scripture where this word is mentioned. . . . For it is a law-term, and alludes to a judge acquitting an accused criminal of the thing laid to his charge.[86]

This is no more than that which happened when one was born again. Whitefield had no doubts about the reality of regeneration. Moreover he was convinced that the regenerate man knew himself to be such and said of his own situation that he had known it "for about thirty-five years as clear as the sun is in the meridian." [87] But he was frankly at a loss to analyze the miracle: "How this glorious Change is wrought in the Soul, cannot easily be explained. For no One knows the Ways of the Spirit, save the Spirit of GOD himself. Not that this ought to be any Argument against this Doctrine." [88] This much was certain: those who had been born again knew it by a "spiritual, as well as a corporeal feeling." [89] There might be some doubt in the minds of the onlookers, but the subject of regeneration himself could brook no uncertainty. "I know I am justified," said Whitefield, "I believe I shall be sanctified, and am assured I shall be everlastingly redeemed." [90]

The inward witness of Whitefield's own experience was corroborated—as well as that experience could ever be outwardly—by what he saw in the throngs who waited to hear him speak. How could Whitefield doubt the inner working of the Spirit when he saw its operations as plainly as he did? (One man even labeled a chapel where Whitefield spoke a *"Soul-Trap."* [91]) Once as Whitefield was praying, he saw a man "dropp'd down, as tho' shot with a Gun" and was assured by that individual (on asking the reason why) that it was none other than "The Power of God's Word." [92] Whitefield had seen the colonists in New England affected by the hundreds. It had been the same at Cambuslang in Scotland. He could not doubt, therefore, that the Spirit spoke to men's hearts and convicted them of sin. And—which was more important—he had seen sinful creatures not only moved to convulsive tears for their guilt; he had seen them made new creatures in the assurance of being born again.

There was, for instance, the case of a great reprobate, almost

a Scandal and Reproach to human Nature. He used to swear to ease his Stomach, and was so fond of new Oaths that he used to go on Board the Transport Ships, and offer a Guinea for a new Oath, that he might have the Honour of coining it.[93]

This man Whitefield knew to be so completely changed as to be willing to stand "like a Lamb" under persecution and abuse. Or again he saw the fear of death removed from those who knew themselves reborn. Of one such he wrote:

The deceased Earl [of Buchan] died like the patriarch *Jacob;* he laid his hands on, and blessed his children, assured them of his personal interest in JESUS, called most gloriously on the Holy Ghost; cried, Happy! happy! as long as he could speak.[94]

The changed character of these and countless other lives, together with the sporadic nature of the spirit, which manifested itself first in one stratum of society and then in another, left no doubt in Whitefield's mind, not only of the reality of regeneration, but of the abiding truth of the doctrine of election.

For Whitefield being born again meant becoming a participant in God's nature. "And O what a privilege is this!" he exclaimed, "to be changed from beasts into saints, and from a devilish, to be made partakers of a divine nature." [95] The Holy Ghost, who accomplished the new birth, continued to dwell in man. In a world that was "nominally Christian" there was need for no outward miracles, "only an inward Co-operation of the *Holy Spirit* with the *Word.*" [96] But this for Whitefield was only logical. After man became a new creature, he began to act like a new creature. It was in the continuing power of the indwelling Spirit, and out of the knowledge of being justified by faith, that the regenerate man now proceeded to do good works. "The Sum of the Matter," wrote Whitefield,

is this: Christianity includes Morality, as Grace does Reason; but if we are only mere Moralists, if we are not inwardly wrought upon, and changed by the powerful Operations of the Holy Spirit, and our Moral actions proceed from a Principle of a new Nature, however we may call ourselves Christians, it is to be feared we shall be found naked at the Great Day, and in the Number of those, who vainly depend on their own Righteousness, and not on the Righteousness of JESUS CHRIST imputed to and inherent in them, as necessary to their eternal Salvation.[97]

This sentiment was one that Whitefield expressed so vigorously and so often that seventy-five years after his death Jothan Sewall, writing his recollection of the great preacher, recalled how he had exclaimed: "Works carry a man to Heaven! It were not more presumptuous than for a person to undertake to climb to the moon by a rope of sand!" [98]

Once redeemed, man found that

this faith will not be dead, idle or inactive: for 'tis . . . continually exciting the possessor of it to shew it forth by his works; not as necessary conditions, but as proofs of his justification in GOD's sight; and as so many tokens of his gratitude and love for what GOD has done for his soul. This is what the apostle stiles a "Faith working by love." [99]

Having arrived at the point of salvation from the hopeless condition of human nature, man could according to Whitefield turn his face toward heaven. Surely a more specific heaven never beckoned to the faithful, nor a more lurid hell ever frightened the sinful. Whitefield's testimony that heaven was "rather a state than a place" [100] was outweighed by the numerous anthropomorphic details which were scattered through his references to the life beyond.

Heaven, Whitefield told his congregations, would be a place where friends would recognize each other and "know the names of every one mentioned in the book of GOD." [101] Eternity would ring with anthems sung to the music of celestial harps.[102] One of the joys that Whitefield imagined belonging to the elect in heaven was a rehearsing of the circumstances of their conversions. He fancied his own name entering such discussions, for he projected himself into the future and heard some of his erstwhile followers saying:

God begat me to himself by your ministry! what a blessing will it be to hear them say, blessed be God, next to the Spirit I owe my coming here to that servant of thine! and with what ravishment will the minister say, behold me and the children thou hast given me! with what holy triumph will they all then cast their crowns at the foot of the Lamb! [103]

With the unfortunate characteristic that seems chronic to those who depict the world to come Whitefield was infinitely more successful in his representation of hell than of heaven. It is of some significance that one of his sermons was entitled "The Eternity of Hell-Torments." [104] He considered it prudent as well as orthodox to believe in hell; for if there was none, he argued, then he was safe, and if there was, he had believed rightly. In one of his sermons he pictured the dying vision of one who was damned and described the condemned man as saying:

I see hell opened for me, I see the damned tormented, I see such a one in hell that I debauched; in the midst of his agony he said, I am coming to thee, I am coming, I must be damned, God will damn my soul, and died. Take care of jesting with God; there is room enough in hell.[105]

Moreover, Whitefield believed that the damned would have a sight of those in heaven, "to let them know what a heaven, what a Christ, what a glory" they had lost.[106] Again he speculated about poetic justice meted out in punishment for sin:

Bishop Usher's opinion was, and I heartily concur in it, that those who value themselves most on their beauty and dress, and do not love God on earth, will be most deformed in hell, and their bodies suffer proportionally there. There is no dressing in hell, nothing but fire and brimstone there, and the wrath of God.[107]

Such preaching as this surely accounted for some of the numerous instances of the awful silence that accompanied Whitefield's sermons. A population that had not yet rejected the belief in witches would be little disposed to give critical examination to homilies of hell. One can imagine the frightening effect of the following excoriation informed by the magic of the field-preacher's voice:

Let me ask . . . what the devil hath wrought in you; O thou unconverted soul, sin has made thee a beast, made thy body, which ought to be the temple of the living God, a cage of every unclean bird; what hath satan wrought in thee? but made thee a nest of vile stinking swine; and what will he give thee? hell, hell, hell.[108]

His auditories may have winced at his grammar. But they could not miss the point of his belief in a burning hell. "O what will you do," he asked,

when the elements shall melt with fervent heat; when this earth, with all its fine furniture, shall be burnt up; when this archangel shall cry, *time shall be no more!* whither then, ye wicked ones, ye unconverted ones, will ye flee for refuge? O, says one, I will fly to the mountains: O silly fool, O silly fool, fly to the mountains, that are themselves to be burnt up and moved. O, says you, I will flee to the sea; O you fool, that will be boiling like a pot: O then I will flee to the elements; they will be melting with fervent heat. I can scarce bear this hot day, and how can you bear a hot element? . . . Will you fly to the moon? that will be turned into blood: will you stand by one of the stars? they will fall away.[109]

Behind his belief in election and redemption, behind his belief in the God-man Christ and the indwelling Holy Spirit, behind his belief in a heaven of bliss and a hell of eternal torments, Whitefield saw the figure of God, less definite than that of Jesus, less real to him than the Holy Spirit, but guarantor of the whole scheme of his theology, at once its foundation and assurance.

Though he did not often bother to say so explicitly, Whitefield was a trinitarian. His commonest statement of the doctrine occurred in the brief ascriptions of praise which were customarily printed at the end of his published sermons. Typically, these were quite explicit about "our LORD JESUS CHRIST . . . with the Father, and the Holy Ghost, three persons and one eternal GOD." [110] Such an expression rarely appeared in the sermons themselves. The single clearest instance of a doctrine of the Godhead (which, incidentally, comes close to tritheism) was announced in a sermon on "Christians, Temples of the Living GOD." in which Whitefield spoke of God as "Father, Son, and Holy Ghost," and added that

they who once held a consultation to create, are all equally concerned in making preparations for, and effectually bringing about the redemption of man. The Father creates, the Son redeems, and the Holy Ghost sanctifies all the elect people of GOD.[111]

In another sermon he referred to the Father and the Son making a covenant together for the redemption of the elect.[112]

As it has been pointed out, Whitefield, who was not technically entitled to be called a Calvinist, was frank to admit that he embraced the "calvinistical scheme, not because *Calvin*, but JESUS CHRIST" had taught it to him.[113] It was not surprising, therefore, that God appeared as a sovereign in his thought. God was a sovereign, moreover, who gave careful attention to every aspect of human existence. Whatever happened in Whitefield's opinion was accomplished by the will of God consciously directed toward concrete circumstances:

Our minute Philosophers, nay, and our Christians, falsely so called, laugh at the Notion of a particular Providence. But to suppose a general, without holding a particular Providence, is as absurd, as to imagine there can be a Chain without being composed of Links.[114]

God was also, as it were, a celestial bookkeeper with ledgers in which he catalogued all the actions of men. "The Captain observed me a little disordered," Whitefield wrote in his *Journal* of the first voyage to America, "and gave Mr. *H.* a Cordial for me: The good LORD note this Favour in his Book." [115]

Cordial or cyclone, it was all one with Whitefield. Whatever happened was by the specific and merciful providence of God. After a successful passage from England he spoke to his fellow travelers in a typical farewell address, confessing that

> GOD who was in that pillar of a cloud, and pillar of fire, which departed not from the *Israelites,* and who has made the sun to rule the day, and the moon to rule the night, has, by his good providence, directed us in our right way.[116]

It was the same God who was "pleased to bring . . . [Whitefield's] body to the very brink of the grave by convulsions, gravel, a nervous cholic, and a violent fever." [117] Whitefield's inability to understand the ways of providence did not invalidate his belief in the eternal goodness. He was confident that inequalities would be adjusted finally and that at the last day God would "take care to repay" all.[118] Even the question of why some were not elect would in the end, he assured his listeners, "be fully cleared up by methods to us, as yet unknown, because unrevealed. However, this we know, that the judge of all the earth will, most assuredly, do right." [119]

Such, then, was the theology that Whitefield professed. It was also the theology that he preached. But as it was not necessarily the theology that informed his actions, it is now pertinent to consider Whitefield's faith.

Chapter VIII

The Faith of George Whitefield

WHITEFIELD'S professed theological creed was not identical with the vigorous faith by which he lived. To say this is not to charge him with duplicity. It is only to observe that Whitefield was a man and like many men believed what he wanted to believe and did what the exigencies of the moment required, thereby betraying a difference between his *fiducia* and *assensus*. The gap was first apparent in Whitefield's practical attitude toward the Bible.

Theoretically he protested a belief in the Bible as the norm of faith and the directive of life:

If we once get above our Bibles, and cease making the written word of GOD our sole rule, both as to faith and practice, we shall soon lie open to all manner of delusion, and be in great danger of making shipwreck of faith and a good conscience. Our blessed LORD . . . fought the devil with, "It is written." [1]

In Whitefield's opinion each part of the Bible was equally inspired and equally valuable. He was, for example, uncertain and timorous in admitting the superiority of the story of the prodigal son, concerning which he said: "Methinks of all the Parables that *Jesus* ever put forth, that which I have now chosen . . . if it be lawful to compare spiritual things with spiritual, . . . excels other Parables." [2] Within the pages of Holy Writ then, of identical value and abiding worth, was to be found a statement of creed and guidance for "all times, circumstances, and places, though never so minute, never so particular." [3] In Whitefield's theology the Scripture was a guide, a norm, a standard. But in his faith it was an instrument, remarkably adapted to vindicating a pattern of behavior or a point of view. Whitefield's particular approach to the Bible in practical life-situa-

115

tions and the operative technique which he employed are adequately demonstrated in the evangelist's relation to the problem of slavery and the manner in which he was able to support his own position.

Early in his career Whitefield had written a pamphlet bearing the deceptively simple title *A Letter to the Inhabitants of Maryland, Virginia, North and South Carolina* (an obvious restraint in one who frequently adorned the title pages of his publications with an outline of the contents). The essay was an attack upon the colonists of these provinces for their treatment of slaves who according to Whitefield fared worse than their owners' dogs.[4] The date of composition, January, 1740, made it impossible that the sentiment expressed was, as is sometimes thought, the result of a recent visit with Anthony Benezet, the great Quaker abolitionist of Philadelphia. Whitefield was guest of the Benezet family more than once on his visits to America, but not until after May of 1740.[5] The sentiment in this message was, presumably, instinctively Whitefield's own.

"I think God has a quarrel with you," wrote the missionary to the slaveholders. And he charged the colonists with giving their servants over to the "inhuman usage of cruel task-masters, who . . . brought them even to death itself." [6] In this pamphlet Whitefield took no definite stand against slavery as an unchristian institution. The suggestion that it was such, however, might easily have been inferred:

> Whether it be lawful for christians to buy slaves, and thereby encourage the nations from whence they are bought to be at perpetual war with each other, I shall not take upon me to determine; but sure I am it is sinful, when bought, to use them as bad as, nay worse than brutes.[7]

Certainly it was not unlikely that people knowing Whitefield's connection with the Georgia colony would normally have supposed him to be antislavery. At the founding of the colony the trustees had forbidden the ownership or employment of slaves. What was more natural than that Whitefield, who was enthusiastic about this godly haven in the new world, this blessed asylum for all the dispossessed, should have agreed with its founders respecting human bondage?

Yet a year later the man who had made open attack on slaveholding colonists and written them grave admonition regarding the abuses to which the institution was liable was using all his influence to persuade the trustees of Georgia to allow legal slavery in the colony. The reason was clear enough: The Bethesda orphanage could not be run without slave labor. "As for manuring more Land than the hired Servants and great Boys can manage," Whitefield reported in 1741, "I think it is impracticable without a few Negroes." [8] Writing to the trustees of Georgia in 1748, Whitefield, after making various observations about life and labor on the Bethesda plantation, added: "This confirms me in the opinion I have entertained for a long time, that *Georgia* never can or will be a flourishing province without negroes are allowed." [9] Even before slaves were allowed in the colony, the philanthropist bought them for the support of his Orphan-House and was pleased to have them. As early as 1747 he was using the profit of a slave-worked plantation in South Carolina, which he had called *Providence,* for the benefit of Bethesda.[10]

Eventually Whitefield came to the point of writing the following rationale:

However . . . , it is plain to a demonstration, that hot countries cannot be cultivated without negroes. . . . And though it is true, that they are brought in a wrong way from their own country, and it is a trade not to be approved of, yet as it will be carried on whether we will or not; I should think myself highly favoured if I could purchase a good number of them, in order to make their lives comfortable, and lay a foundation for breeding up their posterity in the nurture and admonition of the LORD.[11]

Naturally Whitefield could not hold this position without a scriptural crutch to lean on. The difficulty in finding one was slight. "I hear of some [slaves] that were bought with *Abraham*'s money," he remarked.[12] That, of course, made it all right! Actually Whitefield turned out to be one of the two most influential men in effecting the abrogation of the slave prohibition in the colony of Georgia.[13] He bought slaves himself and used them, and at his death he willed his Negroes, along with his buildings, lands, furniture and books, to the Countess of Huntingdon.[14] But he did this in consistency with Holy Writ, as he understood it, through his practiced ability of bending the scripture to his own necessity.

The length to which Whitefield was capable of going in supporting personal prejudice or advantage by the perversion of a biblical text is evidenced in the following excerpts from his catechism on the scriptures:

Q. What may we learn from the disciples wondering that he [Christ] talked with a woman?

A. That men, especially ministers, ought not too frequently to converse with persons of that sex.[15]

Q. What learn you from CHRIST *bidding them, "Gather up the fragments that remained?"*

A. That we ought to be frugal, though not covetous; and that they will certainly have much to answer for, who waste their whole estates in gaming.[16]

It was not surprising that Whitefield, believing that the Bible offered specific directions for every circumstance, resorted on occasion to sortilege, the practice of casting lots with the Bible in order to secure a specific direction from God. It was never a question as to whether the Bible did or did not have a message for a situation— the problem was to find the verse that applied. Whitefield wrote of a gathering of seven "despised *Methodists*" who met in consultation over "Things of very great Importance," and said frankly, "What we were in doubt about, after Prayer, we determined by Lot." [17]

The practice of divination was not one which Whitefield employed frequently; but he did not disapprove of its proper use and said so: "I am no friend to casting lots; but I believe, on extraordinary occasion, when things can be determined no other way, GOD, if appealed to, and waited on by prayer and fasting, will answer by lot now as well as formerly." [18]

John Wesley had brought sortilege into play when he determined to publish his sermon on "Free Grace." That course of action had elicited an impassioned response from Whitefield, who wrote his old friend an open letter of objection. Whitefield's attack, however, was directed primarily against the doctrinal issue and only incidentally against the casting of a lot, because it had been done unnecessarily:

The case (you know) stands thus: When you was at *Bristol,* I think you received a letter from a private hand, charging you with not preaching the gospel, because you did not preach up election. Upon this you drew a lot: the answer was "preach and print." I have often questioned, as I do now, whether in so doing, you did not tempt the LORD. A due exercise of religious prudence, without a lot, would have directed you in that matter. Besides, I never heard that you enquired of GOD, whether or not election was a gospel doctrine? . . . It is plain you had a wrong lot given you here, and justly, because you tempted GOD in drawing one.[19]

The time came when Whitefield rejected for himself the practice of making a *"lottery of the scriptures,* by dipping into them upon every occasion," but he did not doubt that the technique was still practiced by many good men.[20] Whatever Whitefield's creed about the Bible, his practical faith was in a canon which, at least on occasion, became a sanction for expediency and a device for necromancy.

There were areas, however, in which Whitefield's theology and faith converged and became identical. The idea of God (along with the nature of heaven and hell) was a point at which his creed and practice were at one. God, as God, was remote in Whitefield's faith, even as in his theology, and—perhaps—a little more terrifying. He was the stern judge meting out rewards and (more frequently) punishments. Whitefield saw the hand of God directly contending with the inhabitants of South Carolina when their homes were depopulated by the smallpox and fever and their slaves rose up in arms against them during the years of 1738 and 1739.[21] For Whitefield it was God who chastened men "with whips, or light afflictions" and finding them insufficient, sent "scorpions, or greater trials." [22] In a day when conquest made nations adventurous and colonial prosperity often made them predatory, Whitefield admonished his hearers that a sinful society was often delivered by God into the hands of a foreign invader. And nothing, warned Whitefield, would more provoke God to give men as a prey into the enemy's teeth than impenitence and unbelief.[23]

Against this conception of God, whom Whitefield feared and obeyed, stood an idea of Jesus, whom he worshiped and adored. Jesus was the loving advocate, the savior, the redeemer. When Whitefield thought about God, he was likely to end in ill-defined, ontological mysticism, "skipping over all the intermediate stages of beings," as he said, and reuniting his "own soul to Him from whom it came, and in whose image it was created." [24] But his description of the union with Jesus was explicit, intimate, and personal, sometimes embarrassingly so. "JESUS is a precious Master," he writes in a letter. "He, as it were, dandles me upon his knees. He carries me in his arms." [25] Sometimes Whitefield was confronted with obscurity in God; he was not always able to fathom the divine mind. By contrast, whatever obscurity he found in Christ, he considered as self-imposed, occasioned by his own failure to associate with his Savior. "For CHRIST loves to exercise the faith and patience of his disciples," said Whitefield, "and frequently leaves them to find out his meaning by degrees." [26] The important fact here was not that Christ *might* not be known, only that he *was* not if men did not persist.

Certainly it was neither illogical nor unbecoming that Jesus should hold a prominent place in the faith of one who stood within the Christian community. Yet Whitefield's faith gave unique emphasis to what has sometimes been called *Jesusology*, partly because of a conscious effort to imitate the historic figure of the Gospels and partly because of Whitefield's tendency to see himself in a messianic role—a trait which he exhibited to a marked degree.

Whitefield did not ignore the details of his first venture in outdoor preaching. He pointed out that he spoke to a multitude from a mount in Kingswood.[27] He recognized the implicit similarity between Jesus' following and his own when some of his friends came to call on him in the evening in Charleston: "The Lord, who once came to the eleven by Night, and said Peace be unto you," he remarked on that occasion, ". . . spoke to many of them." [28] Whitefield was convinced that if Jesus were to appear on the eighteenth-century English scene, he would "go about the streets, . . . [and] would be a field-preacher." [29] Naturally the evangelist thought of the persecution and rebuke to which he was subjected in terms of the reproach of Christ, as the Christian community had always done. But it was not his own inclination alone that drew the likeness between Whitefield's life and the life of Jesus.

Once after he had experienced difficulty with the commissary of New York, Whitefield went to services and heard scripture read which the congregation predicated of him: "In the Second Lesson in the Morning were these Verses, and some I found made an immediate Application of them, by looking on me; . . . *And many of them said,*

he hath a Devil *and is mad, why hear ye him?"* [30] Another time in
Rhode Island he returned to his lodgings and the woman of the
house saluted him with "Blessed art thou of the Lord." [31] Nor were
these isolated instances of unusual approval. Edward Ellington,
among the many who preached sermons on the occasion of Whitefield's death, in eulogizing the evangelist, spoke of the "near . . .
Resemblance with his blessed Master." [32]

Whitefield saw himself so completely the earthly advocate of
Christ that he felt privileged to warn his listeners that they should
meet him again on the last day: "I summon you," he said, ". . . to
meet me at the judgment-seat of CHRIST, that you may acquit both
my Master and me." [33] Seemingly he saw no impropriety in imper-
sonating Christ in a long exhortation to sinners. It is impossible to
imagine that Whitefield with his skillful sense of theater neglected
any dramatic possibilities when addressing a throng of people in an
impassioned plea of which the following words are only a part:
"Behold my hands and my feet! Look, look into my wounded side,
and see a heart flaming with love." [34]

Whitefield's faith was characterized by the distinctive emphasis
which the field-preacher laid on the historical Jesus. It was by reason
of this stress, therefore, different in a measure from his theology. But
there was real divergence between Whitefield's creed and faith in the
doctrines of election and justification. The plain fact seems to be
that Whitefield lived in the faith that a man himself might turn to
God. Moreover, the unrelieved predestination that he preached,
in which a man had no free will but to sin, was shot through with
enough optimism that the perceptive hearers who stood under
Whitefield's spell might well have refused to abandon completely a
belief in their own abilities.

On hasty examination Whitefield's sermons and writings seem to
say without qualification that there is no ability in man to turn to
God. This is exactly the impression that men often got when they
heard him preach, too. The eager New Englander who rode twelve
miles in little more than an hour in order to hear the renowned
preacher had no doubt about the center of Whitefield's theology.
He wailed:

my old foundation was broken up & i saw that my righteousness
would not save me then i was convinced of ye doctrine of Election

121

& went right to quareling with god about it because all that i could do would not save me & he had decreed from Eternity who should be saved & who not i began to think i was not Elected & that god made some for heaven & me for hell & i thought god was not Just in so doing i thought i did not stand on even Ground with others if as i thought i was made to be damned my heart then rose against god exceedigly [*sic*] for his making me for hell now this distress lasted almost two years.[35]

Whitefield has left records, full and plenty, of such sermons as might easily have driven a man to despair. Surely many who heard him felt the blood run cold and believed themselves hopelessly damned. "I intreat you to come," Whitefield begged, and continued, "but I know no one can come, unless the Father draw him: I will therefore address me to my GOD, and intercede with him to send the Comforter into your hearts." [36] More than one person was brought under conviction from hearing such prophecy as this. Whitefield mentioned once having received in a period of a fortnight almost two hundred letters from people in whose souls the arrows of conviction stuck fast.

Without doubt some people did leave Whitefield's services near-mad with the thought of sins unforgiven and souls unredeemed. He admitted as much. "And supposing some of these multitudes should be unhinged, terrified, distracted, or disturbed a little," he demanded. "Is it not better they should be thus unhinged from off their false foundation here," than that they should go to hell? [37] Surely this is the logic that lies behind his observation of being refreshed on hearing of a poor girl found sitting at his gate in the cold who had followed him home after hearing him preach and remained there for some time crying that "she wanted nothing but Christ." [38] The point here is not that his hearers were convinced of man's inability. The question is whether that was the faith of the preacher. The evidence suggests that it was not.

There was a deep and abiding optimism that informed all of Whitefield's sermons and sparked the feverish activity of his busy life. He never denied the pain of the new birth, only the despair of the heart that believed it beyond attainment:

It must be owned, indeed, that it is a great and difficult Work; but, blessed be GOD, it is not impossible. Many Thousands of happy souls have been assisted by a Divine Power to bring it about, and why should *We* despair of Success? [39]

Ever after his experience at Cambuslang, Whitefield happily recalled the turbulent days there and described them to his congregations. "I remember once I was preaching in Scotland, and saw ten thousand effected in a moment," he said, "some with joy, others crying I cannot believe." [40] Yet the end of the recollection was of the salvation of those who conquered after the bitter experience. With unanswerable logic Whitefield inquired why any should despair if men so convicted could come into the joy of the new birth.

Whatever others thought of him, Whitefield knew that his work was not to disturb men and leave them so, but to bring them and help them bring themselves into the community of the saints. "The distracting people's minds to such a degree as to occasion sudden roarings, agonies, screamings, tremblings, dropping-down, ravings and such like," he wrote, "is by no means the great end proposed." [41] In a desperate effort to bring all who heard him into the liberty of the gospel, Whitefield at times entreated people, in words that left little doubt of his faith, that they themselves could, if they would, turn their hearts to God. He advised them that opportunity was at hand:

O poor souls, that hast been never cast down. . . . Methinks I see the heavens opened, the Judge sitting on his throne, the sea boiling like a pot, and the Lord Jesus coming to judge the world; well, if you are damned, it shall not be for want of calling after. O come, come. [42]

Here Whitefield was plainly implying that subsequently none who had heard him could plead not having had the privilege of coming to Christ. That is but another way of saying that they could if they would. Again, he pictured the day of judgment and saw himself reluctantly testifying against those who heard him and turned away, who did "not improve the divine mercies" and thereby had forced him to "appear as a swift witness against" them. [43]

Completely in character, Whitefield cried out: "I beseech you, therefore, O sinners, be ye reconciled to GOD," [44] with the import that the sinners could themselves effect the agreement. His invitations to accept Christ were clear and democratic: "I invite you all to come to him and receive him as your LORD and Saviour; he is ready to receive you: if you are afraid to go because you are in a lost condition, he came to save such." [45] "Do not say I preach despair," he warned: "I despair of no one, when I consider GOD had mercy on such a wretch as I." [46] He pleaded with incandescent ardor: "Can you bear to think of a bleeding, panting, dying JESUS, offering himself up for sinners, and . . . not accept of him?" [47] He begged men fervently not to "harden" their hearts or "oppose the will" of Jesus. And like a recruiting sergeant drumming up volunteers, he cried "Come, come, if your soul is for Christ, to arms, to arms, put on your cockades, you that have them in your pockets, for fear you should be known to be Christ's." [48] "We don't chuse to come to Christ," he proclaimed, "because we don't chuse to have him as a free gift; we don't like to come to him as poor and needy." [49]

Perhaps Whitefield gave the single most startling instance of faith in man's ability to turn himself toward God in a sermon on the "Marks of Having Received the Holy Ghost." In it he declared that an individual was known to be marked by the Spirit of God when he had a spirit of supplication, an aversion to sin, a spirit of conquest over the world, and a love for others. To this analysis of the Signet of the Holy Ghost, Whitefield added—unbelievable for a Calvinist! —that "whosoever upon an impartial examination, can find the aforesaid marks on his soul, may be as certain, as though an angel was to tell him, that his pardon is sealed in heaven." [50]

What Whitefield said in a variety of ways (as the above instances illustrate) was that man could help to save himself, that his salvation was not utterly dependent on the divine decree of election. Whitefield even went so far as to say that a man should turn to Christ without bothering his head over predestination, and he quoted the eminent Dr. Isaac Watts—philosopher, poet, theologian —in support of his view:

Dr. Watts . . . says "we should go first to the grammar-school of faith and repentance, before we go to the university of presdestination:" whereas the devil would have them go first to the university, to examine whether they were elected or rejected, or no.[51]

Christianity for Whitefield was not a matter of reasoning and logic. The knowledge of salvation came through the heart, not the mind. "I may know I am beloved of the Lord," Whitefield exclaimed. This certainty arose through "experiencing *his love*," [52] and that love was available to those who chose to have it and thereby entitle themselves to "live and reign with him for ever." [53]

The man whose orphic voice charmed the thousands who came to hear his sermons did speak, it is true, of election beyond man's ability. Scattered through his messages, however, there were indications that he believed the picture not so dark as hyper-Calvinism would have it. The implicit, and often articulate, optimism of the field-preacher's sermons was more impressive in the light of the actual pattern of his life.

Whitefield spent his life, quite literally, proclaiming the gospel. He preached some eighteen thousand times during the course of his ministry.[54] The gospel for him was undeniably good news, not a frightening message. "But I will tell you of the love of GOD, the love of GOD in CHRIST," he said, "and surely that must compel you, that must constrain you, whether you will or not." [55] This message which people might hear *and* receive he preached at the expense of his physical well-being. His letters contain such frequent references to poor health and sickness that the reader becomes accustomed, almost calloused, to such observations as this: "By thoughtfulness, frequently preaching, and a crazy tabernacle [that is, his *body*], my nightly rests are continually broken." [56] Deliberately driving himself, Whitefield exchanged the "pretty Preferment" he might have had in a less demanding career in England for the rigorous existence of itinerant preaching and restless moving between two continents. He did so not simply because he felt his message true. Instinctively he knew that his preaching was a means of saving the souls of men. In other words, if men heard the truth, they could accept it. He intended to give as many as possible that opportunity.

Such a conviction of man's ability to co-operate with God in the salvation of his own soul lay behind actions of Whitefield that are easily misunderstood otherwise. His advertising of his own speaking engagements was vulgar when measured by the standard of propriety. Chauncy found it so and complained bitterly. "Might he not be too much encouraged . . . from the *popular Applauses*," he asked, and continued:

If he had not been under too strong a Bias from something or other of this Nature, why so fond of preaching always himself, to the Exclusion, not of his *Brethren* only, but his *Fathers*, in Grace and *Gifts* and *Learning*, as well as *Age?* And why so ostentatious and assuming as to alarm so many Towns, by proclaiming his Intentions, in the *publick Prints*, to preach such a Day in such a *Parish*, the next Day in such a one, and so on, as he past through the Country; and all this, without the Knowledge, either of *Pastors* or *People* in most Places? [57]

Although the nature of itinerant preaching made it necessary that some sort of announcement be given to folk that they might have opportunity to hear, Whitefield's brash and unblushing techniques of publicity were in questionable taste. Yet his behavior was defensible in the light of Whitefield's sense of the frantic immediacy of opening the door of salvation for men. He was compelled to tell them of the times of his preaching, just as he was compelled to preach to them. What matter that men called him mad? He called God to witness that he did not grumble. Immortal souls were at stake. It not only was admissable, it was mandatory, for him to trumpet the news of the gospel far and wide; and any means of confronting sinners with the truth was good. Thus Whitefield could advertise his preaching schedule—almost blatantly—or he could stop in the midst of a sermon to tell his hearers that the angry storm raging without was but the voice of a wrathful God. [58] Somehow he must catch and hold the attention of men and make them know that the gospel was for them. Such actions stemmed from the faith of a man who believed that human effort could avail.

Whitefield's letters contained numerous prayers expressing his deep longing for more time, more opportunity to preach. He cried for a thousand tongues and meant it literally. "O for more time," he pleaded, "and if possible for more souls and bodies! LORD JESUS, twenty times ten thousand are too few for thee." [59] He would have preached a "hundred times a day" had it been a physical possibility. [60] His passionate belief in the power of God did not invalidate his profound faith in the ability of man. He thought the two might work together toward man's salvation. The high destiny of the prophet was to proclaim this eternal truth. It was impossible for Whitefield to preach in all the quarters where this gospel must be told, and impossible to enlist enough companions to spread the message. He poured out his soul in a letter:

O for more labourers. I am told thousands went away last *Sunday* evening from *Tottenham-Court,* for want of room. Every day produces fresh accounts of good being done, and at this end of town the word runs and is glorified more and more.[61]

When he met with people in America imploring him "for CHRIST's sake stay and preach to us," he more than ever wanted a thousand lives [62] This was plainly the prayer of a man who thought that there was some point to his preaching—that it did some good, that it was the means of serving men notice of eternal truth which, having heard, they might appropriate for themselves.

Because he despaired of none, and because he thought any could turn to the love of God, Whitefield addressed any ear, willing or not, with his burning words. He strove with criminals under the very shadow of the gallows. It was not unusual to see men riding to their death "tossing up who should sit on the right hand in the cart"; but those hapless creatures who chose to could listen to Whitefield offering them the chance of heaven, if he had learned of their scheduled execution and if he could reach the fated place in time.[63] He also directed a word to those who had come to watch the public hangings. "A very peculiar providence led me lately to a place, where a horse stealer was executed," he wrote, and continued:

Thousands attended. The poor criminal had sent me several letters, hearing I was in the country. The sheriff allowed him to come and hear a sermon under an adjacent tree. Solemn, solemn! After being by himself about an hour, I walked half a mile with him to the gallows. His heart had been softened before my first visit. He seemed full of solid divine consolations. An instructive walk. I went up with him into the cart. He gave a short exhortation. I then stood upon the coffin, added, I trust, a word in season, prayed, gave the blessing, and took my leave.[64]

This was indeed the essential Whitefield, improving every occasion to preach the gospel, and proclaiming a message which said often by its content and always by its manner and its information that man, any man, every man, could turn to God by his own effort.

An inescapable coimplicate of Whitefield's position on the human ability was his estimate of the value of man's "good works." The ideal of preaching, he said, was to labor "to bring people to a real faith in CHRIST as the LORD their righteousness, and then exhort those that believe, to be careful to maintain and shew forth their faith, by a constant uniform performance of all manner of good works." [65] Whitefield stoutly maintained that the fundamental point at which the Protestant churches differed from Rome was in pleading for "free justification in the sight of GOD, by faith alone, in the imputed righteousness of JESUS CHRIST, without any regard to works, past, present, or to come." [66] But as a matter of fact, he did not reckon men "real converts" until he saw "them bring forth fruits of the Spirit, in doing justly, loving mercy, and walking humbly with their GOD." [67] Moreover, he told them of the unspeakable joy and consolation with which they in heaven would "look back on . . . past sincere and hearty Services, which have procured us so invaluable a Reward!" [68] George Whitefield called his "preaching, praying, &c . . . only *splendida peccata*," [69] but his censure was not convincing. For he saw the Christian life in terms of specific things that were and were not done. Nothing in his view was more certain than that all were to "appear before the judgment-seat of CHRIST, to be rewarded according to the deeds done in the body." [70]

The legalistic conception of the Christian life was evidenced in a score of ways in Whitefield's life and writings. For instance, he spoke approvingly and in glowing terms of the Pharisaical conception of the Sabbath that bound the people of Boston:

> I know of no place upon the face of the earth where the Sabbath is kept as it is in Boston: if a single person was to walk in Boston streets in time of worship, he would be taken up; it is not trusted to poor insignificant men, but the justices go out in time of worship, they walk with a white wand, and if they catch any persons walking in the streets, they put them under a black rod.[71]

Foreseeing the final judgment for eternal life or everlasting death not in terms of faith but with regard to the record of men's deeds, he demanded of his congregation, "Which will stand you best at the day of judgment, so much money expended at a horse-race, at a cockpit, at a play or masquerade, or so much given for the relief of your fellow-creatures?" [72] Whitefield also fulminated against specific sins and so spelled out the errors of commission that it is hard to free him from the charge of Pharisaism. Theaters, those "nurseries of debauchery," were targets for special attack, for they were the "bane of true christianity." [73] The insights of modern psychology make this attitude in Whitefield easily understood in the light of his early love for the stage and the histrionic devices which he used in preaching. His onslaught got results. The following quotation from one of Whitefield's letters needs no comment:

At *Glasgow*, the man who owned the playhouse was made so uneasy by the word preached, that he took down the roof himself. For this Satan owes me a grudge, and therefore it is put in the paper, that a mob was raised.[74]

There were other objects of his righteous wrath. He scored the attendance on "Balls and Assemblies, and all other polite Entertainments." [75] He regretted the "too, too frequent noise of *box and dice*, at the unlawful games of hazard and back-gammon" [76] and railed against "revelling, cock-fighting, and such like." [77]

The success with which this approach to the good life met is indicated by two notices from the public press. The first appeared in the *Virginia Gazette* under a London date line and is in obvious response to Whitefield's particularly galling attack on woman's susceptibility to fad and fashion:

Several fine Ladies who used to wear French Silks, French Hoops of 4 yards wide, Tete de Mouton Heads, (or Bob Wigs) and white Satin Smock-Petticoats, &c. are turned *Methodist,* and Followers of Mr. Whitefield, whose Doctrine of *the New Birth* has so prevail'd over them, that they now wear plain Stuff Gowns, no Hoops, common Night Mobs, and plain Bays for *Jenny's.*[78]

The other notice, leaving no question about certain emphases in Whitefield's sermons preached to throngs at Philadelphia in the spring of 1740, was published by Benjamin Franklin:

Since Mr. Whitefield's preaching here, the Dancing School, Assembly and Concert Room have been shut up, as inconsistent with the Doctrine of the Gospel: And though the Gentlemen concern'd caus'd the Door to be broke open again, we are inform'd that no Company came the last Assembly Night.[79]

The material here introduced indicates no unique quality of Whitefield's faith or personal religion, nor is it intended to. Such a conception of Christianity as is implied by the evidence above was no more unusual in the eighteenth century than it is in the twentieth. But Whitefield's preoccupation with the legalistic does demonstrate that although the evangelist put so little theological emphasis on laws and good works that he was called an Antinomian (a position— incidentally—which was particularly abhorrent to him),[80] his practical faith was informed by an abiding conviction that the works of man were of great worth. The practices against which he inveighed were both those which he called positively debauching per se, at which a modest heathen would blush, and

those seemingly innocent entertainments and meetings, which the politer part of the world are so very fond of, and spend so much time in: but which, notwithstanding, keep as many persons from a sense of true religion, as doth intemperance, debauchery, or any other crime whatever.[81]

It was important, therefore, to eschew the ways of the world not alone because they were evil, but because they kept men from engaging in the works of love. For his own part Whitefield was forever busy with doing the works of mercy.

The charitable and humanitarian projects to which Whitefield gave himself have already been mentioned. He did not claim any distinction in this respect, freely acknowledging, for example, that the original idea for Bethesda was not his own: "Some have thought, that the erecting such a building was only the produce of my own brain; but they are much mistaken. It was first proposed to me by my dear friend the reverend Mr. *Charles Wesley*." [82] What he did was no more than men were doing in other parts of the English-speaking world in the mid-eighteenth century. Between 1720 and 1745 Guy's, Westminster, London, and Middlesex hospitals were all founded in England.[83] Thomas Coram, a retired captain of the merchant marine, who for years had agitated the project of a foundling home, saw such an institution opened in 1745 under the charter of George II and adorned with a painting by Hogarth and an organ that was the gift of Handel.[84] Society had broken out in a rash of philanthropy. The point here insisted is that Whitefield, who was no more than a man of his times as he worked for the care of orphans or the education of youth, believed that these works might —in a measure—justify man before the face of God.

In the last series of sermons which he preached in England, Whitefield stated again his position on faith and works:

I tell you the truth, I am against good works, don't run away before I have finished my sentence; we are against good works being put in the room of Christ, as the ground of our acceptance; but . . . our faith will work by love. Ever since I was a boy, I remember to have heard a story of a poor indigent beggar, who asked a clergyman to give him his alms, which being refused, he said, will you please, sir, to give me your blessing; says he, God bless you: O, replied the beggar, you would not give me that if it was worth any thing. There are many who will talk very friendly to you, but if they suppose you are come for any thing, they will run away as from a pick-pocket.[85]

Here at the very end of his life Whitefield was still saying that works were of nothing worth and adding immediately that they were the certain, possibly essential, index of faith! This parting word he delivered as he started toward America, eager to make a college of Bethesda in order to educate the pious youth of the colony. Whitefield preached a theology in which a totally depraved man was unable to effect his salvation and powerless to resist the pull of electing love. He professed a creed of justification by faith alone. But the faith by which he lived was a lively conviction that man could do much to aid in working out his own salvation. The chronic dilemma of the Calvinist who seeks to justify the validity of his preaching to a humanity that can respond only to the voice of God, Whitefield solved uniquely: he professed Calvinism, lived by an Arminian faith, and preached them both. "It was a maxim in the first reformers time, that though the *Arminians* preached up good works," he said, "you must go to the *Calvinists* for them." [86] In both his writings and his works Whitefield labored to prove this maxim true and identified himself with both positions. The heart of his theology was man's inability. The heart of his faith was man's free will.

The concepts of heaven and hell in Whitefield's theology were identical with those that informed his faith. There was a difference, however, between the practical and theoretical entrance fee. Theoretically, one was given heaven in faith. Actually, faith seemed for Whitefield to have been an available option which afforded man the opportunity to merit salvation. God was a bookkeeper, and the record of one's life determined his future. Both points of view were nicely combined in a quotation from his lecture on "The Prodigal Son." It seems fitting as a concluding comment on Whitefield's faith: "I know you cannot come of yourselves. Are you willing to come? O then, God shall send his Spirit to bring you home, and meet you half-way." [87]

Chapter IX

Conflict Within the
Christian Community

THE Christian community of the eighteenth century, through which Whitefield cut so wide a swath, regarded him variously, but rarely with apathy and usually with prejudice too deep to admit of an objective judgment. It was not a difficult thing to be controversial about religion in those days. Many men were. A traveler of the time says that in England, Christianity was overwhelmed with sects, including—among others—Antinomians, Hederingtonians, Theaurian Joanites, Seekers, Waiters, Brownists, Reevists, Baronists, Wilkinsonians, Familists, Ranters, and Muggletonians.[1] The situation suggests the proverbial French criticism of the English, that they were a people with a hundred religions and only one sauce.

If it was easy then to be controversial about religion, it was even simpler to be controversial about Whitefield. He expressed himself freely, and frequently in such a way that those who heard him could not ignore the fiery revivalist. And though many were rising up early in the morning to hear him speak the word, others were calling him "Dog" and saying he "ought to be whipped at the Cart's Tail." [2]

Many of the clergy of the Church of England took exception to the field-preacher for the quite understandable reason that he vilified them publicly and charged them with being guilty of every fraction of the moral code. Moreover, he did so while he was "wearing ye Garb of her children . . . with solemn declarations of his esteem and admiration" for the church! [3] The clergy, said Whitefield,

frequent play-houses, they go to horse-races, they go to balls and assemblies, they frequent taverns, and follow all the entertainments that the age affords; . . . but, my dear brethren, observe they always go disguised, the ministers are afraid of being seen in their gowns and cassocks; the reason thereof is plain, their consciences inform them, that it is not an example fit for the ministers of the gospel to set.[4]

In this gross hypocrisy, said Whitefield, they were concerned only that the orange women might not know them, and they did not care whether God saw them or not.[5]

But the clergy according to the field-preacher were guilty of worse than sinking into turpitude themselves. They caused others to stumble, and that was monstrous; for Whitefield was convinced that the "greatest curse that God can possibly send upon a people in this world, is to give them over to blind, unregenerate, carnal, lukewarm and unskilful guides." [6] Whitefield had no doubt that on the last day many of the worldly priests would stand "confounded, whilst the poor despised *faithful Ministers* of CHRIST . . . enter[ed], after all their tribulation, into the joy of their LORD." [7] Meanwhile he did not hesitate to censure the faithlessness of the clergy. When he was in New York on his second visit to the colonies, he attended service in an Established church and recorded in his *Journal* great despair over what he found there:

> Went to the *English* Church, both Morning and Evening, and felt my Heart almost bled within me, to consider what blind Guides were sent forth into her. If I have any regard for the Honour of Christ, and Good of Souls, I must lift up my Voice like a Trumpet, and shew how sadly our Church ministers are fallen from the Doctrines of the Reformation. Her Prophets prophesy *Lies*, and I fear many of the People love to have it *so*.[8]

For his own part Whitefield was convinced that in both America and England there were "wolves in sheeps cloathing" [9] mixed in with the faithful ministers. It was of such men that he said boldly, "they cannot preach with the demonstration of the Spirit and with power, unless they preach from experience, and have had a proof of his [Christ's] divinity, by a work of grace wrought upon their own souls." [10] Unless he saw evidence of such a work of grace, Whitefield was likely—as he did in Boston—to take his leave of them on "finding how inconsistent they were." [11]

Whitefield's passion for doctrinal purity directed him to speak disapprovingly of men who were quite respectable morally. John Tillotson, late archbishop of Canterbury, had been a man of spotless reputation, "as lovable as he was learned," [12] and it was, therefore, a double outrage to the clergy of the established church to hear Whitefield announce:

My affirming that Archbishop Tillotson knew no more of Christianity than Mahomet, has been look'd upon as one of the most unjustifiable Expressions that ever proceeded out of my Mouth: . . . I have and do now . . . upon the maturest Deliberation, say again what I have often said before, That Archbiship Tillotson knew no more about true Christianity than Mahomet.[13]

The clergy, thus attacked, retaliated in kind. The most obvious charge which they brought against Whitefield (and the easiest to sustain) was that of enthusiasm. This was a grave accusation in the eighteenth century, for the current usage made the culprit at once suspect as to his sanity and susceptible to ridicule. Dr. Johnson's definition of *enthusiasm* as a "vain belief of private revelation; a vain confidence of divine favor or communication" [14] seemed a perfect description of Whitefield to his enemies. Early observers of the field-preacher had speculated about his possible lunacy. The publication of his *Journals* made the matter quite clear to many: Whitefield was a madman. Bishop Lavington referred frequently to the *Journals* of Whitefield in his *Enthusiasm of Methodists and Papists Compared*. He concluded that the kind of religion practiced and fostered by Whitefield was a conglomerate of shoddy and said that

this *new dispensation* is a *Composition* of *Enthusiasm, Superstition,* and *Imposture.* When the blood and spirits run *high,* inflaming the brain and imagination; it is most properly *Enthusiasm;* which is *Religion run mad:*—when *low and dejected,* causing groundless terrors, or placing the *great duty of man* in little Observances; 'tis *Superstition,* which is *Religion scared out of its Senses:*—when any fraudulent dealings are made use of, and any wrong projects carried on under the mask of piety; 'tis *Imposture,* and may turmed Religion turned *Hypocrite.*[15]

More serious than Lavington's attack had been the earlier one in 1739 by Edmund Gibson, bishop of London, who in his seventieth year wrote a pastoral letter warning the people of his diocese against *lukewarmness* on the one hand and *enthusiasm* on the other.[16] The greater part of this work was devoted to a consideration of enthusiasm among the Methodists, who were charged with nine specific offenses, such as claiming extraordinary guidance or special inspiration from the Holy Ghost. These accusations were supported exclusively by quotations from Whitefield's *Journals*. Gibson was a careful student, the greatest authority in Engand on church law. He was also celebrated for his goodness. That a man of his erudition and piety (whose published letters to this point had been only three in number and concerned with the "Defence of the Gospel-Revelation, and by way of Preservative against the late Writings in favour of Infidelity")[17] should take particular notice of Whitefield is proof of the enormous excitement that the young man had created. The burden of the bishop's attack on Whitefield may be reduced to the denunciation of Whitefield's pretense to preferment as a special sort of Christian. The good Bishop made a strong case.[18]

Whitefield's answer appeared only twelve days after the bishop's letter was published. He agreed with the prelate that "Lukewarmness and enthusiasm . . . [were] certainly the bane of true Christianity," but he thought it most unlikely that he was guilty of either.[19] He said that he "never did pretend to these extraordinary operations or working miracles, or speaking with tongues";[20] rather he had claimed only the ordinary operation of an indwelling spirit which, according to the teaching of the Thirty-nine Articles, he considered the portion of all believers. He admitted to meekness only. "My constant way of preaching," he wrote, "is first, to prove my propositions by scripture, and then to illustrate them by the articles and collects of the church of *England*."[21] And as for the irregularity of surprising effects which resulted from his preaching, Whitefield expressed incredulity that the bishop had been a minister "so many years, and . . . never seen any sudden or surprising effects, consequent" upon his own preaching.[22] To the bishop's exception over Whitefield's rashly censuring the clergy for their practice, the lately ordained priest said that he had never had any ministers in mind except his "indolent, earthly-minded pleasure-taking brethren."[23] Here, of course, Whitefield had his point, for the established clergy of eighteenth-century England became a byword for worldliness and lethargy. In addition to correcting Whitefield for his enthusiasm and reprimanding him for his denunciation of the clergy, the bishop had strenuously objected to his professing to "propagate a new Gospel, as unknown to the generality of ministers and people, in a christian country." [24] To this charge Whitefield pleaded guilty and indicated that he preached the true gospel of salvation by grace which was new to men because they had been misled by an irresponsible or unregenerate clergy. He even said that the bishop "could not well be guilty of a greater inconsistency" than in his position of professing a belief in justification by faith and exhorting his priests to commend good works as a necessary condition to salvation.[25]

The time came when the chief objection the Church of England made to Whitefield was that of his being an itinerant. Whitefield was never more aggrieved than in answering such a cavil:

They say, it is not regular our going out into the Highways and Hedges, and compelling poor Sinners to come in. We ought not so to beseech them to be reconciled to GOD. They desire to know by what Authority we preach, and ask, what Sign shewest thou that thou dost these Things? But alas! what further Sign would they require? We went not into the Fields till we were excluded the Churches.[26]

Attacked on this score in an anonymous pamphlet which he supposed also written by the Bishop of London, Whitefield said proudly that if preaching in the fields was to "be vile," then he chose to "be more vile." [27] Whitefield ignored such practical objection as complaint over the damage that the terrain suffered from his hearers, those

Multitudes of the Rabble from all Parts [who] . . . in their March back [from preaching service], committed such Devastations in the Farmers Grounds, by breaking up Inclosures, trampling down the Grain, pilfering Turneps, &c. that the Estates, for a few Miles round *London,* were in a manner ruined by them.[28]

And as for the illegality of gathering in the fields to hear preaching, the evangelist said that laws incorrectly interpreted as applying to such a situation were intended only "to supress *seditious conventicles,"* and to thwart the plots of *"disloyal persons,* who, under pretence of tender consciences, have, or may, at their meetings *contrive insurrection."*[29] It was axiomatic, in fact, with Whitefield that real religion and true patriotism were inseparable, even though the irreligious and disloyal could not perceive the union: "The devil always wants to make it believed that God's people, who are the most loyal people in the world, are rebels to the government under which they live." [30] If itinerant preaching were breaking the law, Whitefield insisted, then all ministers who exchanged pulpits were equally irregular, at least as real violators of their ordination commission as these journeying preachers.[31] In the following summary and apology for the itinerants the put-upon Whitefield implied pointedly that the objection to their field-preaching was not primarily over its legality:

> And being without cause denied the use of their brethren's pulpit . . . they [the itinerants] continue to this day, witnessing. . . . In doing thus, they know of no "wholesome rules, wisely and piously established by the powers spiritual and temporal," which they have violated. And though for so doing, they should be mobbed, as they frequently have been . . . yet they know of one who was mobbed himself upon a like account, and commanded *Timothy* to approve himself a minister of GOD *in tumults.* Being sensible of the indolence and unorthodoxy of the generality of the clergy, they think they are sufficiently warranted by the example of the Prophets of the Old, and of JESUS CHRIST and his Apostles in the New-Testament . . . to bear a faithful testimony against them. And being called by the Providence of GOD abroad, after their unworthy labours had been blessed at home, they have judged it meet, right, and their bounded duty, from time to time, to publish accounts of what GOD had done for their own and other people's souls: which, though despised by some, and esteemed enthusiastical by others, have been owned to the instruction and edification of thousands. But whether this may be properly called "open and public boasting, unbecoming the modesty and self-denial of a minister of the gospel, especially one who would be thought to carry on his ministry under the immediate guidance of the blessed Spirit," . . . or whether they were written with a single eye to the Redeemer's glory, they are willing to leave to the determination of that GOD, to whom all hearts are open.[32]

The disputation with the Church of England that like a nimbus surrounded Whitefield all his days was dramatized in his conflict with Alexander Garden, Commissary of South Carolina, Rector of St. Philip's in Charleston.[33] When the two first met, the representative of the Bishop of London received the young prophet "in a most Christian Manner" and was "more than civil" to him. At that time Whitefield had stopped in Charleston as he was returning to England to take priest's orders. The parishioners of Garden, too, hospitably brought Whitefield presents of "Wine, Ale, Cake, Coffee, Tea, and other Things proper" for his passage. That was in the summer of 1738.[34]

Their paths did not cross again until the spring of 1740, and—considering what had happened in the interim—it is not to be wondered at that Whitefield met with a cool reception. The interview between the commissary and the firebrand is reproduced from Whitefield's own account, the details of which are richly suggestive of the intensity of the raging quarrel:

Friday, March 14. Arrived last Night at *Charles-Town.* . . . Waited on the Commissary . . . but met with a cool Reception.—After I had been there a little while, I told him that I was informed he had some Questions to propose to me, and that I was now come to give him all the Satisfaction I could in answering them.—Upon this I immediately perceived Passion begin to arise in his Heart.—Yes, Sir, says he, I have several Questions to put to you.—But, added he, you are got above us, . . . Then he charged me with Enthusiasm and Pride, for speaking against the generality of the Clergy, and desired I would make my Charge good. —I told him I thought I had already: But as yet I had scarce begun with them—He then asked me where in the Clergy were so much to blame?— I answered, they did not preach up Justification by Faith alone: And upon talking with the Commissary, I found he was as ignorant of it as any of the rest.—He then sneer'd me with telling me of my Modesty. . . . Charged me with breaking Canons and Ordination Vow: And notwithstanding I told him I was ordained by Letters Dismissory from the Bishop of *London,* yet in a great Rage he told me, if I preached in any public Church in that Province, he would suspend me.—I replied, I shall regard that as much as I would a Pope's Bull.—But, Sir, said I, why should you be offended at my speaking against the generality of the Clergy; for I always spoke worthily of you? . . . Sir, you did not behave thus when I was with you last.—No, says he, you did not speak againt the Clergy. . . . Because, replied I, more Light has been given me since that Time.—But, Sir, said I, if you will make an Application to yourself, be pleased to let me ask you one Question.—"Have you delivered your Soul by exclaiming against the Assemblies and Balls here?"— What, Sir, says he, must you come to catechise me?—No, . . . I have not exclaimed against them; I think there is no Harm in them.—Then,

Sir, said I, I shall think it my Duty to exclaim against you.—Then, Sir, replied he in a very great Rage, Get you out of my House.—I made my Bow, and with my Friends took my leave, pitying the Commissary, who I really thought was more noble than to give such Treatment.[35]

With bad blood definitely between them, the two now carried their differences into the pulpit. While the commissary was expatiating on the text "Those who have turned the world upside down are come hither also," Whitefield retaliated with a homily on "Alexander the coppersmith hath done me much evil; the Lord reward him according to his works." [36]

Whitefield left Charleston and went to Savannah, and soon thereafter Garden published a pamphlet of six letters addressed to Whitefield, airing his grievances publicly. The attack was caustic. The commissary was exasperated beyond endurance before he began writing the letters. Whitefield had said publicly that were he, as Garden, inclined to dispute, he "would stay till the Cool of the Day," and the commissary, accordingly, stated at the outset that he was under perfect control.[37] He taxed Whitefield (along with the offenses Garden had mentioned in their interview) with a want of "common Decency or good Manners" and accused him of knowing how, while "pretending the Cause of God . . . to insult and abuse." [38]

When Whitefield returned to Charleston in the summer, he heard Garden on Sunday, July 6, preach a "virulent, unorthodox and inconsistent" [39] sermon against the Methodists in general and himself in particular and was denied the sacrament.[40] On the following Friday he was "cited to appear before the Commissary and his court in a judicial way." The court sat at St. Philip's church, and Whitefield was formally charged with breaking the canon law.[41] He made an appeal to his Majesty in the High Court of Chancery, explaining it thus to a friend:

The commissary's detaining me here, has much tended to the furtherance of the gospel. I put in my exceptions against his sitting as my judge, and they were repelled; so that I have appealed home, and all other proceedings here are stopped.[42]

After a year and a day Whitefield was again summoned to appear before the ecclesiastical court at St. Philip's. When he did not put in an appearance, nor send any word, the court judged him guilty as charged and in the following document sentenced him to suspension:

We, therefore, pronounce, decree, and declare that the said George Whitefield, for his excesses and faults, ought duly and canonically, and according to the exigence of the law in that part of the premises, to be corrected and punished, and also to be suspended from his office; and, accordingly, by these presence, we do suspend him, the said George Whitefield; and, for being so suspended, we also pronounce, decree, and declare him to be denounced, declared, and published openly and publicly in the face of the Church.[43]

The pronouncement was of doubtful legality; and Stephens, reporting the trial and sentence in his *Journal,* observed—probably correctly, "To all which Mr. *Whitefield* gave but little heed." [44]

There was evidently a misunderstanding somewhere. The blame seems to have been with English authorities, both ecclesiastical and civil, rather than with Whitefield, who intended to apply to the proper persons and get a hearing. But he did not, and so the suspension was not removed, and only the lack of authority prevented Garden from excommunicating the evangelist, who persisted in disregarding the suspension.[45]

Garden subsequently regretted his loss of control in dealing with Whitefield when this difficulty first arose. He said that in the defense of the "Cause of Truth, against the Franticks" he wished that his "Pen agt. W—d had run in somewhat smoother a Stile."[46] But he did not change his opinion about the evangelist and eventually attacked Whitefield in even more telling fashion in the following comment on Bethesda:

Bad also is the present State of the poor Orphan House in *Georgia;* that Land of Lies, & from wch we have no Truth, but what they can neither disguise nor conceal.—The whole Colony is accounted here one great L-e from beginning to this Day; & the Orphan House, you know, is a part of the whole—A scandalous Bubble! Many of the poor Orphans (as the Cant runs) some under 15, some above 20 year of age (idle Fellows & Hussies) are starved out, & the few remaining are in a starving Condition, while yet their Founder has been reaping a double Harvest for them in *Scotland.* . . . His Managers there keep all things as dark as an Inquisition.[47]

A history of such a difficult relationship as that contained and typified in the episodes above might well suggest that there was no one in the Established Church to speak a good word for Whitefield. This was not the case. To begin with, the fact of Whitefield's ordination speaks for something. It is true that he was not a field-preacher when he came to take orders, but he was already identified with the Oxford Methodists. Actually, he was looked upon as rather a special individual and was assured of the church's particular regard by Bishop Benson, who said to him, "Notwithstanding I have declared I would not ordain any one under three and twenty, yet I shall think it my Duty to ordain you whenever you come for Holy Orders." [48]

Between the time of his ordination as a deacon and that at which he became a priest of the church, Whitefield had written his first *Journal*. Moreover, Thomas Cooper and James Hutton, rival printers, had carried on so open a squabble over their respective rights to the manuscript (which both published) that more than normal interest was directed to the remarkable book before it was even available to the public.[49] Such questionable, if not unseemly, publicity and the notoriety which the publication occasioned, however, did nothing to interfere with Whitefield's ordination in January of 1739. The stamp of his sermons and the pattern of his popularity were well defined by that time. Bishop Benson had already commended the evangelist's peculiar type of madness, and when subsequently he found it necessary to correct his young protégé, he did so "affectionately," by Whitefield's own confession.[50] It is worthy of note that "Bishop Benson, on his dying bed, sent ten guineas to Whitefield, as a token of his favour and approbation, and begged to be remembered by him in his prayers." [51] As a matter of fact, Whitefield could not have been ordained at all had not the Bishop of London given him dismissory letters; [52] and although Gibson found it necessary to warn his parishioners against the enthusiast, he treated him personally "with great tenderness and moderation." [53] Official approval of Whitefield was implicit in contributions to the Orphan-House made by Dr. Benson and by Dr. Butler, Bishop of Bristol.[54] If Alexander Garden frowned on the upstart, Whitefield, James Blair, Commissary in Virginia, welcomed him gladly and prompted a warm entry in Whitefield's *Journal*: "Paid my respects to Mr. Blair the *Commissary* of *Virginia*, and by far the most worthy Clergyman I have yet conversed with in all *America*.—He receive me with Joy, asked me to preach and wished my Stay was to be longer." [55]

Whitefield was repeatedly denied access to the pulpits of the Established Church, but the Church of England did not disown him officially. The Bishop of London had told Whitefield that he needed no license when he first announced his intention of going to Georgia. A year before he died, Whitefield reminded his hearers of ecclesiastical sanction in high places:

A late bishop of Lincoln, who has not been dead a long while, said to his chaplain, You are not a minister of Cicero, or any of the heathen philosophers; you are not to entertain your people with dry morality, but remember you are a minister of Christ; you are, therefore, to preach the gospel and if you will not preach the gospel in the church, you must not be angry for the poor people's going out into the fields where they hear the gospel.[56]

More than one bishop came to hear Whitefield preach. In Lady Huntingdon's chapel at Bath there was a special curtained bishop's seat immediately inside the door. The witty and eccentric Lady Betty Cobbe, daughter-in-law of the Archbishop of Dublin, who used to smuggle the prelates into this place from which they might hear without being seen, termed it *Nicodemus' Corner*.[57] Clearly, Whitefield was neither ignored nor disowned by the church. And no more did he disown her.

In a letter to the Bishop of Bristol, Whitefield attested genuine regret at having been forced into an unsympathetic course of action:

But, my Lord, what can I do? When I acted in the most regular manner, and when I was bringing multitudes even of Dissenters themselves to croud the churches, without any other reason being given than that too many followed after me, I was denied the use of them.[58]

That circumstance, however, did not embitter the young minister toward his spiritual mother. It only heightened his concern while it deepened his love. "I still continue to use her liturgy, wherever a church or chapel is allowed me," he said, and "unless thrust out, I shall never leave her." [59] Not only that, he was horrified when Charles Kinchin, Rector of Dummer and Fellow and Dean of Corpus

Christi College, one of his most zealous friends, did decide to leave the church. There was nothing spurious about Whitefield's grief for the state of religion in the church of his birth. He spoke of it with deep feeling:

GOD knows my Heart, I do not speak out of Resentment—I heartily wish all the LORD's servants were Prophets—I wish the Church of *England* was the Joy of the whole Earth—But I cannot see her sinking into *Papistical* Ignorance, and Deism resigned, and not open my Mouth against those, who by their sensual lukewarm Lives, and unscriptural superficial Doctrines, thus cause her to err—.[60]

To find that most of the clergy hated to be reformed confused and baffled Whitefield,[61] and that his own actions could be completely misunderstood disturbed him. "If I talk of the Spirit, I am a Quaker; if I say Grace at Breakfast, and behave *seriously,* I am a Presbyterian. Alas! what must I do to be accounted a Member of the *Church of England?*" [62]

Soon after he began preaching, it was suggested in jest that the church's embarrassment over Whitefield might be solved by making him a bishop:

Sept. 5 [1739] The Rev. Mr. Whitefield's Preaching is become so very offensive to the Clergy of this Kingdom, that 'tis said one of my Lords the Bishops a few Day since, went to the King to desire his Majesty to silence him: Upon which his Majesty enquired whether he preach'd Treason, Sedition, &c. but none of these Things being allegd'd against him, his Majesty seem'd at a Loss how to satisfy the Bishop; which a Noble Duke present observing, humbly proposed, that in order to prevent Mr. Whitefield's preaching for the future, his Majesty would be graciously pleased to *make him a Bishop.*[63]

Thirty years later, as the *Virginia Gazette* attests, the same possibility was being considered in grave earnest:

It is thought that the Rev. Mr. Whitefield would be more acceptable to the Americans for a Bishop, than the Rev. Mr. Apthorpe, not only on account of his pious and unwearied labours in those parts, but the vast numbers of friends he hath among the dissenting party, who principally oppose this establishment.[64]

The Church of England, however, never gave Whitefield approval so lavish or criticism so scathing as that which came to him from the ranks of the dissenters. The power of his preaching which roused Boston sinners to a sense of conviction elicited praise from those already awakened. Thomas Prince, whom Chauncy pronounced the most learned man in New England, Cotton Mather excepted, said that Whitefield's visit to New England was so successful that Boston had "never seen any Thing like it before, except at the Time of the general Earthquake." [65] That judgment seems correct in the light of Benjamin Colman's voluntary witness:

Our *dear People,* Your *Ministers* have with Pleasure seen you in the Weeks past, Old and Young, Parents and Children, Masters and Servants, High and Low, Rich and Poor together, gathering and passing as *Clouds* in our Streets, and as *Doves* on the Wing in Flocks flying to the Doors and Windows of our Place of Worship; and hovering about the same, those that could not get in.

The *Fame* of a singular servant and holy Youth, an extraordinary Servant and Minister of JESUS CHRIST . . . had prepared you . . . and . . . we receiv'd him, even as an Angel of GOD . . . .

For though we are *Elder Ministers,* and have been many Years before him in the Service of Souls, and *He* like *David* going against *Goliath,* in the Sight of the *Armies of Israel,* has been seen to be but a Youth & Stripling; yet we are not unwilling or ashamed to come and serve *after Him,* in the Battles of our LORD. . . . You have seen, as it were, a young *Elias,* or the *Baptist* risen again, a burning and shining *Light.*[66]

In the same Bostonian setting Charles Chauncy considered Whitefield young "in *Christian Experience,* as well as *raw Acquaintance with Divinity,*" and found him guilty of a *"monstrous Spirit of censorious Judging."* [67] He took a dim view of Whitefield's protested love for the orphans, since the Englishman visited them infrequently and tarried briefly.[68] Chauncy also thought Whitefield remiss in his administration of the affairs of Bethesda. And as for enthusiasm (which Chauncy judged productive of "more and greater blasphemies and abominations" than "POPERY"),[69] the Boston pastor said with considerable restraint that Whitefield had a *"Turn of Mind* too much disposing him this Way." [70]

New England ministers found it hard to forgive the visiting awakener for his attack on their universities as centers of darkness.

The president and faculty of Harvard published a testimony calling him an "enthusiast, a censorious, uncharitable person, and a deluder of the people." [71] Whitefield's reply was definitely conciliatory:

And I am come to *New-England,* with no intention to meddle with, much less to destroy the order of the New England churches, or turn out the generality of their ministers, or re-settle them with ministers from *England, Scotland,* and *Ireland.* . . . This leads me to ask forgiveness, Gentlemen, if I have done you or your society, in my journal, any wrong. . . . And if you have injured me . . . it is already forgiven without asking.[72]

Forgiveness was not immediate. Yale produced a hostile pamphlet, too.[73] New Englanders did not relish the evangelist's sharp words about the lack of religion and vital piety in their colleges. But in the end Whitefield won them to himself. Eventually he heard the New Haven students calling for him to preach and sending by the president of the college to entreat him to give them just one more quarter of an hour in the chapel.[74] He received the public thanks of the town of Boston; [75] and he was restored even to the good graces of Harvard, which affirmed its change of heart in the following record:

At a meeting of the President and Fellows of *Harvard* College, *August* 22, 1768. The Rev. Mr. *George Whitefield* having, in addition to his former kindness to *Harvard* College, lately presented to the Library, a New Edition of his Journals, and having procured large benefactions from several benevolent and respectable gentlemen; VOTED, That the Thanks of the Corporation be given to the Rev. Mr. *Whitefield,* for these instances of Candour and Generosity.[76]

And long before the Harvard community had forgiven him, the College of New Jersey had dignified Whitefield in the eyes of American colonists by conferring on him an honorary Master of Arts degree.[77]

The objection to Whitefield on the part of Dissenters was not confined to America. Attack was directed against the revivalist by the self-styled "suffering REMNANT of the *Anti-Popish, Anti-Lutheran, Anti-Prelatick, Anti-Whitefieldian, Anti-Erastian, Anti- Sectarian,* true *Presbyterian* Church of CHRIST in Scotland," [78] which scored Whitefield bitterly for his methods, his doctrine, his practices, and his success. Nothing was left unsaid in an official "Protestation, Witness and Testimony against *George Whitefield.*" The Presbyterians renounced him as an "abjured prelatick Hireling, of as lax Toleration-Principles as any that ever set up for the advancing of the Kingdom of Satan." [79] Ralph Erskine, the man who had first invited Whitefield to come to Scotland, bluntly called the preacher a liar. Although these exclusive Scots seemed most disturbed over the fact that Whitefield was not a Presbyterian, they also pointed out that he was unscriptural! He was, they said, a greedy man "making Merchandize of his pretended Ministry" and in all truth a "Son of the Church of *Rome.*" [80] The work at Cambuslang they called a "mere Delusion of Satan," and Scotland, they announced to the world, had sinned in giving him a kind reception.[81]

Whitefield's controversial role in the Christian community was not limited to his association with the Church of England or the more prominent bodies of dissenters. He found life complicated in any quarter. His relationship with the Moravians was but another aspect of a personality with whom the quarrel was often quick and the combat sometimes severe. On his second visit to America, Whitefield projected a utopian scheme for establishing at once a school for Negroes and a refuge for some of his English friends. On April 22, 1740, he wrote in his *Journal:*

This Day I bought 5000 Acres of Land on the Forks of the *Delaware.* Ordered a large House to be built thereon for the Instruction of these poor Creatures. The Land, I hear, is exceeding rich. It is a Mannor, and pays only a White-Rose yearly for Chief Rent.[82]

It is unnecessary to consider here any reasons for the failure of this project beyond the immediate one of the death of William Seward, who had pledged himself and his means to the assistance of this undertaking. Six days after the land was bought, Whitefield "Took a Sorrowful Leave of" Seward. (As he added in a footnote to the 1756 edition of his *Journals,* this was the last time he saw his worthy friend, who before Whitefield's return to England "was entered into his Rest.") [83] It was in October of 1740 that Seward, accompanying the Welsh evangelist Howell Harris on a preaching tour, was blinded by a mob at Caerleon and then "ruthlessly slain on the Green at Hay beneath the ancient town wall." [84]

While he was still ignorant of the fate of Seward and, therefore, still working toward the realization of this project (which he had named *Nazareth*), Whitefield hired some Moravians to erect the necessary buildings.[85] It would have seemed natural for Whitefield to have made cause with these members of the Unitas Fratrum who were in the area and shared a common interest in evangelistic zeal with the great revivalist. On May 5 he made arrangements for them to do all the carpenter work and requested Peter Bohler to take general superintendence. The venture was not successful. Trouble, however, arose over theology, not architecture. After engaging the brethren in the spring, Whitefield had not seen them again until the fall. But the construction itself was impeded, first by continual rain for a month and then by want of labor. "Three hundred pounds sterling were expended before the cellar-walls were finished in September." [86] Meanwhile Whitefield had argued heatedly with a Moravian in Georgia, whose name was Hagen, over the doctrine of predestination:

Whitefield returned to Pennsylvania in November, 1740, nursing his wrath against Hagen, and finding Bohler to be of the same mind, he peremptorily ordered the Moravians to leave his land. Neighbors interfered, and cried shame on him for turning the little company adrift in the depth of winter, and he finally agreed to let them stay for a while in the log cabin which was sheltering them while they were building the large stone house.[87]

Yet the Moravians had first come to their sanctuary in Pennsylvania through the help of Whitefield. When the English demanded military assistance of the pacifist Brethren at the time of the threatened Spanish invasion, Bohler and his Moravian followers accepted Whitefield's gracious invitation to use his sloop, the "Savannah," for passage to Philadelphia.[88] No later than the April before he broke with the Moravians, Whitefield had called Bohler a "dear Lover of our LORD JESUS CHRIST" and had told how he preached the gospel. This judgment, incidentally, Whitefield reconsidered and omitted the compliment in the 1756 revision of his *Journals*.[89]

Whitefield had gone freely to meetings of the Moravians in earlier days and had been a frequent visitor at their Fetter Lane Society.[90] But in 1753 he published an expostulatory letter addressed to Count Zinzendorf, in which he accused the count and the other leaders of the Brethren with having

been unhappily instrumental in *misguiding* the real, simple, honest-hearted christians; of *distressng*, if not *totally ruining* numerous families, and introducing a whole *farrago* of superstitious, not to say *idolatrous* fopperies, into the English nation.[91]

When Whitefield's *Journals* were first published, it was the Moravian James Hutton who had printed them and, moreover, had contended for the privilege of doing so. In 1740, however, he refused to accept manuscripts from Whitefield because of the doctrines they expressed.[92] And after Whitefield published his letter to Zinzendorf, it was Hutton—Whitefield's former friend—who championed the count because there were "so many bulls of Bashan" who roared "so madly against him." [93] John Syms, for some time Whitefield's confidant and quasi secretary, deserted Whitefield for the Moravians and said that the "bulk" of the letter was untrue; Peter Bohler said less guardedly that it was all a lie.[94]

Four years after this storm of accusation and name-calling, Whitefield wrote mildly concerning Count Zinzendorf:

O to be an *Israelite* indeed, in whom there is no guile! Simplicity and godly sincerity is all in all. A want of this, I fear, hath led the Count into all his mistakes. With great regret I speak or write of any people's weaknesses; but I did and do now think, that divine Providence called me to publish what you mention. The Redeemer gave it his blessing. I do not find that their fopperies are continued, and I hear also that they have discharged many debts.[95]

The uneven tenor of the relationship between Whitefield and the Moravians was but another facet of his debated status in the Christian community.

The Orphan-House in Georgia was a continual source of contention, and Whitefield—as the spirit and force behind Bethesda—was alternately maligned and praised for this charity. The offerings that he took raised the question of his honesty, and he had to defend himself against the charges of being a "bold man and importunate beggar," [96] who had "collected Monies for *himself* in his Journies, under the Pretext of doing it for the Poor." [97] Indeed, people went so far as to say that Whitefield's orphanage was chimerical and his collections fraudulent, accusations which a traveler in America gladly refuted after a visit to Bethesda:

> It gave me much Satisfaction to have an Opportunity to see this *Orphan-House,* as the Design had made such a Noise in *Europe,* and the very Being of such a Place was so much doubted every where, that, even no farther from it than *New England,* Affidavits were made to the contrary.[98]

Whitefield was a stormy figure, even within Methodism although the disputation that he occasioned in Christendom was likely to be regarding the Methodist characteristics that he bore. His break with Wesley has already been noted. The breach, however, was by no means final. The man who withheld the right hand of fellowship from Wesley at the time of the conflict over free grace lived to write him, frankly importuning a reunion and begging for his old friend's prayers.[99] He died eulogized by the founder of Methodism, who said in his funeral oration on Whitefield:

> How few have we known of so kind a temper, of such large and flowing affections? Was it not principally by this, that the hearts of others were so strangely drawn and knit to him? Can any thing but love beget love? This shone in his very countenance, and continually breathed in all his words, whether in public or private.[100]

When Whitefield preached, the Methodists heard praises for themselves from his lips. "I will assure you," he said (and this only shortly before his death), "Moses was a Methodist." [101] He found Methodism's sanction and similarity, too, in Paul, Barnabas, Luther, and Zwingli.[102] Perhaps his loftiest tribute was given in his "true portrait of a Methodist":

> He is one of those whom GOD hath chosen in CHRIST out of mankind, to bring them by CHRIST to everlasting salvation, as vessels made to honour; wherefore they, who be endued with so excellent a benefit of GOD, are called according to GOD's purpose by his spirit working in due season: they, through grace, obey the calling; they be justified freely;

and made the sons of GOD by adoption: they are conformed to the image of his only begotten Son JESUS CHRIST; they walk religiously in good works; and at length, by GOD's mercy, they attain everlasting felicity.[103]

It was the Methodists, however, who once passed by Whitefield while he was preaching in Moorfields with their fingers stuck in their ears that they might not hear so much as a word of his false doctrine of divinity.[104]

Whitefield has been associated with the Calvinistic Methodists, but his connection with this organized branch of Methodism was tenuous. Indeed, it was a characteristic of the free soul, Whitefield, that he had no commerce with organized religion and religious organizations as such. It was only incidentally that he worked with them. Certainly he had no zeal to build his own organization. "I should but weave a *Penelope's* webb, if I formed societies," he said; "and if I should form them, I have not proper assistants to take care of them." [105] Whatever organized form he gave to the results of his labors was as circumstance compelled him. The moderatorship of the Calvinistic Methodist conference to which he was elected in Waterford, South Wales, in January of 1743,[106] he subsequently resigned,[107] although he went to such meetings as he could when he was not in America.[108] And after his death it was the Welsh Calvinist Methodists and Lady Huntingdon's connection that lasted; [109] Whitefield Methodists were for the most part "absorbed" by the Congregational Independents.[110]

The fact seems to be that the controversial Whitefield was in marked degree truly catholic. Again and again he gave utterance to an intense passion for the vitality of Christianity rather than the institution which mediated that gospel to men: "Christianity will never flourish, till we are all of one heart and of one mind; and this would be the only means of seeing the gospel of JESUS to flourish, more than ever it will be persecuting those who differ from us." [111] His catholicity of spirit was given specific expression in a sermon on "Spiritual Baptism":

I don't care whether you go to church or meeting; I am, I profess, a member of the church of England, and if they will not let me preach in the church, I will preach any where; all the world is my parish, and I will preach wherever God gives me an opportunity, but you will never find me disputing about the outward appendages of religion; don't tell me you are a Baptist, an Independant, a Presbyterian, a Dissenter, tell me you are a Christian, that is all I want.[112]

In a profound conviction that the strength of Christianity lay not in forms and ceremonies, he expressed real charity toward Rome. The man who deplored the excesses of Lisbon said that a "Papist" and a Protestant who had the *"Piety* of an Apostle and the *impartial Love"* of the first Christians "would not want *half a sheet* of Paper to hold their Articles of Union, nor be half an Hour before they were of one Religion." [113] Perhaps it was knowing this of him which once prompted Catholics of Dublin to tell Whitefield that they would leave their priests if he would remain in Ireland.[114]

Although Whitefield was called upon to defend himself against the charge of exclusiveness, he seemed actually so little guilty of the indictment that one of his defenders was shocked that any should doubt his catholicity.

Here I cannot but confess my Astonishment at an *Objection* rais'd against him by some Gentlemen, That in *England* he is a *Churchman,* in *Scotland* a *Kirkman,* here he is a *Dissenter,* and there *Anabaptist:* That is, he has Communion with *all* those Churches, and therefore ought to have Communion with *none.*[115]

Whitefield's "one sole question" was always *"Are you a christian?"* [116] Almost legendary is the story of Whitefield gazing toward heaven during one of his sermons and calling out to Father Abraham to inquire if there were any Presbyterians, Baptists, Methodists, or Independents in heaven. And being repeatedly told that such were not there, Whitefield cried, "Why, who have you then?" to which Abraham replied: "We don't know those names here. All that are here are Christians." [117] Whitefield's persistence in this paramount concern (with its attendant indifference to the liturgy of the Church of England) was largely responsible for his failure to make a college of his beloved Bethesda. Ecclesiastical approval of his plan was denied when the archbishop realized that Whitefield had been sincere when on having been "frequently asked, 'Upon what bottom the intended College was to be founded,'" always answered, "Un-

doubtedly upon a *broad bottom*." [118] Had the roving evangelist with
the catholic spirit been willing to establish a sectarian college, he
could have found support. But this was not Whitefield. To the end
of his days he contended that

it cannot be an unchristian Spirit to be as glad to see Truths in one
Party of Christians as in another; and to look with Pleasure upon any
good Doctrines that are held by any Sect of Christian People, and be
thankful to God, that they have so much of the genuine, saving Truths of
the Gospel amongst them.[119]

The Christian community never came to a unanimity about
Whitefield—even approximately so. In many ways he was an im-
ponderable as long as he lived. He took care that the times of his
outdoor preaching services should not interfere with those of the
Established Church, and once when through error he transgressed
this self-imposed rule, "he shortened his Sermon, and dismiss'd his
Meeting, and came to the said Church himself, and his Hearers along
with him." [120] Though he attacked the clergy of the Church of England, he defended its articles valiantly. He died in its fold, but he
was buried beneath a dissenting pulpit. There were prominent dissenters of his day who "showed publicly but little sympathy with
Whitefield, though they acknowledged much privately." [121] Robert
Philip devoted a chapter to this strange circumstance in his biographical study of Whitefield and ascribed it to an unwillingness of
English dissenters to show any official sympathy toward Methodism
for fear of compromising themselves with the Establishment, whose
favor they were seeking.[122] And as for Methodism, Whitefield defended the movement ardently (prosecuting rioters who persecuted
the faithful [123] and championing students whose Methodism got
them expelled from Oxford [124]) while reserving for himself the right
to deplore a Methodism grown respectable. Little wonder that he
became for them not one to contend *with* but one to contend *over*
in an effort to secure his worth in the eyes of Christendom.

The essentially controversial character of Whitefield as a member
of the Christian community, as well as the community's acknowledg-
ment of that status, was well expressed in an article entitled
"Memoirs of the Rev. Mr. George Whitefield," published in *The
London Magazine* in the month that news of Whitefield's death

reached England. After giving a history of Whitefield's life and quoting rather extensively from his writings, the unsigned essay concluded with the following paragraphs:

And though in the pulpit he often found it necessary by the terrors of the Lord to persuade men, he had nothing gloomy in his nature, being singularly charitable, and tender-hearted; and, in his private conversation chearful, communicative, and entertaining. To the very meanest he was always easy of access . . . a faithful steward of the extensive charities he drew from his numerous and compassionate hearers. . . . For this, and for his other labours, the name of George Whitefield will long be remembered with esteem and veneration, not only by his personal acquaintance, by those who were awakened by his ministry, but by all true christians of every denomination, whilst vital and practical religion hath a place in the British dominions.

Such is the portrait drawn of Mr. Whitefield by the Methodists; the enemies of that sect however, particularly the very learned author of *The Enthusiasm of Methodists and Papists compared,* are so far from admitting his pre-tensions to an extraordinary portion of sanctity, that they positively pronounce him a most profligate hypocrite; his piety they attribute to avarice; his zeal to pride; and his very humility to ostentation. They tell us, that during life he was continually boasting of his poverty, yet at his death they talk of his being immensely rich.—This is not all, his late progress to America is set down to the grossest account; an attachment to a woman, by whom he had a child while his wife was living; and it is even added that this child was the first infant ever entered into his orphan-house in Georgia. How far the character on either side may be just, we do not by any means pretend to affirm; the chief particulars of his history we have extracted from his own writings, and as we have given the most flattering eulogium that has been published by his friend, we can't be deemed partial in mentioning the opinion of his enemies.[125]

Chapter X

℥

Conflict Within the Secular Community

AT the opening of the century in which Whitefield was born, Richard Steele published a work attacking the "Fashionable Vice of Exploding Religion," entitled *The Christian Hero: an Argument Proving that no Principles but Those of Religion Are Sufficient to Make a Great Man.*[1] The appearance of this book which was to enjoy a new edition in every decade save one of the eighteenth century was a portent of the times in which to be moral was fashionable. *The Spectator,* a newspaper that first appeared in England on March 1, 1711, was launched expressly to "enliven Morality with Wit, and to temper Wit with Morality."[2]

Generally speaking, there was a reaction in the eighteenth century against the extreme licentiousness of the Restoration (just as a certain laxity of morals had resulted in the rebellion against a rigid Puritanism). The Puritan was typified now by the tradesman-journalist, rather than the embattled warrior or the hymn-singing prisoner. Yet the England of Anne and the Georges was an England that liked being exposed to what was called a lesson, as the immediate and substantial popularity of Hogarth's "The Harlot's Progress" proved.[3] That series of prints, and the others from the facile hand of the same artist, exhibits a world that is grossly imperfect in many ways. In a Hogarth print, there occurs over the door of a gin shop the well-known advertisement:

> Drunk for a Penny
> Dead drunk for two pence
> Clean Straw for Nothing[4]

155

Hogarth's *haut monde* is peopled with more than its share of fops and fools, and his pictures teem with pickpockets, thieves, cutpurses, and prostitutes—plying their trades or taking a last ride to Tyburn. In Hogarth's London, men are entertained by the antics of pet monkeys and dancing masters or diverted by attending public executions at which "Friends or relations . . . pull the dying Person by the Legs, and beat his Brest to dispatch him as soon as possible." [5] Whitefield was born into this world as well as into Wesley's.

There is religion in Hogarth's world—to be sure. But its power is to disgust or repel, not to attract. A congregation sleeps under the dull monotony of a clerical drone; a tipsy curate disgraces himself at a wake; a cynical clergyman marries a dissolute rake to a lecherous crone. Hogarth's is a world in which religion is fashion, not a world that is fashioned by religion.[6] For this sphere to ignore Whitefield was no more possible than for the realm of priests and prelates to do so.

The consideration of Whitefield as a provocative figure in the secular world that was so chary of professional religion and yet so pathetically eager for the genuine will be considered for the most part from English sources and, consequently, in the evangelist's English setting. America had not yet enjoyed the leisure sufficient to create a literature, for the young country was still in the midst of undistinguished, plebeian years that sowed what later times were to reap. American writers were preponderantly ministers[7] whose opinions have already been noted. Yet even in the colonies, if one can judge by the scanty testimonies of the secular press that are available, the field-preacher was a personality to occasion altercation and dispute beyond that in the religious community.

In the Augustan age of English letters Dr. Johnson was arbiter. James Boswell, the mentor's biographer, considered Whitefield's eloquence powerful,[8] but Johnson thought the popular preacher no orator.

He would not allow much merit to Whitefield's oratory. "His popularity, sir," said he, "is chiefly owing to the peculiarity of his manner. He would be followed by crowds were he to wear a nightcap in the pulpit, or were he to preach from a tree." [9]

Johnson persisted in this rather unflattering estimate of Whitefield's abilities. According to the eccentric doctor the evangelist merely "vociferated and made an impression" [10] and did not actually draw as much attention as a mountebank. Johnson insisted that Whitefield gathered his following not by excellence of performance but

by doing what was strange. Were Astley [a celebrated horse rider] to preach a sermon standing upon his head on a horse's back, he would collect a multitude to hear him, but no wise men would say he made a better sermon for that.[11]

In spite of such caustic evaluation of Whitefield's merit Johnson did not treat Whitefield's ministry "with contempt," but thought "he did good." [12] Indirectly Johnson acknowledged Whitefield's influence in a tribute to Dagge, the jailer at Newgate. Indeed, it is not impossible that Johnson knew that Dagge was a convert of Whitefield's. This estimate of Whitefield as something of a show-off, but at the same time as an instrument of genuine religion, cannot be lightly taken from a man whose spiritual sensitivity was plainly shown in a prayer occasioned by the death of his wife:

And may [I] remember that I am punished for my sins, and hope for comfort only by repentance. Grant, O merciful God, that by the assistance of thy Holy Spirit I may repent, and be comforted, obtain that peace which the world cannot give, pass the residue of my life in humble resignation and cheerful obedience; and when it shall please Thee to call me from this mortal state, resign myself into thy hands with faith and confidence, and finally obtain mercy and everlasting happiness, for the sake of Jesus Christ our Lord. Amen.[13]

Johnson was alive to the world of the spirit, and he could recognize its spokesmen.

Another figure of English letters, Horace Walpole, however, had only insult for Whitefield. Methodism itself he found nothing short of madness, and Whitefield he considered the wildest of a disordered lot:

This nonsensical new light is extremely in fashion, and I shall not be surprised if we see a revival of all the folly and cant of the last age. Whitefield preaches continually at my Lady Huntingdon's at Chelsa; my Lord Chesterfield, my Lord Bath, my Lady Townshend, my Lady

Thanet and others have been to hear him; what will you lay that next winter he is not run after instead of Garrick? [14]

Walpole thought the sought-after preacher more than a pied piper. He regarded him as a fiend. In 1768 he wrote to a friend:

I hope the Methodist your neighbour does not like his patriarch Whitefield encourage the people to forge, murder, etc., in order to have the benefit of being converted at the gallows. That arch-rogue preached lately a funeral sermon on one Gibson hanged for forgery, and told his audience that he could assure them Gibson was now in heaven, and that another fellow, executed at the same time, had the happiness of touching Gibson's coat, as he was turned off. As little as you and I agree about an hundred years ago, I don't desire a reign of fanatics. Oxford has begun with the rascals, and I hope Cambridge will wake—I don't mean that I would have them persecuted, which is what they wish—but I would have the clergy fight them and ridicule them.[15]

With obvious relish and his customary acrid wit Walpole noted that Lord Ferrers, Lady Huntingdon's insane nephew who was executed for a particularly cold-blooded murder, was with "all the frenzy in his blood . . . not mad enough to be struck" with Methodism, "though Whitefield prayed for him and preached about him." [16] Although Walpole was quick to admit the support that Whitefield commanded, he did not consider it of ultimate significance. In 1758 he lamented society's loss of Lady Fanny Shirley to the Methodists:

> Where Fanny, ever-blooming fair,
> Ejaculates the graceful pray'r,
> And, scap'd from sense, with nonsense smit,
> For Whitefield's cant leaves Stanhope's wit.[17]

But after the death of Whitefield and of Lady Huntingdon, Walpole announced his confidence that the sect would decline, observing that the "second crop of apostles seldom acquire the influence of the founders." [18]

Horace Walpole was shrewd enough to know that martyrdom often lends dignity to a cause that well-aimed raillery can kill. The profane world heaped ridicule upon Whitefield, full and plenty.

Alexander Pope called him a *braying ass*.[19] This was the kind of attack which Whitefield sustained, albeit the blows, though not mortal, were serious. Perhaps the most celebrated instance of such abuse was the production of Samuel Foote's play *The Minor*.

Samuel Foote was wellborn and Oxford-educated. He turned to the stage after making a failure of both marriage and law. But he was enormously successful as actor-playwright. It was his habit to introduce real characters into his works and to expose them to the lash of his satire in merciless caricature.[20] In *The Minor*, which appeared at the height of Foote's popularity, the Methodists were made the butt of his wit, and Whitefield was referred to as *Dr. Squintum*, a name attributed to him by folk who made light of his crossed eye.

The drama was first acted in July, 1760. A month later Whitefield wrote to a friend: "Satan is angry. I am now mimicked and burlesqued upon the public stage." [21] The piece prompted by Satan scandalized the Methodists—particularly Lady Huntingdon, who waited on both the Duke of Devonshire, who was then Lord Chamberlain, and David Garrick, in an effort to have the license canceled and the production suppressed.[22]

The ribald farce by the English Aristophanes was mainly a vehicle for the extraordinary ability of the author-mimic, who used the stage for social comment. An unsigned introduction to Foote's published plays commended him for his service to the community:

As the principal merit of all our author's writings consists in the drawing of peculiar characters well known in real life, which he heighteened by his own manner of personating the originals on the stage, it will be necessary to inform posterity, that . . . in the conclusion, or rather epilogue to the piece, spoken by Shift, which the author performed . . . he took off, to a great degree of exactness, the manner and even person of that noted preacher, and chief of the Methodists, Mr. George Whitefield. Indeed, so happy was the success of this piece, in one respect, that it seemed more effectually to open our eyes, those of the populace especially, in regard to the absurdities of that set of enthusiasts, than all the more serious writings that had ever been published against them.[23]

Two scenes from the play are sufficient to convey the character attributed to Whitefield by Foote. The first is the epilogue referred to above. Shift, a conniving rascal whose schemes have not paid off, determines to become an itinerant preacher:

> Near the mansions of Moorfields I'll bawl;
> Friends, fathers, mothers, sisters, sons, and all,
> Shut you your shops, and listen to my call.
> With labour, toil, all second means dispense,
> And live a rent-charge upon Providence.
>
> .   .   .   .
>
> Aye, that might be, ye cry . . .
> But we ne'er had a rasher for the coals.
> And d'ye deserve it? How d'ye spend your days?
> In pastimes, prodigality, and plays!
> Let's go see Foote! Ah, Foote's a precious limb!
> Old-nick will soon a football make of him!
> Oh, what you snivel? Well, do so no more,
> Drop, to atone, your money at the door,
> And, if I please,—I'll give it to the poor.[24]

More libelous in its attack on Whitefield is that criticism which is implicit in a scene which is dominated by the character of Mrs. Cole. The woman is an outrageous bawd who, forced by illness and age into retirement from the active life of easy virtue, has become a procuress, fashioned, presumably, on the famed Mother Douglas[25] of the times. Mrs. Cole is an ardent convert of Dr. Squintum. On her way to a tabernacle service Mrs. Cole stops for an interview with Sir George Wealthy, for whom she is engaged to secure a mistress. Her talk of business is frequently interrupted with references to her religion—so completely one of justification by faith that it occasions no conflict with the demands of her occupation. She twits a former customer with his not having visited her establishment since his arrival in London:

Mrs. *Cole*. And never once call'd upon old Cole. No, no, I am worn out, thrown by and forgotten, like a tatter'd garment, as Mr. Squintum says. Oh, he is a dear Man! But for him I had been a lost sheep; never known the comforts of the new birth; no,—There's your old friend, Kitty Carrot, at home still. What, shall we see you this evening? [26]

Mrs. Cole expresses a thousand pities that a certain woman of her acquaintance is such a reprobate. "But she'll mend; her time is not come," says the old harridan and adds, "all shall have their call, as Mr. Squintum says, sooner or later; regeneration is not the work of a day. No, no, no." [27]

The benevolent Mr. Squintum had indeed been the agent of Mrs. Cole's salvation. Romanism she judged inconsiderate, refusing to give her absolution, she said, "without I quitted my business." It was at this point in Mrs. Cole's career that tabernacle religion and Squintum saved her. The testimony is explicit: "O no, it would not do. So, in my last illness, I was wish'd to Mr. Squintum, who stept in with his saving grace, got me with the new birth, and I became as you see, regenerate, and another creature." [28] The utter perversion of Mrs. Cole's religion is seen in her encouragement to a young girl who is reluctant to enter the life of prostitution. "Don't you remember what Mr. Squintum said?" Mrs. Cole asks. "A woman's not worth saving, that won't be guilty of a swinging sin; for then they have matter to repent upon." [29]

The point at which this study impinges on the material quoted above is not that of persecution of the Methodists. Rather it is the underlying skepticism concerning Whitefield's work and religion that informs the play. There was just enough truth in the caricature of Whitefield to create doubts in serious minds. Without question certain folk of Mrs. Cole's sort had become followers of the field-preacher. Englishmen seemed to inquire with tongue in cheek, but they actually asked in grave earnest: What kind of religion admits a Mrs. Cole without necessity of reformation into a tabernacle society? Londoners may or may not have known that Whitefield, thinking it wrong for the "devil's house to have all the good tunes," had appropriated some popular airs from favorite stage operas of the day and set sacred words to them. Even so, when strains of such music-hall ballads as "Love in a Village" or "Maid of the Mill" floated from the Moorfields Tabernacle, the popular mind found it easy to associate the melodies and, consequently, the Methodists who sang them with the disreputable tavern life that had created the airs.[30] What kind of religion sings this kind of song? asked London. This, of course, was only another way of asking the basic question: What kind of person is Whitefield, and what sort of religion does he teach? The secular community had a ready answer, but not a unanimous one.

Mrs. Cole's fictional counterpart (who embodied the same ill-concealed attack on Whitefield) was found in Mrs. Snarewell, a character of another drama of the 1760's, *The Register-Office*.[31] Here Whitefield was plainly intended by the "Mr. Watchlight," who had taken the reprobate Mrs. Snarewell into his fold and managed to get himself named chief beneficiary in her will. Of more significance was a real life individual discovered at Whitefield's tabernacle and reported by Frances Brooke in her account of attending service there:

I asked a very pious orange-woman who sat near me, and who, to the great annoyance of one of my senses, had raised her devotion with the noble spirit of juniper, whether it was usual with him to keep them so long in expectation? [Whitefield was late arriving.] She told me, no; and that she was afraid the dear man was ill: and went on: "Madam, did you ever hear Mr. *W—f—d?* O! he is a sweet creature, a charming man! ah! would they were all like him! Thank God, I have followed him these twenty years." [32]

Miss Brooke's description of the preacher and of his religion substantiated that of Foote:

THIS charming man at last ascended the reading-desk, and began with an earnestness which pleased me, but accompanied with such antick gesticulations as soon took off the effect. His tone of voice is vulgar and unnatural, his pronunciation provincial and harsh: . . . he began in the pulpit with a form of devotion of his own, which lasted the best part of an hour; with the folly of which I should have been diverted, had I not been shocked by the blasphemy of some passages, in which he addressed himself to the Saviour of the world with the same familiarity as to one of his own congregation. But this is the less surprising when one considers, that he modestly receives from his followers not respect but worship; that they kiss the edge of his robe, and follow the wheels of his chariot (for this humble self-denying man is master of a very neat equipage) with uplifted hands and all the marks of adoration. His sermon, which lasted about two hours, was a confused heap of unmeaning rhapsody, and unentertaining, uninstructive stories; and the tendency of it, if such unconnected trash can be said to have any, was to persuade his hearers, that the way to gain heaven at last was to repent the two evenings of his lecture, and be very wicked all the week besides; and that virtue and morality were hateful to the Supreme Being.[33]

On the other hand, according to Benjamin Franklin (a man not noted for excessive compliment or impulsiveness in judgment) charm seems to be a characteristic that Whitefield definitely possessed. Moreover, Franklin believed that Whitefield was of unquestioned integrity. In his autobiography he paid high tribute to the field-preacher's wholesome effect on Philadelphia:

The multitudes of all sects and denominations that attended his sermons were enormous, and it was a matter of speculation to me, who was one of the number, to observe the extraordinary influence of his oratory on his hearers, and how they admir'd and respected him, notwithstanding his common abuse of them, by assuring them they were naturally *half beasts and half devils*. It was wonderful to see the change soon made in the manners of our inhabitants. From being thoughtless or indifferent about religion, it seem'd as if all the world were growing religious, so that one could not walk thro' the town in an evening without hearing psalms sung in different families of every street.[34]

Though Franklin told an amusing story of resolving to give nothing toward a collection for the orphans in Georgia and then in response to Whitefield's matchless oratory emptying his pockets,[35] he spoke firmly in behalf of Whitefield's honesty. Reports were circulated that these offerings were used for Whitefield's "private emolument." Franklin, who—by his own confession—"was intimately acquainted with him" never had the "least suspicion." [36] On the basis of a practical experiment which he reported in careful detail, the publisher of Philadelphia even verified the extravagant claims regarding the number of people who could hear Whitefield.

He preach'd one evening from the top of the Court-house steps, which are in the middle of Market-street, and on the west side of Second-street, which crosses it at right angles. . . . I had the curiosity to learn how far he could be heard, by retiring backwards down the street . . . and I found his voice distinct till I came near Front-street. . . . Imagining then a semicircle, of which my distance should be the radius, and that it were fill'd with auditors, to each of whom I allow'd two square feet, I computed that he might well be heard by more than thirty thousand. This reconcil'd me to the newspaper accounts of his having preach'd to twenty-five thousand people in the fields.[37]

Indeed, Franklin's acceptance of the legend and his approval of the man were such that, searching for some enterprise with which his life might "finish handsomely," he could think of no better (though impossible) project than being with Whitefield "jointly employ'd by the Crown, to settle a Colony on the Ohio." [38]

Less appreciative of the evangelist than Franklin was Henry Fielding, the novelist, who dealt briefly but belligerently with Whitefield in a reference to the Bell Inn at Gloucester. "The master of it is a brother to the great preacher Whitefield," he said, "but is absolutely untainted with the pernicious principles of Methodism." [39] How noxious Fielding considered the teachings of Whitefield, he had set forth in a novel published seven years earlier:

"Sir," answered Adams, "if Mr. Whitefield had carried his doctrine no farther than you mention, I should have remained, as I once was, his well-wisher. I am myself as great an enemy to the luxury and splendor of the clergy as he can be. I do not, more than he, by the flourishing estate of the Church understand the palaces, equipages, dress, furniture, rich dainties, and vast fortunes of her ministers. Surely those things, which savour so strongly of this world, become not the servants of one who professed his kingdom was not of it: but when he began to call nonsense and enthusiasm to his aid, and set up the detestable doctrine of faith against good works, I was his friend no longer; for surely, that doctrine was coined in Hell, and one would think none but the Devil himself could have the confidence to preach it. For can anything be more derogatory to the honour of God, than for men to imagine that the all-wise Being will hereafter say to the good and virtuous, 'Notwithstanding the purity of thy life, notwithstanding that constant rule of virtue and goodness in which you walked upon earth, still as thou didst not believe everything in the true orthodox manner, thy want of faith shall condemn thee?' Or on the other side, can any doctrine have a more pernicious influence on society, than a persuasion, that it will be a good plea for the villain at the last day; 'Lord, it is true, I never obeyed one of thy commandments, yet punish me not, for I believe them all?' " [40]

Another pioneer in the English novel, Tobias Smollett, was even more caustic. In a history of England he said that "weak minds were seduced by delusions of a superstition stiled Methodism, raised upon the affectation of superior sanctity, and maintained by pretensions to divine illumination." [41] Whitefield he dismissed as an obscure preacher. Oddly, Smollett showed evidence later, at least by implication, of having modified his own view of the controversial Whitefield. His *History* was written early in his career. *Humphry Clinker,* far and away his mellowest novel, was not published until the year of the author's death. By that time, 1771, the tide of romanticism was running strong in England. The return to warmth in English letters was part of a larger force that was operative in all of English life:

Romanticism, which sought to evoke from the past a beauty that it found wanting in the present, was but one phase of that revolt against the coldness and spiritual deadness of the first half of the eighteenth century which had other sides in the idealism of Berkeley, in the Methodist and Evangelical revival led by Wesley and Whitefield, and in the sentimentalism which manifested itself in the writings of Richardson and Sterne.[42]

Methodism in the character of Clinker, the humble convert, gained the involuntary respect of Smollett. Bitter scorn was poked at the Methodists in the wonderfully ignorant letters of Winifred Jenkins, who lived by "God's grease," and read her "byebill." But the presentation of the patience and goodness with which the uncomplaining Clinker suffered rebuke and injustice because of his Methodism betrayed Smollett's real, if grudging, admiration for his simple hero and the religion which he represented. By implication, at least, there was a certain approval of Whitefield.[43]

Of Whitefield's contemporaries William Cowper had the refreshing distinction of offering the evangelist a genuine tribute, expressed in some measure of literary excellence. Whitefield's *Journals* never drew a closer parallel between his life and that of the great missionary of the early church than the comparison that the poet Cowper made:

> Paul's love of Christ, and steadiness unbribed,
> Were copied close in him, and well transcribed
> He follow'd Paul; his zeal and kindred flame,
> His apostolic charity the same,
> Like him, cross'd cheerfully tempestuous seas,
> Forsaking country, kindred, friends, and ease;
> Like him he labor'd, and like him, content

165

To bear it, suffer'd shame where'er he went,
Blush, Calumny! ...

. . . .

And say, Blot out my sin, confess'd, deplored,
Against thine image in thy saint, O Lord! [44]

This was not the tribute of a man who gave his praise lightly or who used words loosely; it was the confession of a deeply sensitive individual. Cowper was attracted to the kind of religion Whitefield proclaimed, partly—according to his biographer—because the poet "was a 'gentleman' and a disliker of Nonconformity!" [45]

Whitefield did not appear as a pivot of controversy solely in literature that made self-conscious pretensions to merit. He was attacked in some pamphlets that were specifically designed to represent him as ridiculous while pandering to the low taste of a public whose literary preference was often restricted to the chapbooks of the century.

The Methodists, a burlesque poem, tells of how the devil, searching for an advocate on earth, finds Whitefield the most satisfactory instrument of accomplishing the satanic will. It relates how the fiend joyfully surveys the Oxford club "And gladly hugs each holy BOY." Whitefield, the *"Ape of Grace,"* becomes the model for the rake:

> Cease ye Town Rakes old ways t'explore,
> Or aim at Gaiety to Wh—re
> Alter your *Rules,* new *Methods* try,
> To your Instructor *W—tf—d* fly;
> There learn to ogle, whine, and cant,
> For Love and for Religion pant;
> And while *one* Eye to Heav'n ye send,
> The *other* on your Mistress bend,
> She'll chearfully obey your Task,
> Hid under such a *Visor Mask;*
> Put on a formal Gown and Band,
> Then take her gently by the Hand,
> Tell her no *earthly* Thoughts employ
> Your Mind, but heavenly joy,
> That all you mean by't in the Whole
> Is *Care* for her *immortal Soul,*
> She yields to the delusive Dream.[46]

Only in consideration of coarse material in such questionable taste as this does the intensity of feeling about Whitefield become evident. Even more objectionable than *The Methodists* is the volume of Whitefield's *Secret Memoirs* which, following closely the autobiographical *Short Account* that had produced the storm of protest against Whitefield's spiritual pride, accuses him of insanity, sexual perversion, fraud, stupidity, and plagiarism.[47] In a concluding outburst Whitefield is taxed with being devil-possessed:

Who but *Satan* could advise him, that there was no Religion in our going to Church? Doing Hurt to no one? Being constant in the Duties of the Closet? And giving Alms to our poor Neighbours? Who but *Satan* could induce him to strole about the Fields like an *Ignis Fatuus,* and entice poor Artificers to neglect their Employments and follow him . . . whilst their Creditors remained *unpaid,* and their *Families starving?* [48]

Such extravagant attacks on Whitefield by those technically outside the community of the church are not confined to writers. One of Hogarth's cruelest prints represents Whitefield in a picture called "Credulity, Superstition and Fanaticism." [49] The artist's work is "somewhat more than a satire on Methodism" but certainly no less.[50] The scene is the meeting of a religious society. Prominent in the gathering is a cross-eyed clerk who, flanked by cherubim, stands at a lectern which is draped with a copy of a "Hymn *by* G. Whitfield." The words from the hymn correspond to those in the edition of Whitefield's hymnbook. On a nearby hassock there is a basket containing Whitefield's *Journals.* The clerk is surrounded by evidences of the worst manifestation that alleged religion has ever produced. The worshipers are plainly fanatic, possibly insane. It is truly an illustration of Thomas Nevile's fond zealots who forsook all "To doat on Whitefield with ecstatic look." [51] The procedure is watched from outside by a bemused Moslem who looks through the window at the antics of the followers of the popular preacher.

"Credulity, Superstition and Fanaticism," published in 1762, is the extension of another print, "Enthusiasm Delineated," [52] which was engraved in 1761 but withheld from the public until 1798. In the earlier picture Whitefield appears in even less attractive light. The setting and most of the figures are the same as those already described. The clerk, however, is of grosser aspect, and beneath his lectern there is a dog (with "Whitefield" inscribed on his collar) adding his howls to the general confusion. This monstrous commentary, although produced by the secular community, is nevertheless the creation of one who endeavored to "give a lineal representation of the strange effects of literal and low conceptions of Sacred Beings." [53] William Hogarth's work was informed by a puritanical morality. That the missionary of the fields should appear so repulsive a figure to the social critic is but another evidence of the highly debatable character of Whitefield's words and works. People would remember the bedlamite quality of gatherings which Whitefield addressed, for their "paroxysms and epilepsies of enthusiasm" [54] had been caught for all time by Hogarth's graphic skill. He was, however, not the only one from the art world of his day to depict Whitefield. Woolastan's idealized likeness of the preacher at twenty-seven hangs in the National Portrait Gallery in London.[55] In direct contrast to Hogarth's delineation, Woolastan's Whitefield is benign and gentle, and is obviously guided by the instinctive goodness that shines in his face.

Among the secular personalities of Whitefield's time were those who took notice of the phenomenal success of the field-preacher and yet saw in him neither a saint nor a devil. Some, indeed, admitted his talents and resisted them without feeling it necessary to damn him in the bargain.

Edward Shuter, a celebrated comic actor, took great delight in listening to Whitefield's oratory, a compliment that was not lost on the preacher, who mentioned it in a letter to a friend, adding that he understood Shuter was "much impressed" and had brought others with him.[56] David Garrick, the peerless tragedian, heard Whitefield with somewhat less than uncritical detachment. His approbation for the preacher's technique was genuine and

like Franklin, [he] distinguished between his new and his old sermons, saying that his eloquence advanced up to its fortieth repetition before it reached its full height, and that Whitefield could make his audiences weep or tremble merely by varying his pronunciation of the word Mesopotamia. Garrick once said, "I would give a hundred guineas if I could only say 'O!' like Mr. Whitefield." [57]

The novel of Whitefield's day also had a considerably more objective estimate of the evangelist to offer than that of either Fielding or

Smollett. Richard Graves' *The Spiritual Quixote* is far less critical of Methodism in general and Whitefield in particular than the subtitle, *The Summer's Ramble of Mr. Goeffrey Wildgoose; A Comic Romance,* might lead one to imagine.

Graves' novel is a picaresque treatment of the Methodist convert. Instead of Smollett's humble footman, Clinker, Goeffrey Wildgoose, the country squire, is the hero who gives over a summer to the madness of Methodism. Whitefield is pictured in two ways. He is one of the individuals whom Wildgoose meets in his travels. The celebrity is also the obvious model for Wildgoose himself, whose comments and sermons are easily traced to their wellspring in the *Journals* and other writings of Whitefield.[58] Graves' spirit is never cruel. But Whitefield—as Whitefield—appears slightly ridiculous. The portrait of him is amusing; but the pen that draws it is indulgent, not sardonic:

As Wildgoose was . . . expostulating with his friend, they arrived at Mr. Whitefield's lodgings; and, upon inquiring for him, they were shewn up one pair of stairs by the Maid of the house, who tapping at the door, the two Pilgrims were immediately admitted to Mr. Whitefield's presence.

Mr. Whitefield was sitting in an elbow chair, in an handsome dining room, dressed in a purple night-gown and velvet cap; and, instead of a Bible or a Prayerbook as Wildgoose expected, he had a good bason of chocolate, and a plate of muffins well-buttered, before him.[59]

The famous preacher of the new birth inquired about the specific details of Wildgoose's conversion, asking pompously, "when and where were you converted? . . . in what year, what month, what day, and in what manner." [60] These are pointed questions reminiscent of those drawn up by Whitefield for use of the women belonging to religious societies and published in *The Gentleman's Magazine* in May, 1739. Certainly the new-birth emphasis is familiar. Graves' picture is of a recognizable Whitefield, but hardly the roving pilgrim of the fields. This man is surrounded by the amenities of city life.

As the model for Wildgoose, however, the squire turned Methodist preacher, Whitefield is the passionate itinerant who proclaims the gospel while enduring shame happily and suffering fools gladly. By his "smoothing eloquence, and the earnestness of his manner," Wildgoose converts many.[61] A visit to Bath is attended with some success, and an interview with Mrs. Placket (blood sister to Mrs. Cole of *The Minor* and Mrs. Snarewell of *The Register-Office*) creates the overwhelming impression of Wildgoose's naïve, but appealing, innocence. The very fact that Wildgoose is unknowing of the vice of the old procuress, rather than winking at her profession as Whitefield's counterparts do in the plays mentioned above, suggests a gentler treatment for the evangelist at the hands of Graves than was served him by the dramatists. Graves portrays a character who is neither so fine as Cowper's Leuconomus (a name under which the poet represented Whitefield "pilloried on Infamy's high stage") [62] nor yet so pernicious as Foote's Squintum. In the end the Methodist activity of Wildgoose, though ill-advised, turns out to have been utilized by Providence, and Wildgoose assumes a certain heroic cast of stature. Here in a single novel is a controversial picture of the field-preacher who is variously the self-important celebrity or the lovable dupe of society, depending on whether he is called *Whitefield* or *Wildgoose*.

Current periodicals, reporting the phenomenal career of the popular preacher, depicted (if unwittingly) an equally paradoxical individual. The *Pennsylvania Gazette,* normally friendly to Whitefield, published soon after his first visit to Philadelphia a tribute announcing that if ever a minister of the gospel endeavored to make Christ Jesus his great example, the excellent visitor was the man;[63] five months later the paper ran a long letter accusing Whitefield and Seward with unchristian and illegal actions in connection with closing the local Concert Room. Seward had with the help of the owner locked the door and taken away the "Keys of the *Assembly-Room, Dancing-School,* and *Music-Meeting.*" For this behavior, which some considered outrageous, certain "Gentlemen threaten'd to Cane" Seward and publicly charged him with having acted contrary to the law. Whitefield naturally was included in the same indictment, and the complaint also alleged falsification in the report of the vast multitudes said to have heard Whitefield preach.[64] Certainly there was here no recognizable editorial policy of publishing only news friendly to Whitefield. The columns of the Pennsylvania newspaper printed the intelligence both of his refusal to preach to the prisoners in New York and of his personal contribution to their relief some years later, on which occasion his conduct was commended in the following hearty fashion:

Last Friday in the Afternoon, the Rev. Mr. Whitefield visited the Gaol of this City; and preached. . . . That truly Reverend Man delivered an excellent Discourse. . . . Then the good Man, being informed that no Provision was made for the Support of Debtors, he generously gave, out of his Purse, enough to purchase ten Cords of Wood for the Use of the poorest Prisoners, and promised to make a Collection for their Relief. . . . What a Pity, that such a Godlike Man's Constitution is almost worn out by Apostolick Labours! [65]

Whitefield's name occurred frequently in the pages of the *Virginia Gazette,* sometimes as the hypocrite who deserved to be "Thunderstruck with divine Vengeance" [66] and sometimes as the angel of Moorfields.[67] In the Boston press he was alternately blessed [68] and damned.[69]

The disparate views which the colonial newspapers expressed about Whitefield are, of course, no more than other aspects of the secular community's inability to fit the awakener into a single slot and keep him there. The controversy over his significance which was reflected in British literature and articulated in the American press was vastly more pointed in English periodicals.

The London Magazine took notice of the young Whitefield when he first became a subject of popular interest. In May of 1739 a writer looked with jaundiced eye at the progress of the preacher and inquired: "But if one Man, like the Rev. Mr. *Whitefield,* should have it in his Power, by his Preaching, to detain 5 or 6000 of the Vulgar from their Daily Labour, what a Loss, in a little Time, may this bring to the Publick?" [70] The June issue of the magazine following his ordination carried a facetious attack on Whitefield in the guise of a proposal from a quack doctor that the two professional men join forces in fleecing the poor. "When men talk to be understood," the charlatan pointed out, "the very Vulgar themselves can examine their Principles, and unravel their Arguments." But, he asked logically, "when we wrap ourselves round with Obscurity, who can expose? who can reprove?" [71] In the next month this publication scored the preacher with doggerel verse on one page and praised him in the same medium on another. The approving poet encouraged Whitefield's colonial venture:

Plow the rough seas, the *Georgian* mountains trace;
Teach the *American,* how good his claim,
Learn him to lisp his bleeding Saviour's name.[72]

Later *The London Magazine* printed an interview between Whitefield and a visitor who, seeking to uphold the preacher's honesty,
was summarily dismissed by the outraged parson who *"excessively
reddening, and turning toward the Objector"* cried out, "Sir, I
shall not shew my accounts to you." [73] Still, to this periodical Whitefield was indebted for circulating a vindication of Bethesda written
by an objective visitor. A traveler, having returned from the colonies,
wrote of the staff at the Georgia orphanage and published his observations in the magazine:

And whatever Opinion I may have of the Absurdity of some of their
religious Notions, Tenets, and Practices, yet so far as they conduce to in-
culcate Sobriety, Industry and Frugality, they deserve Encouragement
from all Well-Wishers of their Country: and indeed, I could not
here perceive any Thing of that Spirit of Uncharitableness, and
enthusiastick Bigotry, their *Leader* is so fam'd for.[74]

The Gentleman's Magazine showed no more pronounced editorial
conviction on the true nature of the man, Whitefield, than did *The
London Magazine,* but it carried numerous items about him, includ-
ing both vitriolic attack [75] and impassioned defense.[76] Less than six
months before Whitefield died, the periodical published some
*"Flowers culled from an unpublished sermon of Mr. Whitefield's.
. . . Taken down in short hand by one who heard it preached."*
Typically, the selections ended on a note of implicit controversy:

In conclusion, he drew a most lively picture of Mary Magdalen's person and attire in her unregenerate state, and when she was, as he expressed himself, a *Fille de joie,* or a Town-Lady. A like picture has lately
been drawn by a preacher at Huntingdon, not a Methodist; the publication of which was extorted by the unjust clamour that was raised against
it.[77]

The secular community came to no single mind about Whitefield
even after his death. As a figure of an age which saw sincere piety
often accused of moroseness and severity,[78] Whitefield was subject in

any case to uncritical judgment. And as the dissonant character of two communities, he would hardly be correctly evaluated by the majority. David Hume may or may not have had the Methodists (and their prophet ,Whitefield) in mind when he wrote of the marks of decline which made him fear the fall of philosophy and decay of taste.[79] He was said, at second or third hand, to have heard Whitefield and commented that he surpassed anything he ever saw or heard from any other preacher. The authenticity of this compliment is uncertain, and there is room to doubt whether the sentiment commends Whitefield. But there is no uncertainty about William Hazlitt's contempt when in derision he called Whitefield "that burning and shining light," and denounced him for having disseminated a religion that was "carte blanche for ignorance and folly" and too often a combination of the "turbulence of a drunken brawl at an alehouse, with the indecencies of a bagnio." [80] Yet even Hazlitt admitted that Cowper's tribute to Whitefield was "one of his most spirited and striking things . . . written *con amore.*" [81]

George Eliot exhibited an almost mischievous attitude toward the field-preacher when she placed a veiled bust of him in the study of Dr. Lyon, the minister in *Felix Holt,* and had the good doctor give the following explanation:

. . . that is the eminent George Whitefield, who, you well know, had a gift of oratory as one on whom the tongue of flame had rested visibly. But Providence . . . ordained that the good man should squint; and my daughter has not yet learned to bear with this infirmity.[82]

There is sly humor, too, in Robert Southey's point of view as expressed in *Espriella's Letters from England.* In his biography of John Wesley, Southey treated Whitefield gently, if not sympathetically. But in the fictional work which purports to be a series of letters written by a Spanish Roman Catholic, visiting in England, Southey suggested that when Whitefield preached in the chapels of his patroness, the feeling incited was not the exclusive work of the Holy Spirit:

I know a lady who was one day questioning a beggar woman concerning her way of life, and the woman told her she had been one of my lady's groaners, which she explained by saying that she was hired at so much a week to attend at Lady Huntingdon's chapel, and groan during the sermon.[83]

As a balance to any such levity as that expressed in the quotations immediately above, or to the implication contained in them that Whitefield was regarded as increasingly insignificant by the secular community that outlived him, there is the testimony of William Blake, a man who believed himself a divinely appointed agent. In gravest earnest he wrote:

No Faith is in all the Earth: the Book of God is trodden under Foot.
He sent his two Servants, Whitefield & Wesley: were they Prophets,
Or were they Idiots or Madmen? Shew us Miracles!
Can you have greater Mircles than these.[84]

Half a century later John Greenleaf Whittier, another poet in another land, looked on the "Whitefield Church" in Newburyport and sang to America of the preacher buried beneath the pulpit there who, though he blundered at times, was an advocate of the angels and still hallowed the town by his memory:

He erred: shall we count His gifts as naught?
Was the work of God in him unwrought?
The servant may through his deafness err,
And blind may be God's messenger;
But the errand is sure they go upon,—
The word is spoken, the deed is done.
Was the Hebrew temple less fair and good
That Solomon bowed to gods of wood? [85]

The controversial character that Whitefield bore in the ecclesiastical mind in his own times was not one that he sustained within the confines of the Christian community alone. The secular world in his day, and afterward, looked on him with mixed feelings and expressed itself in passion and prejudice.

Chapter XI

The Evangelist's Secret

IT is not easy to discover the secret of Whitefield's appeal to the multitudes who followed him and under the spell of his preaching stood silent and awed (or sobbed their conviction in mortal agony) in numbers impressive even if only a half, or a fraction, of those reported can be accepted. His popularity was obvious but difficult of explanation.

A strong case can be made for Whitefield as a devil or a saint. To draw a picture of the man in warped perspective and untrue color is simple. Such distortion has been the besetting characteristic of those who have written about him. Critics of Whitefield have often been, if not eighteenth century in fact, eighteenth century in attitude. That is, they have looked on Whitefield as a figure to champion or a mountebank to denounce. In such an approach it is possible only to say that his appeal was the magnetism of eternal truth, or to admit that he defrauded a trusting public. Neither of these extremes catches the essence of the man.

The character of Whitefield assumes clarity only as investigation searches beneath his surface history to the wellspring of his actions.

An approach to the understanding of Whitefield can be made by reference to the personality of the apostle Paul. It is not sufficient to say that Whitefield admired Paul extravagantly and sought to emulate him, although this is quite true. He was not a second Paul, but he and the missionary to the Gentiles shared more than the record of weathering storms at sea and knowing personal abuse.

The fact is that Whitefield (like Paul) considered himself called by a divine power to a great destiny, chosen before the foundation of the world. The greatness lay in the magnitude of the power that commanded him and his unbelievable opportunity to co-operate with such a creative force. The destiny was rooted in the irresistible

175

strength of the constraining love that summoned him. Whitefield's theology admitted of such an election. The experience of personal conversion sealed him in the faith that it had happened to him, that he was of the redeemed. The mission to Georgia was the beginning of a life devoted to the testimony that these things were true.

Like Paul, Whitefield was a paradox in the truest sense of the word. He was not so much a contradiction as he was a civil war, fighting within himself far more than he battled with the world. Admittedly, there is a measure of the melodramatic in Whitefield's autobiography and in the outbursts that punctuate his writings with self-depreciation or embarrassingly frank confessions. The fact that he employed transparent devices in the perfectly human tendency to draw attention to himself, however, does not mean that he was a charlatan. Fraud and naïveté are not the same thing. His spiritual struggle, about which he spoke too freely, was real enough.

The inward conflict that Whitefield suffered came partly from his odd combination of humility and pride. Habitually careful to acknowledge that the power which moved upon the multitudes to whom he preached was of God and that he himself was no more than an instrument of grace beyond personal control, Whitefield was childishly interested in "how many" and "how much." He noted whether the crowd was large or small, how they reacted, and what they said. But he did not miss the ability of James Blair, the basically sacrificial spirit of William Tennent, or the intellectual superiority of Edwards; and in the presence of these titans he was modest.

He showed an insolence unbecoming to the apostle of charity and brotherly love in insisting that his rights were denied him when, young, inexperienced, and insulting, he was refused access to the pulpits whose ministers did not elect to aid him in their own castigation. But the spirit of real tolerance breathed in his willingness to work in any communion where men were inclined to ignore externals and agree on essentials. That his conception of essentials was less flexible than our own is a characteristic of his century, not of his creed. His supreme arrogance in bringing a *new* gospel to a nominally Christian land was mitigated by the profound conviction that it was not *a* gospel, but *the* gospel.

Whitefield was a man of weak constitution who endured, and transcended, the frailty of the flesh. He wailed in mixed metaphor that God had sent a "thorn in the flesh to buffet him," but he rose

176

valiantly above bodily handicap. His continual bouts with sickness hardly interrupted his physically depleting preaching schedules in England or his long circuits through the colonial wilderness.

Whitefield was a ravaging fire that consumed his enemies, searing them with the intense heat of a sulphurous passion. He was also the glowing flame that warmed the hearts and lighted the way of friends whose loyalty was freely given, bravely maintained. Seemingly given to fawning before those nobly born or persons of rank, Whitefield actually asked no odds to cross theological swords with a commissary, or a bishop, or an archbishop. He admired Lady Huntingdon as an elect and noble mother in Israel, but he did not withhold censure of the frivolous world of London or Bath.

This paradoxical character of Whitefield is not seen in any single fact. It is apparent only when his theology and faith, together with the evaluation that his world put upon them, are measured against the panorama of his personal history. At this distance Whitefield seems often to have had more turbulence than depth, especially if judged by his writings, which are rarely profound and often dull. He must, however, be seen in his own setting.

There is no denying that Whitefield appealed to men by his histrionic ability and his unerring flair for the dramatic. Yet to say that his main attraction in America was that he brought the colonists their first taste of theater leaves unexplained the man's popularity in the old world. In a deeper sense, however, Whitefield's unique power over men may be illuminated in terms of the theater.

The greatness of any enduring drama rests finally on a scene of identification, a point at which the piece upon the boards achieves reality in the life of the man in the pit, because he looks on it and says this could happen to me, this has happened to me. When the genius of a great actor informs such a scene, the one who watches recognizes universality and instinctively reponds. The place at which Whitefield's dramatic ability touched the lives of his audiences was that of the human predicament. He spoke to man's eternal question: What shall I do to be saved? The individual in the pit heard the strange man on the boards speaking of a restlessness that any man knew and of a certainty that every man sought. The situation to which Whitefield addressed himself was ruthlessly democratic: it embraced the colliers at Kingswood, the fan painters at Bath, sailors at sea, and slaves in Georgia. Whitefield was insured an audience because he played to man's dilemma, not because he acted. Only the setting changed. The drama was always the same.

Whitefield's faith and his theology were both rooted in the human situation. His faith overcame what his theology professed. His theology was not new. Men had previously heard all that he had to say. They had not, however, heard it said quite in the idiom that he used. The difference was not in his technique. The difference was in the spokesman. And here, seemingly, is the real secret of Whitefield's attraction: the intensely confessional character of his preaching—the intensely confessional character of the man who preached.

The paradoxical nature of his personality could not defeat the attraction of the testimony that he gave. However trite, the word must be said: Whitefield was appealing, not because of this circumstance, but in spite of it. By the Pauline cast of his make-up he could, and often did, obscure the horizon against which he stood. Too much of the time he was a theological cuttlefish. But in the end it was of no matter, because beneath the surface of what he said was the solid stratum of what he was—a man who knew himself called of God and redeemed.

In a sense Whitefield *was* dead to the world. None could doubt it who heard him speak. His sermons are said to have lost much between the pulpit and the press; somehow they were subtly changed, even when the words were identical, because they had been taken down in shorthand. What the printed page lacked was the burning passion that made his often ordinary words incandescent with a power that transformed them, because the man *was* what he was saying. There was a measure in which Whitefield achieved that exceedingly rare quality of the prophet—he could preach what he practiced, instead of trying to practice what he preached.

Although not within the scope of this work to trace Whitefield's influence, or lack of it, on succeeding generations, it can be remarked in this connection that his fate was not a singular religious phenomenon. Many shone in the reflected glory of his own brightness. Thousands were warmed, but few were ignited.

The advantages which Whitefield held over the regular clergy were not his novelty, nor the cobweb distinctions of theology which many of his followers probably failed to comprehend completely. His advantage over other preachers was the earnestness with which he said even questionable things because they were not questioned by him.

Unwittingly Whitefield was illustrative of his basic theology— that some are moved by a power beyond themselves. This he could never deny in the face of his decision to go to Georgia and his subsequent history which ran far beyond the time he would have thought and wished himself dead. Nor could Whitefield deny the new birth when he remembered the days before he knew himself redeemed. Such an assurance was inescapable in his preaching, and in the face of such testimony men could only scoff or succumb.

Whitefield was also illustrative of his basic faith—that man can turn himself toward the eternal. None had pressed toward the kingdom with greater zeal than he. His tenacity had outlasted his despair, and he had lived to see the dawn for which he had prayed.

Wherever he went, whatever he preached, Whitefield was himself. That self was the paradoxical, Pauline personality that was rife with conflict. But he was free and honest to own that self and, more important, to acknowledge the power in which he lived. This highly confessional preaching affected men as dramatics and novelty could never do alone and as unsupported homilies could never do at all. People were drawn to Whitefield, because they recognized in him one who had solved the riddle of human existence. In desire and longing they listened to him, hoping to work out their own difficulties, although neither he nor they would have defined the circumstances with quite the same words that are used here.

The hard basic core of the Whitefield personality was the fact that he had experienced the new birth. That was more important than why or how it had happened. His mind explained it in one way, and his heart accepted it in another. A hiatus between his theology and his faith was unavoidable, just as it was inevitable that there should have been controversy over the man himself. But beneath the theology and the faith, there was the ground of Whitefield's being, an abiding conviction that he knew God. His theology and his faith sprang from that certainty. If Whitefield was a charlatan, then he deceived himself more than he ever duped those who heard him. His basic honesty was one factor that made it possible for many to gloss over or forgive his surface errors and faults, however grave.

The heated controversies that surrounded Whitefield were unavoidable. Some argued with him because of his faith and some because of his theology. Some took issue with this or that facet of his paradoxical personality or with a conflict between two of its clashing traits. But even his bitterest enemies proclaimed by their very hostility that he was a person of significance. The reason for this lay in the central fact of the faith that he affirmed. He was a confessional individual. Encountering him, one could attack, flee, or surrender, but it was impossible to come into his presence and remain neutral about him, for his faith could not be ignored. Either controversy or conversion was inescapable.

Whitefield's distinctive ability to hold one creed while preaching another faith was lost to his less intoxicated followers, who found themselves compelled to go one way or another and so could not—as he—embrace the conflicting forces of existence in a way of life that held, but was not undone by, inevitable tensions. For that reason even Whitefield's most ardent admirers often lacked his basic appeal for others.

Admittedly, the stage was well set for Whitefield's appearance. He was ably equipped with natural talents, and in his time men begged or dared the church to give them faith—a challenge, incidentally, that was rarely met. George Whitefield preached a theology that was easily understood and a faith that was easily accepted. Moreover, there was wide enough variance between the two to satisfy diverse tastes. Yet beyond the outward factors that disposed men to his favor and fitted him for their acceptance was the basic fact of his confessional testimony. Men who were searching for a standard to which they might pin their colors appropriated—when they could— the banner that he offered. When they could not, they were grateful for the respite of standing by to look at one who "knew whom he had believed."

Notes

Whitefield's *Journals* are referred to by number, included parenthetically in the bibliography. His collected writings are referred to as *Works*.

Chapter I

1. John Gillies, *Memoirs of the Life of the Reverend George Whitefield* (London and Edinburgh, 1772), p. 274.
2. Luke Tyerman, *The Life of the Rev. George Whitefield* (New York, 1877), II, 599.
3. *Virginia Gazette*, No. 1015 (Purdie and Dixon), November 1, 1770, p. 1. (Editors' names are parenthetically included in citations from issues during periods when more than one publication bore the same name.)
4. Abel Stevens, *The History of the Religious Movement of the Eighteenth Century, Called Methodism* (New York, 1858-61), I, 466.
5. Joseph Beaumont Wakeley, *The Prince of Pulpit Orators* (New York, 1871), p. 384.
6. *Journal* VII, 39; *Works*, II, Letter DCL, 151.
7. *Virginia Gazette*, No. 464, June 20, 1745, p. 3.
8. *Works*, III, Letter MCCCXXXI, 327-28.
9. *Virginia Gazette*, No. 1015 (Purdie and Dixon), November 1, 1770, p. 1.
10. William Jay, *Memoirs of the Life and Character of the Late Rev. Cornelius Winter* (New York, 1811), p. 80. Winter became Whitefield's assistant in 1767.
11. *Virginia Gazette*, No. 1016 (Purdie and Dixon), January 17, 1771, p. 1.
12. Stevens, *op. cit.*, p. 467. Also see *Pennsylvania Gazette*, No. 2182, October 18, 1770, p. 3, and No. 2183, October 25, 1770, p. 2.
13. Charles Wesley, *An Elegy on the Late Reverend George Whitefield* (Bristol, 1771), p. 3.
14. John Wesley, *A Sermon on the Death of the Rev. Mr. George Whitefield*. Facsimile (Atlanta, 1953), p. 1. Hereinafter cited as Wesley's *Sermon on Whitefield*.
15. Gillies, *op. cit.*, pp. 276-77.
16. John Wesley, *The Journal of the Rev. John Wesley* (London, 1909-16), V, 397-99. Hereinafter cited as Wesley's *Journal*.
17. *Virginia Gazette*, No. 1032 (Purdie and Dixon), May 9, 1771, p. 1.
18. Ebenezer Pemberton, *Heaven the Residence of the Saints* (London, 1771), p. 31.
19. *Virginia Gazette*, No. 1053 (Purdie and Dixon), October 3, 1771, p. 2.
20. Gillies, *op. cit.*, p. 1.
21. George Whitefield, *A Short Account of God's Dealings with the Reverend Mr. George Whitefield* (London, 1740), p. 8. Hereinafter cited as *Short Account*.
22. Charles G. Harper, *The Oxford Gloucester and Milford Haven Road* (London, 1905), II, 1.
23. *Short Account*, pp. 9-10.
24. Thomas Brown, *The Works of Mr. Thomas Brown* (London, 1715), III, 277-78.

25. *Short Account,* p. 11.
26. Ola Elizabeth Winslow, *Jonathan Edwards* (New York, 1941), p. 181.
27. *Short Account,* p. 13.
28. *Ibid.,* p. 18.
29. *Ibid.,* p. 23.
30. *Ibid.,* p. 12.
31. Gillies, *op. cit.,* p. 2.
32. *Short Account,* p. 12.
33. *Ibid.,* p. 14.
34. Henry Fielding, *The History of Tom Jones a Foundling* (New York, 1931), p. 350. Hereinafter cited as *Tom Jones.*
35. *Short Account,* p. 15.
36. *Ibid.,* p. 17.
37. *Ibid.,* pp. 18-19.
38. *Ibid.,* p. 23.
39. *Ibid.,* p. 24.

Chapter II

1. *Short Account,* p. 24. See James Woodforde, *The Diary of a Country Parson* (London, 1926), I, 13-15, for record of eighteenth-century student vice.
2. *Short Account,* p. 25.
3. *Ibid.,* p. 40.
4. *Ibid.,* p. 26.
5. *Ibid.,* p. 27.
6. *Ibid.,* p. 29.
7. *Ibid.,* pp. 37-38.
8. George Whitefield, "All Men's Place," *Eighteen Sermons* (Newburyport, 1797), pp. 290-91. Hereinafter cited as *Eighteen Sermons.*
9. *Short Account,* pp. 38-39.
10. Jay, *op. cit.,* p. 63.
11. *Short Account,* pp. 48-49.
12. Approximate date set by Whitefield's reference to Lent, *ibid.,* pp. 47-48.
13. *Works,* I, Letter VII, 10.
14. *Short Account,* pp. 50-59. For discussion of prisons see Walter Besant, *London in the Eighteenth Century* (New York, 1903), pp. 534-45.
15. In a letter "From Mr. Whitefield, to Mr. J. Wesley," written in April, 1737, for which see *The Methodist Magazine,* XXI (July, 1798), 358.
16. *Works,* I, Letter XIX, 23.
17. *Short Account,* p. 53; Rezeau Brown, *Memoirs of Augustus Hermann Francke* (Philadelphia, [1830], pp. 116-17.
18. *Short Account,* p. 56.
19. *Ibid.,* p. 64.
20. *Ibid.,* p. 57; "Sermon XXXVII: The Duty of searching the Scriptures," *Works,* VI, 85.
21. *Short Account,* pp. 63-64.
22. T. G. Bonney, ed., *Cathedrals, Abbeys and Churches of England and Wales* (London, 1898), I, 206-15.
23. *Short Account,* p. 68.
24. *Works,* I, Letter XIII, 15.
25. *Short Account,* p. 69.
26. *Works,* I, Letter XIII, 16; "Answer to the Bishop of London's Last Pastoral Letter," *ibid.,* IV, 13.
27. *Ibid.,* I, Letter XIII, 15.
28. *Short Account,* p. 71.
29. *Works,* I, Letter XV, 17.
30. James A. H. Murray and others, eds., *A New English Dictionary* (Oxford, 1888-1928), I, Pt. I, 504.

31. *Works*, I, Letter XVI, 18.
32. William Wale, ed., *Whitefield's Journals, to Which is Prefixed His "Short Account" and "Further Account."* (London, 1905), p. 69. Hereinafter cited as Wale.
33. Gillies, *op. cit.*, p. 279.
34. George Whitefield, *The Two First Parts of His Life, with His Journals, Revised, Corrected and Abridged* (London, 1756), p. 24. Hereinafter cited as *Life, with Journals, Revised*.
35. "Sermon VIII: The Necessity and Benefits of Religious Society," *Works*, V, 120.
36. *Ibid.*, I, Letter XVI, 19.
37. Wale, p. 68.
38. *Ibid.*, p. 69.
39. *Ibid.*, pp. 69-72.
40. Robert Wright, *A Memoir of General James Oglethorpe* (London, 1867), pp. 48-55.
41. Wale, p. 72. Delamotte was the son of a London merchant. Wesley's *Journal*, I, 106.
42. Wale, pp. 69-85, *passim*.
43. *Works*, I, Letter XXVII, 30.
44. *Journal* I, 25.

Chapter III

1. H. D. Traill, ed., *Social England* (New York, 1902), V, 345.
2. Wesley's *Journal*, I, 401.
3. *Ibid.*, I, 407.
4. Wale, p. 72.
5. *Life, with Journals, Revised*, p. 29.
6. Wale, pp. 72-73.
7. *Life, with Journals, Revised*, p. 30.
8. "A Letter to the Reverend Mr. John Wesley: In Answer to his Sermon, entituled, *Free Grace*," *Works*, IV, 56. Hereinafter cited as "Letter to Wesley."
9. Thomas Jackson, *The Life of the Rev. Charles Wesley* (New York, 1842), p. 95.
10. "Remarks on a Pamphlet, Entitled, The Enthusiasm of Methodists and Papists compared," *Works*, IV, 242. Hereinafter cited as "Remarks on Methodists and Papists."
11. *Journal* I, 52.
12. *Ibid.*, pp. 28-29.
13. *Ibid.*, p. 33.
14. *Ibid.*, p. 38.
15. *Ibid.*, p. 36.
16. *Ibid.*, pp. 47-48.
17. *Ibid.*, p. 57.
18. William Stephens, *A Journal of the Proceedings in Georgia* (London, 1742), I, 199. Hereinafter cited as Stephens' *Journal*.
19. *Ibid.*, I, 204.
20. *Ibid.*, I, 222.
21. *Virginia Gazette*, No. 72, December 16, 1737, p. 3.
22. *Ibid.*, No. 75, January 6, 1738, p. 4.
23. Wesley's *Journal*, I, 413.
24. *Ibid.*, I, 422.
25. *Journal* II, 12.
26. *Ibid.*, p. 2.
27. *Journal* I, 56; *Journal* II, 2; Stephens' *Journal*, I, 200.
28. *Journal* II, 2-3.
29. *Journal* III, 20.
30. *Short Account*, pp. 11-14.
31. Gillies, *op. cit.*, p. 271.

32. Stephens' *Journal*, I, 211.
33. "A Letter to the Revd. Thomas Church," *Works*, IV, 120. Hereinafter cited as "Letter to Church."
34. Stephens' *Journal*, I, 283.
35. *Ibid.*, I, 308.
36. *Ibid.*, I, 330.
37. *Ibid.*
38. *Ibid.*, II, 14.
39. *Ibid.*, II, 243.
40. *Ibid.*, II, 304.
41. From a letter "To the Inhabitants of Savannah," *Works*, III, 429.
42. *Journal* I, 40.
43. *Works*, III, Letter MCLXXXVII, 222.
44. *Ibid.*, III, Letter MCCCV, 307.
45. Wale, p. 81.
46. *Ibid.*, p. 85.
47. *Journal* II, 5.
48. *Ibid.*, p. 3.
49. Wale, p. 78.
50. *Journal* II, 11.
51. Gillies, *op. cit.*, p. 25.
52. *Works*, I, Letter XL, 44.
53. *Ibid.*, I, Letter XLI, 45.
54. *Journal* III, 5.

Chapter IV

1. *Journal* II, 13.
2. *Ibid.*, p. 21.
3. *Ibid.*, p. 25.
4. *Ibid.*, p. 31.
5. *Ibid.*, p. 36.
6. *Ibid.*, p. 1.
7. George L. Lam and Warren H. Smith, "Two Rival Editions of George Whitefield's *Journal*, London, 1738," *Studies in Philology*, XLI, No. 1 (January, 1944), 86-93.
8. *Journal* III, 5.
9. John Brown, *An Estimate of the Manners and the Principles of the Times* (London, 1757), p. 85.
10. *Journal* III, 11.
11. *Ibid.*, pp. 11-14.
12. A. Barbeau, *Life & Letters at Bath in the xviij th Century* (New York, 1904), p. 158.
13. Aaron Seymour, *The Life and Times of Selina, Countess of Huntingdon* (London, 1839-40), I, 24-25, 98-99, 179, 463-64, 478. Hereinafter cited as Seymour's *Life*.
14. *Ibid.*, I, 196.
15. Edith Sitwell, *Bath* (London, [1932]), p. 125.
16. *Journal* III, 17.
17. *Ibid.*, pp. 23-25.
18. *Weekly Miscellany*, February 10, 1739 (n.v.), for citation of which see Tyerman, *op. cit.*, I, 172.
19. *Journal* III, 21.
20. *Ibid.*, p. 25.
21. *Ibid.*
22. *The London Magazine*, VIII (July, 1739), 342.
23. *Journal* III, 25-26.

Notes

24. *Ibid.*, p. 26.
25. Seymour's *Life*, II, 357.
26. Samuel Johnson, *Lives of the English Poets* (Oxford, 1905), II, 423.
27. John Wesley in a letter published in *The London Chronicle*, IX, No. 630 (January 8, 1761), 32.
28. *Journal* III, 44.
29. *Ibid.*, p. 28.
30. Thomas Southcliffe Ashton and Joseph Sykes, *The Coal Industry of the Eighteenth Century* (Manchester, 1929), p. 150.
31. *Journal* III, 28.
32. Gillies, *op. cit.*, pp. 37-38.
33. *The London Magazine*, VIII (May, 1739), p. 239.
34. *Journal* III, 28-31.
35. *Ibid.*, p. 45.
36. *Ibid.*, pp. 33-35.
37. *The Gentleman's Magazine*, IX (March, 1739), 162.
38. *Journal* III, 71-72.
39. *Works*, I, Letter XLVI, 49.
40. Tyerman, *op. cit.*, I, 207; Besant, *op. cit.*, p. 124.
41. Besant, *op. cit.*, pp. 244, 554.
42. *Journal* III, 77.
43. Seymour's *Life*, I, 92.
44. *Journal* III, 77.
45. Tyerman, *op. cit.*, I, 226.
46. *Journal* III, 80.
47. *Ibid.*, pp. 83-84.
48. *Pennsylvania Gazette*, No. 558, August 23, 1739, p. 2.
49. This was the period of the publication of the anonymous *The Methodists, an Humorous Burlesque Poem* (London, 1739).
50. *Works*, I, Letter LXV, 63.
51. *Journal* V, 23.
52. *Pennsylvania Gazette*, No. 570, November 15, 1739, p. 3.
53. *Journal* V, 31.
54. Benjamin Franklin, *The Life of Benjamin Franklin* (Philadelphia, 1916), I, 265.
55. *Journal* V, 35.
56. John Nichols, *Literary Anecdotes of the Eighteenth Century* (London, 1812), II, 547.
57. *Journal* V, 35.
58. *Ibid.*, p. 37.
59. *Ibid.*, pp. 44-45.
60. *Pennsylvania Gazette*, No. 571, November 22, 1739, p. 4.
61. *Journal* V, 52.
62. *Ibid.*, p. 59.
63. *Ibid.*, p. 64.
64. *Ibid.*
65. *Virginia Gazette*, No. 177, December 21, 1739, p. 3.
66. *Journal* V, 85.
67. *Ibid.*, p. 70.
68. *Ibid.*, pp. 77-78.
69. *Journal* VI, 4.
70. *Journal* V, 86.
71. *Ibid.*, 82.
72. Stephens' *Journal*, II, 244.
73. *Ibid.*, p. 246.
74. *Virginia Gazette*, No. 181, January 18, 1740, p. 3.

Chapter V

1. *Journal* VI, 3.
2. *Ibid.*
3. *Works,* I, Letter CLXX, 157.
4. Stephens' *Journal,* II, 248.
5. Francis Moore, *A Voyage to Georgia* (London, 1744), p. 25.
6. *Journal* VI, 5.
7. Patrick Tailfer and others, *A True and Historical Narrative of the Colony of Georgia in America* (Charles-Town, South Carolina, 1741), p. 113.
8. *Works,* I, Letter CLIX, 147.
9. Stephens' *Journal,* II, 319.
10. *Ibid.,* II, 418. Thaddeus Mason Harris, *Biographical Memorials of James Oglethorpe* (Boston, 1841), p. 199.
11. Tyerman, *op. cit.,* I, 440. *Works,* III, 465.
12. Stephens' *Journal,* II, 271. Also see Amanda Johnson, *Georgia as Colony and State* (Atlanta, [1938]), p. 67.
13. Wright, *op. cit.,* p. 270.
14. Stephens' *Journal,* II, 323.
15. *Ibid.,* II, 324.
16. Wright, *op. cit.,* p. 272.
17. Thomas Gamble, Jr., *Bethesda* (Savannah, 1902), p. 16; Gamble quotes Whitefield without citing source.
18. "Continuation of the Account . . . of the Orphan-House," *Works,* III, 465.
19. Stephens' *Journal,* II, 375.
20. *Ibid.,* II, 328-29.
21. *Journal* VII, 63-64.
22. Stephens' *Journal,* II, 255-56.
23. *Ibid.*
24. *Ibid.,* II, 269.
25. *Ibid.,* II, 305.
26. "A Letter to the Inhabitants of Maryland, Virginia, North and South-Carolina," *Works,* IV, 35-49. Hereinafter cited as "Letter to Inhabitants."
27. *Works,* I, Letter CLXIX, 156.
28. William Seward, *Journal of a Voyage from Savannah to Philadelphia* (London, 1740), p. 1. Hereinafter cited as Seward's *Journal.*
29. *Ibid.,* p. 3.
30. *Journal* VI, 17.
31. Wesley's *Journal,* II, 395 n.
32. *The Christian History . . . for the Year 1743* (Boston, 1744-45), II, 361. Hereinafter cited as *Christian History.*
33. "The Gospel a Dying Saint's Triumph," *Eighteen Sermons,* p. 72, supplies the information in a footnote.
34. Joseph Smith's sermon prefixed to George Whitefield's *Fifteen Sermons* (Philadelphia, 1794), p. 20.
35. Charles Wesley, *op. cit.,* p. 17.
36. Winslow, *op. cit.,* pp. 134-35.
37. *Journal* I, 2.
38. *Journal* III, 17.
39. *Journal* VII, 57.
40. *Christian History,* II, 361.
41. Wakeley, *op. cit.,* pp. 225-26.
42. *Journal* VI, 43.
43. Jay, *op. cit.,* p. 21.
44. "A Letter to the Reverend Dr. Durell, Vice-Chancellor of the University of Oxford. Occasioned by a late Expulsion of Six Students from Edmund-Hall," *Works,* IV, 339. Hereinafter cited as "Letter to Durell."

45. *Ibid.,* IV, 340.
46. Jay, *op. cit.,* p. 21.
47. *Ibid.,* p. 18.
48. "Sermon III: *Abraham's* offering up his Son Isaac," *Works,* V, 46.
49. Seymour's *Life,* I, 208.
50. Wakeley, *op. cit.,* pp. 196-97.
51. Franklin, *op. cit.,* I, 265-72.
52. *Journal* VI, 27.
53. *Ibid.,* p. 30.
54. *Ibid.,* p. 38.
55. *Ibid.*
56. *Ibid.,* p. 44.
57. *The Wesleyan-Methodist Magazine,* 4th ser., V (February, 1849), 165.
58. *Journal* VI, 54.
59. *Journal* VII, 28.
60. Nichols, *op. cit.,* II, 547.
61. *Journal* VII, 40.
62. Wakeley, *op. cit.,* p. 142.
63. *Journal* VII, 41.
64. *Ibid.,* p. 44.
65. *Ibid.*
66. Jay, *op. cit.,* p. 26.
67. *Journal* VII, 53.
68. *Ibid.,* pp. 47-49.
69. *Ibid.,* pp. 42, 53.
70. *Ibid.,* p. 57.
71. *Ibid.*
72. *Ibid.,* p. 61.
73. Franklin, *op. cit.,* I, 267-68.
74. George B. Wood, *Early History of the University of Pennsylvania* (Philadelphia, 1896), p. 10.
75. *Journal* VII, p. 66.
76. *Ibid.,* p. 73.
77. *Ibid.,* p. 78.
78. George L. Walker, *Some Aspects of the Religious Life of New England* (New York, 1897), pp. 89-91.
79. *Journal* VII, 83.
80. *Ibid.,* p. 85.
81. Quoted from a private MS by Gillies, *op. cit.,* p. 69.

Chapter VI

1. *Works,* I, Letter CLXXI, 158.
2. *Ibid.,* IV, 479.
3. *Ibid.,* I, Letter CLXXI, 158.
4. Jay, *op. cit.,* p. 62.
5. *Works,* I, Letter CLXXII, 159. Tyerman, *op. cit.,* I, 369-70, identifies the woman as Elizabeth Delamotte.
6. *Works,* I, Letter CLXXIII, 161.
7. *Short Account,* pp. 12, 15.
8. *Journal* I, 15.
9. "Sermon VII: Thankfulness for Mercies received, a necessary Duty," *Works,* V, 102.
10. *Ibid.,* I, Letter CCIII, 194.
11. *Ibid.,* I, Letter CCCLXXVI, 344.
12. *The Gentleman's Magazine,* XI (November, 1741), 608.

13. *Works,* I, Letter CCCLXX, 338.
14. James Patterson Gledstone, *George Whitefield* (New York, 1901), p. 179. Tyerman, *op. cit.,* I, 530.
15. *Works,* I, Letter CCCLXXI, 339.
16. *Ibid.,* II, Letter DCLIV, 155.
17. Jay, *op. cit.,* p. 62.
18. *Ibid.,* pp. 62-63.
19. Wesley's *Journal,* II, 509. Also see p. 506.
20. Griffith T. Roberts, *Howell Harris* (London, [1951]), p. 60.
21. *Works,* II, Letter DLXVIII, 77.
22. *Ibid.,* III, Letter DCCCCLXXV, 13.
23. *Ibid.,* II, Letter DLIX, 68.
24. Leslie Stephen and Sidney Lee, eds., *The Dictionary of National Biography* (Oxford, 1937-38), XXI, 89.
25. *Works,* II, Letter DLXI, 70.
26. *Virginia Gazette,* No. 483, October 31, 1745, p. 1.
27. "A Faithful Minister's Parting Blessing," *Eighteen Sermons,* p. 18.
28. *Works,* II, Letter DCCCLXX, 387.
29. *Ibid.,* III, Letter MCCCCVI, 382.
30. *Ibid.,* II, Letter DXXXIV, 39.
31. *Caledonian Mercury,* No. 3598, October 11, 1743, p. 2.
32. *Works,* II, Letter DXLVII, 50-51.
33. *Ibid.*
34. *Ibid.,* II, Letter DLXXIII, 83. Also see *ibid.,* II, Letter DCCCLXVIII, 384, and Letter DCCCLXXV, 391.
35. *Virginia Gazette,* No. 995 (Purdie and Dixon), September 7, 1769, p. 1. Also see *Works,* III, 373 n.
36. *Journal* III, 39-43.
37. *Ibid.,* p. 41.
38. *Works,* I, Letter CCCXXXVII, 304.
39. *Ibid.*
40. *Ibid.,* I. Letter CCLXXXVIII, 268.
41. Dugald Butler, *John Wesley and George Whitefield in Scotland* (Edinburgh and London, 1898), pp. 15-25.
42. *Works,* I, Letter CCCXXXIX, 308.
43. *Ibid.,* I, Letter CCCXXXIX, 307.
44. Robert Philip, *The Life and Times of the Reverend George Whitefield* (London, 1837), p. 401.
45. Butler, *op. cit.,* p. 58.
46. *Works,* I, Letter CCCCXXXI, 409-10.
47. *The Scots Magazine,* IV (September, 1742), 437.
48. *Works,* I, Letter CCCXXXVII, 305.
49. *Pennsylvania Gazette,* No. 819, August 23, 1744, p. 1.
50. *Works,* III, Letter MCCCLXXXVII, 370.
51. *Ibid.,* III, Letter MCCCLXXXVIII, 370.
52. *Ibid.,* I, Letter CCXXI, 210-12.
53. Wesley's *Journal,* II, 421-22.
54. *Works,* IV, 54 ff.
55. Cited by Tyerman, *op. cit.,* I, 472.
56. *Works,* I, Letter CCCCLXIII, 448.
57. Wakeley, *op. cit.,* pp. 170-73.
58. William E. H. Lecky, *A History of England in the Eighteenth Century* (New York, 1888-91), II, 626-27.
59. *Works,* II, Letter DLVII, 64.
60. *Ibid.,* II, Letter DLXI, 70.
61. *Ibid.,* II, Letter DCXXI, 125.

Notes

62. *Ibid.*, III, "An Account of the Orphan-House in Georgia," 468.
63. Charles Chauncy, *Seasonable Thoughts on the State of Religion in New England* (Boston, 1743), p. 37. Hereinafter cited as Chauncy's *Thoughts.*
64. Benjamin Trumbull, *A Complete History of Connecticut* (New Haven, 1818), II, 244.
65. Chauncy's *Thoughts,* p. 250.
66. *Ibid.*, p. 189.
67. *Works,* II, Letter DCXL, 144.
68. Robert Southey, *Selections from the Letters of Robert Southey* (London, 1856), I, 410-11. Southey came by the *Journals* with difficulty.
69. *Works,* I, Letter CCCCXII, 388.
70. *Ibid.*, I, 387.
71. *The Gentleman's Magazine,* XL (April, 1770), 542.
72. *Works,* III, Letters MCXXVII, MCXXVIII, MCXXIX, 171-73.
73. *Ibid.*, I, Letter CCCCXII, 387-88.
74. *Ibid.*, II, Letter DCCLXXV, 278.
75. *Ibid.*, II, Letter DLI, 60.
76. *Ibid.*, III, Letter MCLXX, 207.
77. Robert Southey, *The Life of Wesley* (London, 1820), II, 357-58. Hereinafter cited as Southey's *Life.*
78. *Ibid.*, II, 358.
79. Sitwell, *op. cit.*, p. 85.
80. Barbeau, *op. cit.*, p. 190.
81. Seymour's *Life,* I, 196-97.
82. *Works,* II, Letter DCLXX, 167-68.
83. Seymour's *Life,* I, 445.
84. *Works,* II, Letter DCCCVIII, 317.
85. P. D. S. Chesterfield, *Letters of Lord Chesterfield to Lord Huntingdon* (London, 1923), p. 109.
86. Seymour's *Life,* I, 477. The description is Walpole's.
87. *Ibid.*, I, 468.
88. *Works,* III, Letter MCCCXXXVII, 332.
89. *Ibid.*, I, Letter CCLXXXVI, 267.
90. Seymour's *Life,* I, 202-3.
91. *Works,* III, Letter DCCCCLXVIII, 6.
92. *Ibid.*, III, Letter DCCCCLXXVIII, 17.
93. *Ibid.*, III, Letter MCXXXIV, 177.
94. *Ibid.*, III, Letter MCLII, 193.
95. *Ibid.*, III, Letter MCLXXXVII, 222.
96. Benjamin Rush, *The Autobiography of Benjamin Rush* ([Princeton, N.J.], 1948), p. 55.
97. Tyerman, *op. cit.*, II, 291.
98. *Works,* II, Letter DCCCCVII, 424.
99. *Ibid.*, II, Letter DCCCCXI, 427.
100. Tyerman, *op. cit.*, II, 280-81.
101. *Works,* II, Letter DCCCCXXVI, 440.
102. *Ibid.*, II, Letter DCCCCXL, 453.
103. *Ibid.*, I, Letter CCXLI, 230.
104. George Whitefield, *An Extract of the Preface to the Reverend Mr. Whitefield's Account of the Orphan-House in Georgia* (Edinburgh, 1741), pp. 6-7. Hereinafter cited as *Preface to Orphan-House.*
105. *Works,* I, Letters CCCXVI, CCCXVII, CCCXVIII, 288-89.
106. *Preface to Orphan-House,* pp. 19-21.
107. "Soul Prosperity," *Eighteen Sermons,* pp. 55-56.
108. *Preface to Orphan-House,* pp. 14-15.
109. *Ibid.*, p. 16.

110. *Works*, III, 447-48.
111. *Preface to Orphan-House*, p. 11.
112. *Works*, III, Letter MXVII, p. 55.
113. Charles Hodge, *The Constitutional History of the Presbyterian Church in the United States of America* (Philadelphia [1851]), Pt. II, 243.
114. Gillies, *op. cit.*, p. 208.
115. *Works*, III, Letters MXXVII-MXLV, 65-92.
116. Francis Moore, *op. cit.*, pp. 30, 56.
117. *Works*, III, Letter MXXXV, 75.
118. *Ibid.*, III, Letter MXLI, 86.
119. *Ibid.*, III, Letter MXL, 83.
120. *Ibid.*, III, Letter MXLI, 88.
121. *Ibid.*, III, Letter MXLV, 92.
122. *Ibid.*, III, Letter MLXXVI, 117.
123. Union Society, Savannah, Ga., *Minutes of the Union Society* (Savannah, 1860), p. [247].
124. *Works*, III, Letter MCCCIX, 310.
125. *Ibid.*, III, Letter MCCXLII, 263.
126. *Pennsylvania Gazette*, No. 1837, March 8, 1764, p. 2.
127. *Works*, III, Letter MCCCIV, 306.
128. *Pennsylvania Gazette*, No. 1838, March 15, 1764, p. 2.
129. *Works*, III, Letter MCCCV, 307.
130. *Ibid.*, III, Letter MCCCXII, 312.
131. *Ibid.*, III, Letter MCCLXXXVIII, P.S., 294.
132. *The London Chronicle*, XVII, No. 1285, March 16, 1765, p. 262; No. 1297, April 13, 1765, p. 353. "Continuation of the Account . . . of the Orphan-House," *Works*, III, 469.
133. *Works*, III, Letter MCCCXXII, 320.
134. *Ibid.*, III, 475-84.
135. Seymour's *Life*, II, 255.
136. Rush, *op. cit.*, p. 56.
137. *Works*, III, Letter MCCXXV, 251.
138. *Ibid.*, III, Letter MCCCCXV, 387.
139. "Soul Prosperity," *Eighteen Sermons*, p. 59.
140. Seymour's *Life*, II, 128.
141. *Ibid.*, p. 129.
142. *Works*, III, Letters MCCCCXL-MCCCCXLI, 406-9.
143. *Ibid.*, III, Letter MCCCCXLIII, 410.
144. *Ibid.*, III, Letter MCCCCLXV, 427.
145. *London Chronicle*, XXVIII, No. 2169, November 8, 1770, p. 448.

Chapter VII

1. *Christian History*, I, 284.
2. *Works*, I, Letter CCXIV, 205; Letter CCCCLVIII, 442.
3. *Ibid.*, I, Letter CCXIV, 205.
4. "The Gospel a Dying Saint's Triumph," *Eighteen Sermons*, p. 63
5. "Sermon IX: The Folly and Danger of being not righteous enough," *Works*, V, 135.
6. "Sermon XLI: *Saul's* Conversion," *ibid.*, VI, 156.
7. "Sermon LIX: The True Way of beholding the LAMB of GOD," *ibid.*, VI, 425.
8. "A Faithful Minister's Parting Blessing," *Eighteen Sermons*, p. 5. "Letter to Durell," *Works*, IV, 329.
9. Jay, *op. cit.*, p. 54.
10. Perry Miller, *Jonathan Edwards* (New York, 1949), p. 133.
11. "The Good Shepherd," *Eighteen Sermons*, p. 360.

Notes

12. *Journal* I, 47. Cf. Supra. III, note 16.
13. *Works,* III, Letter MCCCCX, 385.
14. "Sermon L: Christians, Temples of the living GOD," *ibid.,* VI, 274.
15. "Sermon I: The Seed of the Woman, and the Seed of the Serpent," *ibid.,* V. 4-5.
16. George Whitefield, *The Indwelling of the Spirit* ([n.p.], 1741), p. 12. Hereinafter cited as *Indwelling Spirit.*
17. "Jacob's Ladder," *Eighteen Sermons,* p. 343.
18. "Neglect of Christ the Killing Sin," *ibid.,* p. 256.
19. George Whitefield, *The Nature and Necessity of Our New Birth* (London, 1737), p. 9. Hereinafter cited as *New Birth.*
20. *Works,* I, Letter CXLII, 231.
21. *Ibid.,* II, Letter DCCLIII, 254.
22. *Ibid.,* I, Letter XXII, 25.
23. *Ibid.,* I, Letter CCLXVII, 250.
24. "Observations on Select Passages of Scripture turned into Catechetical Questions," *ibid.,* IV, 347. Hereinafter cited as "Catechetical Questions."
25. "Sermon XIII: The Potter and the Clay," *ibid.,* V, 202, 206.
26. "Sermon XXXIX: The Resurrection of *Lazarus,*" *ibid.,* VI, 123.
27. *Journal* VII, 30.
28. *Fifteen Sermons,* p. 12.
29. *Journal* IV, 37.
30. "Sermon I: The Seed of the Woman, and the Seed of the Serpent," *Works,* V, 9.
31. "Sermon LI: CHRIST the only Preservative against a Reprobate Spirit," *ibid.,* VI 292.
32. "Sermon IX: The Folly and Danger of being not righteous enough," *ibid.,* V, 128.
33. "Repentance and Conversion," *Eighteen Sermons,* p. 97.
34. "Neglect of Christ the Killing Sin," *ibid.,* pp. 261-62.
35. "All Men's Place," *ibid.,* p. 281.
36. "Sermon XXXVII: The Duty of searching the Scriptures," *Works,* VI, 81.
37. *Ibid.,* II, Letter DCCCCXXXVII, 450.
38. "Neglect of Christ the Killing Sin," *Eighteen Sermons,* pp. 259-61.
39. *Journal* VI, 49.
40. "Sermon XLVI: Of Justification by CHRIST," *Works,* VI, 217-18.
41. "Sermon XIII: The Potter and the Clay," *ibid.,* V, 211.
42. *Ibid.,* I, Letter XCIV, 90.
43. "Sermon I: The Seed of the Woman, and the Seed of the Serpent," *Works,* V, 13.
44. "A Faithful Minister's Parting Blessing," *Eighteen Sermons,* pp. 6, 7.
45. "Sermon I: The Seed of the Woman, and the Seed of the Serpent," *Works,* V, 20.
46. *Ibid.,* I, Letter LXXXII, 79.
47. John Whitehead, *The Life of the Rev. John Wesley* (London, 1793), pp. 359-60.
48. *Ibid.,* p. 360.
49. John Wesley, *The Works of the Rev. John Wesley* (London, 1829-31), VII, 375-76. Hereinafter cited as Wesley's *Works.*
50. "Letter to Wesley," *Works,* IV, 67.
51. *Ibid.,* p. 58.
52. John Overton, *The English Church* (New York, 1906), pp. 173-74.
53. *Works,* III, Letter MCLXXXIV, 220.
54. "The Furnace of Affliction," *Eighteen Sermons,* pp. 128-29.
55. *Works,* I, Letter CCCLVII, 324.
56. *Journal* IV, 9-10.
57. "All Men's Place," *Eighteen Sermons,* p. 290.
58. "The Burning Bush," *ibid.,* p. 211.
59. "Sermon XIV: The LORD our Righteousness," *Works,* V, 219.
60. "Sermon XXIV: What think ye of CHRIST?" *ibid.,* V, 356.
61. *Eighteen Sermons,* p. 328.

62. "Sermon LI: CHRIST the only Preservative against a Reprobate Spirit," *Works,* VI, 293.
63. "Catechetical Questions," *ibid.,* IV, 356.
64. "Sermon III: *Abraham's* offering up his Son *Isaac,*" *ibid.,* V, 45.
65. "Sermon XXIV: What think ye of CHRIST?" *ibid.,* V, 359.
66. "Sermon XIV: The Lord Our Righteousness," *ibid.,* V, 221.
67. "Sermon IX: The Folly and Danger of being not righteous enough," *ibid.,* V, 138.
68. "Sermon I: The Seed of the Woman, and the Seed of the Serpent," *ibid.,* V, 9.
69. *Journal* V, 46.
70. *Virginia Gazette,* No. 483, October 31, 1745, p. 1.
71. "The Method of Grace," *Fifteen Sermons,* p. 278.
72. "A Letter to the Religious Societies of *England,*" *Works,* IV, 27. Hereinafter cited as "Letter to Societies."
73. "Sermon CVIII: Of the Nature of Regeneration, and Its Necessity, in Order to Justification and Salvation," John Tillotson, *The Works of the Most Reverend Dr. John Tillotson* (London, 1743), VI, 1776.
74. Stephens' *Journal,* II, 320.
75. *Pennsylvania Gazette,* No. 591, April 10, 1740, p. 1.
76. Stephens' *Journal,* II, 307.
77. *Virginia Gazette,* No. 483, October 31, 1745, p. 1.
78. Richard Allestree, supposed author, *The Whole Duty of Man* (London, 1703), unnumbered forepages.
79. "Sermon I: The Seed of the Woman, and the Seed of the Serpent," *Works,* V, 15.
80. George Whitefield, *The Unbeliever Convicted* (Edinburgh, 1742), p. 10.
81. "Neglect of Christ the Killing Sin," *Eighteen Sermons,* p. 269.
82. "Sermon XIII: The Potter and the Clay," *Works,* V, 202.
83. George Whitefield, *The Happy Mourner Comforted* (Edinburgh, 1742), p. 23.
84. "Sermon XXIV: What think ye of CHRIST?" *Works,* V, 361.
85. "Sermon XXIII: Marks of a True Conversion," *ibid.,* V, 352.
86. "Sermon XLVI: Of Justification by CHRIST," *ibid.,* VI, 216.
87. "God a Believer's Glory," *Eighteen Sermons,* p. 306.
88. *New Birth,* p. 8.
89. "Sermon XXIV: What think ye of CHRIST?" *Works,* V, 369.
90. *Ibid.,* I, Letter CXIX, 114.
91. *Ibid.,* III, Letter MCLVII, 196.
92. *Journal* VII, 15.
93. *Ibid.,* p. 67.
94. *Works,* III, Letter MCCCLXXIX, 363.
95. "Sermon XLIV: CHRIST the Believer's Wisdom, Righteousness, Sanctification, and Redemption," *ibid.,* VI, 193.
96. *Indwelling Spirit,* p. 5.
97. *New Birth,* p. 21.
98. William B. Sprague, *Annals of the American Pulpit* (New York, 1859), V, 107-8.
99. "Letter to Societies," p. 29.
100. "Sermon XIII: The Potter and the Clay," *Works,* V, 209.
101. "Sermon XXX: CHRIST's Transfiguration," *ibid.,* V, 453.
102. "The Gospel a Dying Saint's Triumph," *Eighteen Sermons,* p. 77.
103. "All Men's Place," *ibid.,* p. 293.
104. *Works,* V, 392-403.
105. "Soul Prosperity," *Eighteen Sermons,* pp. 60-61.
106. "All Men's Place," *ibid.,* p. 288.
107. "The Lord our Light," *ibid.,* p. 160.
108. "Self-Enquiry Concerning the Work of God," *ibid.,* p. 197.
109. "Christ the Believer's Refuge," *ibid.,* pp. 35-36.
110. "Sermon XLVIII: Satan's Devices," *Works,* VI, 255.
111. "Sermon L: Christians, Temples of the living GOD," *ibid.,* VI, 274.

112. "Sermon I: The Seed of the Woman, and the Seed of the Serpent," *ibid.*, V, 15.
113. *Ibid.*, I, Letter CCCCLVIII, 442.
114. *Journal* III, 76-77.
115. *Journal* I, 29.
116. "Sermon VII: Thankfulness for Mercies received, a necessary Duty," *Works*, V, 98.
117. *Ibid.*, II, Letter DCIII, 110.
118. "Glorifying God in the Fire; or, the Right Improvement of Affliction," *Eighteen Sermons*, p. 178.
119. "Sermon XLVI: Of Justification by CHRIST," *Works*, VI, 224.

Chapter VIII

1. "Sermon II: Walking with God," *Works*, V, 27.
2. George Whitefield, *The Prodigal Son* (Glasgow, 1741), p. 4.
3. "Sermon XXXVII: The Duty of searching the Scriptures," *Works*, VI, 85.
4. "Letter to Inhabitants," *ibid.*, IV, 35-41.
5. *Journal* VI, 35.
6. "Letter to Inhabitants," *Works*, IV, 38.
7. *Ibid.*, IV, 37.
8. *Preface to Orphan-House*, p. 8.
9. *Works*, II, Letter DCCXIV, 209.
10. *Ibid.*, II, Letter DLXXXII, 90.
11. *Ibid.*, II, Letter DCCCLXXXVII, 404-5.
12. *Ibid.*, II, 404.
13. Justin Winson, ed., *Narrative and Critical History of America* (Boston and New York, 1887), V, 387.
14. Gillies, *op. cit.*, p. 349.
15. "Catechetical Questions," *Works*, IV, 357.
16. *Ibid.*, p. 360.
17. *Journal* III, 8.
18. "A Letter to Some Church-Members of the Presbyterian Persuasion, in Answer to Certain Scruples lately proposed . . . ," *Works*, IV, 48. Hereinafter cited as "Letter to Presbyterians."
19. "Letter to Wesley," *Ibid.*, IV, 55-57.
20. "Remarks on Methodists and Papists," *ibid.*, IV, 244.
21. "Letter to Inhabitants," *ibid.*, IV, 41. Edward McCrady, *The History of South Carolina under the Royal Government, 1719-1776* (New York, 1901), pp. 185-86.
22. "Catechetical Questions," *Works*, IV, 360.
23. "Letter to Inhabitants," *ibid.*, IV, 41.
24. "An Act of Praise," *ibid.*, IV, 489.
25. *Ibid.*, I, Letter CCCXXII, 293.
26. "Sermon XXXIX: The Resurrection of *Lazarus*," *ibid.*, VI, 115.
27. *Journal* III, 33.
28. *Journal* VII, 17.
29. *"Soul Dejection,"* *Eighteen Sermons*, p. 225.
30. *Journal* V, 39.
31. *Journal* VII, 23.
32. Edward Ellington, *The Reproach of Christ the Christian's Treasure* (London, 1771), p. 14.
33. "Sermon LII: The heinous Sin of Drunkenness," *Works*, VI, 312.
34. "Sermon XXXV: The Conversion of *Zaccheus*," *ibid.*, VI, 62.
35. Walker, *op. cit.*, pp. 91-92.
36. "Sermon XL: The Holy Spirit convincing the World of Sin, Righteousness, and Judgment," *Works*, VI, 141.
37. "An Answer to the Second Part of an Anonymous Pamphlet, entitled 'Observation upon . . . Methodists,'" *ibid.*, IV, 159. Hereinafter cited as "Second Letter."
38. *Journal*, VII, 42.

39. *New Birth*, pp. 25-26.
40. "Soul Dejection," *Eighteen Sermons*, p. 232.
41. "Second Letter," *Works*, IV, 160.
42. "Soul Dejection," *Eighteen Sermons*, p. 233.
43. "Sermon VII: Thankfulness for Mercies received, a necessary Duty," *Works*, V, 100.
44. "Sermon XXIV: What Think Ye of CHRIST?" *Ibid.*, V, 370.
45. "Sermon XXII: The Folly and Danger of parting with CHRIST for the Pleasures and Profits of Life," *ibid.*, V, 333-34.
46. "Sermon IX: The Folly and Danger of being not righteous enough," *ibid.*, V, 138.
47. *Ibid.*, V, 139.
48. "Spiritual Baptism," *Eighteen Sermons*, p. 251.
49. "Neglect of Christ the Killing Sin," *ibid.*, p. 270.
50. "Sermon XLII: Marks of having received the Holy Ghost," *Works*, VI, 170.
51. "The Beloved of God," *Eighteen Sermons*, p. 112.
52. *Ibid.*, p. 113.
53. "Sermon XLVII: The great Duty of Charity recommended," *Works*, VI, 240.
54. Rush, *op. cit.*, p. 255.
55. "Sermon XXXIII: The Gospel Supper," *Works*, VI, 34.
56. *Ibid.*, III, Letter MCXCV, 228.
57. Chauncy's *Thoughts*, p. 36.
58. Daniel Newell, *The Life of the Rev. George Whitefield* (New York, 1846), p. 160.
59. *Works*, III, Letter MLXXI, 113.
60. *Ibid.*, III, Letter MCIV, 147. Also see *ibid.*, III, Letter ML, 96.
61. *Ibid.*, III, Letter MCLXXXII, 218.
62. *Ibid.*, III, Letter MCCCXXIX, 326.
63. "Improvement of Afflictions," *Eighteen Sermons*, p. 176.
64. *Works*, III, Letter MCCCCLXIII, 425.
65. "Second Letter," *ibid.*, IV, 156-57.
66. "Letter to Church," *ibid*, IV, 116.
67. "Second Letter," *ibid.*, IV, 161.
68. George Whitefield, *The Almost Christian* (London, 1738), p. 20. The same sermon in *Works*, VI, 186, omits reference to reward.
69. *Works*, I, Letter CXXX, 123.
70. "Sermon XXXIII: The Gospel Supper," *ibid.*, VI, 20.
71. "God a Believer's Glory," *Eighteen Sermons*, p. 313.
72. "Sermon XLVII: The great Duty of Charity recommended," *Works*, VI, 230.
73. *Ibid.*, I, Letter CVIII, 103.
74. *Ibid.*, III, Letter DCCCCXXXIX, 27. Also see *Pennsylvania Gazette*, No. 594, May 1, 1740, p. 3; No. 595, May 8, 1740, p. 2.
75. *Journal* III, 58.
76. "Letter to Durell," *Works*, IV, 318.
77. "An Answer to the First Part of an Anonymous Pamphlet, entitled 'Observations upon . . . Methodists,'" *ibid.*, IV, 138. Hereinafter cited as "First Letter."
78. *Virginia Gazette*, No. 160, August 24, 1739, p. 1.
79. *Pennsylvania Gazette*, No. 594, May 1, 1740, p. 3.
80. *Fifteen Sermons*, introduction, p. 14. *Journal* V, 4. "Sermon I: The Seed of the Woman, and the Seed of the Serpent," *Works*, V, 16.
81. "Sermon VIII: The Necessity and Benefits of Religious Society," *Works*, V, 120.
82. "Continuation of the Account . . . of the Orphan-House," *ibid.*, III, 463.
83. Traill, *op. cit.*, V, 48, 49, 425, 428.
84. Besant, *op. cit.*, p. 156. G. M. Trevelyan, *Illustrated English Social History* (London, [1951]), III, 52. Also see Rosamond Bayne-Powell, *The English Child in the Eighteenth Century* (New York, [1939]), pp. 61-67, for splendid pictures of charity schools.
85. "Soul Prosperity," *Eighteen Sermons*, p. 57.

86. "The Good Shepherd," *ibid.*, p. 353.
87. *The Prodigal Son*, p. 28.

Chapter IX

1. François Misson, *Memoires et Observations Faites par un Voyageur en Engleterre* (La Haye, 1698), p. 366.
2. *Journal* III, 52.
3. Albert H. Hoyt, quoting Thomas Bradbury Chandler (1726-90), *New England Historical and Genealogical Register and Antiquarian Journal*, XXVII, No. 3 (July, 1873), p. 232.
4. "Sermon IX: The Folly and Danger of being not righteous Enough," *Works*, V, 129.
5. "Spiritual Baptism," *Eighteen Sermons*, p. 252.
6. "The Method of Grace," *Fifteen Sermons*, p. 278.
7. *Works*, II, Letter DCCLVIII, 261.
8. *Journal* V, 39.
9. "Answer to the Bishop of London's Last Pastoral Letter," *Works*, IV, 18. Hereinafter cited as "Answer to the Bishop."
10. "Sermon XLI: *Saul's* Conversion," *ibid.*, VI, 156.
11. *Journal* VII, 27.
12. A. S. Tuberville, *English Men and Manners in the Eighteenth Century* (Oxford, 1926), p. 295.
13. *Pennsylvania Gazette*, No. 591, April 10, 1740, p. 1.
14. Samuel Johnson, *A Dictionary of the English Language* (London, 1773), I, pages unnumbered.
15. George Lavington, *The Enthusiasm of Methodists and Papists, Compar'd* (London, 1749-1751, I, Pt. I, 81-82.
16. "Answer to the Bishop," *Works*, IV, 16. Also see *Journal* V, 7, 12.
17. Edmund Gibson, *The Bishop of London's Three Pastoral Letters to the People of His Diocese* (London, 1732).
18. Tyerman, *op. cit.*, I, 292.
19. "Answer to the Bishop," *Works*, IV, 6.
20. *Ibid.*, IV, 9.
21. *Ibid.*, IV, 10.
22. *Ibid.*, IV, 13.
23. *Ibid.*, IV, 16.
24. *Ibid.*, IV, 15.
25. *Ibid.*
26. *Journal* IV, 10.
27. "Answer to the Bishop," *Works*, IV, 139.
28. *Genuine and Secret Memoirs Relating to the Life and Adventures of that Arch Methodist, Mr. G. W—fi-d* (Oxford, 1742), pp. 25-26. Hereinafter cited as *Secret Memoirs*.
29. "First Letter," *Works*, IV, 131.
30. "The Good Shepherd," *Eighteen Sermons*, p. 350.
31. "Second Letter," *Works*, IV, 145.
32. *Ibid.*, IV, 168-69.
33. Tyerman, *op. cit.*, I, 358-59. Also see Arthur Lyon Cross, *The Anglican Episcopate and the American Colonies* (Cambridge, 1924), p. 49.
34. *Journal* II, 12.
35. *Journal* VI, 10-11.
36. Wright, *op. cit.*, p. 268.
37. Alexander Garden, *Six Letters to the Rev. Mr. George Whitefield* (Boston, 1740), pp. 6-7.
38. *Ibid.*, p. 32.
39. *Journal* VII, 6.
40. *Works*, I, Letter CCVI, 197.
41. *Ibid.*, I, Letter CCXVI, 206-7.

42. *Ibid.*, I, Letter CCX, 200.
43. *Nashville Christian Advocate*, n.s. XXXI, No. 9, March 4, 1871, p. 2.
44. Stephens' *Journal*, II, 457.
45. Cross, *op. cit.*, p. 86.
46. *New-England Historical and Genealogical Register and Antiquarian Journal*, XXIV, No. 2 (April, 1870), 117.
47. *Ibid.*, p. 118.
48. *Short Account*, p. 26.
49. Lam and Smith, *op. cit.*, p. 86.
50. *Journal* IV, 17.
51. Tyerman, *op. cit.*, I, 159 n.
52. Seymour's *Life*, I, 196.
53. *Ibid.*, I, 197.
54. "Continuation of the Account . . . of the Orphan-House," *Works*, III, 465.
55. *Journal* V, 64.
56. "The Gospel a Dying Saint's Triumph," *Eighteen Sermons*, p. 68.
57. Alfred H. New, *The Coronet & the Cross* (London, 1857), p. 225.
58. *Works*, III, Letter MCXIX, 159.
59. *Ibid.*, III, 160.
60. *Journal* IV, 31.
61. *Journal* VII, 57.
62. *Journal* V, 63. Also see "An Unpublished Journal of George Whitefield," transcribed and edited by Earnest Edward Eells, *Church History*, VII, No. 4 (December, 1938), 34.
63. *Pennsylvania Gazette*, No. 571, November 22, 1739, p. 2. Also see *Virginia Gazette*, No. 181, January 18, 1740, p. 2.
64. *Virginia Gazette* (Rind), No. 151, March 30, 1769, p. 2; *ibid.* (Purdie and Dixon), No. 953, August 24, 1769, p. 2.
65. *Christian History*, II, 14.
66. *Ibid.*, II, 382-84.
67. Chauncy's *Thoughts*, p. 144.
68. *Ibid.*, p. 48.
69. Charles Chauncy, *Enthusiasm Described and Caution'd Against* (Boston, 1742), p. 15.
70. Chauncy's *Thoughts*, p. 178.
71. "A Letter to the Reverend the President, and Professors, Tutors, and Hebrew Instructor, of Harvard-College in Cambridge," *Works*, IV, 203.
72. *Ibid.*, IV, pp. 225-26.
73. *Ibid.*, IV, p. 225.
74. *Ibid.*, III, Letter MCCCXII, 312.
75. *The London Magazine*, XXXIII (May, 1764), 269.
76. Gillies, *op. cit.*, p. 241.
77. *Works*, III, Letter MLX, 104.
78. Church of Scotland, *The Declaration of the True Presbyterians within the Kingdom of Scotland* ([n.p.], 1742), p. 3.
79. *Ibid.*, p. 6.
80. *Ibid.*, p. 21. Also see pp. 12-21, *passim*.
81. *Pennsylvania Gazette*, No. 819, August 23, 1744, p. 1.
82. *Journal* VI, 24.
83. *Life, with Journals, Revised*, p. 348 n.
84. Wesley's *Journal*, II, 395, n.
85. *Journal* VI, 24.
86. Levin Theodore Reichel, *The Early History of the Church of the United Brethren* (Nazareth, Pa., 1888), p. 80.
87. Adelaide Fries, *The Moravians in Georgia, 1735-1740* (Raleigh, N. C., [1905]), pp. 221-22.

Notes

88. Mabel Haller, *Early Moravian Education in Pennsylvania* (Nazareth, Pa., 1953), pp. 6-7.
89. *Journal* VI, 25. Also see Seward's *Journal*, p. 13, and *Life, with Journals, Revised*, p. 345.
90. *Journal* V, 5.
91. "An Expostulatory Letter, Addressed to Nicholas Lewis, Count Zinzendorff," *Works*, IV, 254.
92. James Hutton, *Memoirs of James Hutton* (London, 1856), pp. 55, 69.
93. *Ibid.*, p. 579.
94. *Works*, III, Letter DCCCCLXXV, 13-14.
95. *Ibid.*, III, Letter MCLXII, 201.
96. "A Vindication and Confirmation of the Remarkable Work of God in New-England," *Works*, IV, 80.
97. *Christian History*, II, 373.
98. *The London Magazine*, XIV (August, 1745), 603.
99. *Works*, II, Letter DCLXXII, 170.
100. Wesley's *Sermon on Whitefield*, p. 13.
101. "The Burning Bush," *Eighteen Sermons*, p. 202.
102. "Remarks on Methodists and Papists," *Works*, IV, 247.
103. "Letter to Durell," *ibid.*, IV, 327-28.
104. *Ibid.*, I, Letter CCCXC, 362.
105. *Ibid.*, II, Letter DCLXXII, 170.
106. Roberts, *op. cit.*, p. 49.
107. Tyerman, *op. cit.*, II, 190.
108. *Works*, II, Letter DVI, 13.
109. John Stoughton, *Religion in England Under Queen Anne and the Georges* (London, 1878), II, 150-51.
110. Stevens, *op. cit.*, I, 476.
111. "Sermon IX: The Folly and Danger of being not righteous enough," *Works*, V, 131.
112. "Spiritual Baptism," *Eighteen Sermons*, p. 249.
113. George Whitefield, *A Letter from the Rev. Mr. Whitefield to the Religious Societies* (London, 1740), p. 23. The passage does not occur in the edition of the letter in the *Works*. Hereinafter cited as *Letter to Societies*.
114. *Works*, II, Letter DCCCXCVI, 414.
115. William Hobby, *An Enquiry into the Itineracy, and the Conduct of the Rev. Mr. George Whitefield* (Boston, 1745), p. 7.
116. *Works*, I, Letter CXXXV, 126.
117. Gamble, *op. cit.*, pp. 10-11.
118. "Continuation of the Account and Progress, &c. of the Orphan-House," *Works*, III, 481.
119. *Letter to Societies*, pp. 21-22. The passage does not occur in the edition of the letter in the *Works*.
120. *Christ Riding in His Chariot of Salvation* (Edinburgh, 1742), p. 22.
121. Stevens, *op. cit.*, I, 170 n.
122. Philip, *op. cit.*, Chapter X, 252-63.
123. "A Brief Account of the Occasion, Process, and Issue of a Late Trial at the Assize held at Gloucester, *March* 3, 1743, Between Some of the People called Methodists, Plaintiffs, and Certain Persons of the Town of Minchin-Hampton, in the said County, Defendants," *Works*, IV, 101-9. Also see *ibid.*, II, Letters DXXVI, DXXVII, DXXIX, DXLV, DXLIX, DL, 31-36, 49, 54-59.
124. "Letter to Durell," *ibid.*, IV, 311-41, *passsim*.
125. *The London Magazine*, XXXIX (November, 1770), 552-53.

Chapter X

1. Richard Steele, *The Christian Hero* (London, 1932), p. 1.
2. Joseph Addison, Richard Steele, and others, *The Spectator* (London, 1911), I,

No. 10, 38-39.

3. Robert Etheridge Moore, *Hogarth's Literary Relationships* (Minneapolis and London, 1948), p. 28.

4. "Gin Lane," engraved 1751, for which see William Hogarth, *The Works of William Hogarth* (London, 1872), II, plate 74. Hereinafter cited as Hogarth's *Works*.

5. John Ashton, *Social Life in the Reign of Queen Anne* (London, 1897), pp. 407-10.

6. "The Sleeping Congregation," engraved 1736, Hogarth's *Works*, I, plate 38; "The Harlot's Progress," (Plate VI), *ibid.*, I, plate 27; "The Rake's Progress," (Plate V: "Marries an Old Maid,") *ibid.*, I, plate 33.

7. Vernon Louis Parrington, *Main Currents in American Thought* (New York, 1930), I, 1-130.

8. James Boswell, *The Life of Samuel Johnson* (London, 1831), I, 45.

9. *Ibid.*, II, 81.

10. *Ibid.*, II, 271-72.

11. *Ibid.*, IV, 285-86.

12. *Ibid.*, IV, 286.

13. Samuel Johnson, *The Works of Samuel Johnson* (London, 1816), XII, 443.

14. Horace Walpole, *Correspondence with George Montagu, I* (New Haven, 1941), pp. 73-74. Hereinafter cited as *Correspondence with Montagu*.

15. Horace Walpole, *Correspondence with the Rev. William Cole*, I (New Haven, 1937), p. 134.

16. *Correspondence with Montagu*, pp. 283-84. Also see Tyerman, *op. cit.*, II, 425.

17. Horace Walpole, "The Parish Register of Twickenham," *Fugitive Verses* (New York, 1931), p. 48.

18. Horace Walpole, *Correspondence with Mary and Agnes Berry and Barbara Cecelia Seton*, I (New Haven, 1944), p. 297.

19. Alexander Pope, "The Dunciad," *The Works of Alexander Pope* (London, 1797), V, 156.

20. *Biographia Dramatica* (London, 1782), I, 170-71.

21. *Works*, III, Letter MCCXL, 262.

22. Seymour's *Life*, I, 209. Also see David Garrick, *Private Correspondence* (London, 1781), I, 120.

23. Samuel Foote, *The Dramatic Works of Samuel Foote* (London, 1788), I, 12.

24. *Ibid.*, II, 79-80.

25. *Biographia Dramatica* (London, 1812), III, 44.

26. Foote, *op. cit.*, II, 38.

27. *Ibid.*, II, 39.

28. *Ibid.*, II, 43.

29. *Ibid.*, II, 65.

30. Tate Wilkinson, *The Wandering Patentee* (York, 1795), I, 110-13.

31. Joseph Reed, *The Register-Office* (London, 1771), pp. 33-34. Also see p. 48.

32. Mary Singleton, ed., *The Old Maid*, No. 22, April 10, 1756, new edition (London, 1764), p. 186.

33. *Ibid.*, pp. 186-88.

34. Franklin, *op. cit.*, I, 266-67.

35. Wakeley, *op. cit.*, p. 125.

36. Franklin, *op. cit.*, I, 269-70.

37. *Ibid.*, p. 271.

38. Benjamin Franklin, *The Writings of Benjamin Franklin* (New York, 1905-7), III, 339.

39. *Tom Jones*, Bk. VIII, ch. viii, p. 350.

40. Henry Fielding, *The Adventures of Joseph Andrews* (New York, [1930]), Bk. I, ch. xvii, pp. 86-87.

41. Tobias Smollett, *The History of England* (London, 1790), V, 376.

42. Henry A. Beers, *A History of English Romanticism in the Eighteenth Century* (New York, 1899), p. 31.
43. Tobias Smollett, *The Expedition of Humphry Clinker* (London, 1895), I, 198.
44. "Hope," *The Poetical Works of William Cowper* (Edinburgh, 1854), I, 102-3.
45. Gilbert Thomas, *William Cowper and the Eighteenth Century* (London, 1935), p. 179.
46. *The Methodists, an Humorous Burlesque Poem* (London, 1739), pp. 20-21.
47. *Secret Memoirs*, pp. 18-19, 38-44, 48, 17, 68, 80-81.
48. *Ibid.*, p. 78.
49. Hogarth's *Works*, II, plate 100, engraved 1762.
50. John Nichols, *Biographical Anecdotes of William Hogarth* (London, 1782), p. 300.
51. William Henry Irving, *John Gay's London* (Cambridge, 1928), p. 276.
52. Hogarth's *Works*, II, plate 99, engraved 1761, published 1798.
53. *Ibid.*
54. [Robert Southey], *Letters from England: by Don Manuel Alvarez Espriella* (London, 1814), II, 358. Hereinafter cited as Southey's *Espriella*.
55. Edward Summerfield Ninde, *George Whitefield* (New York, 1924), pp. 9, 48.
56. *Works*, III, Letter MCLXIII, 202.
57. Jay, *op. cit.*, p. 226.
58. Richard Graves, *The Spiritual Quixote* (London, 1774), I, 38, 129, 273, and II, III, *passim*.
59. *Ibid.*, II, 102-3.
60. *Ibid.*, II, 106.
61. *Ibid.*, I, 130.
62. Cowper, *op. cit.*, I, 102.
63. *Pennsylvania Gazette*, No. 574, December 13, 1739, p. 1.
64. *Ibid.*, No. 595, May 8, 1740, p. 2. Also see Seward's *Journal*, p. 6.
65. *Pennsylvania Gazette*, No. 1828, January 5, 1764, p. 2.
66. *Virginia Gazette*, No. 483, October 31, 1745, p. 2.
67. *Ibid.*, No. 872 (Purdie and Dixon), February 4, 1768, p. 2.
68. *Boston Gazette*, No. 1080, September 29, 1740, p. 3.
69. *Ibid.*, No. 1026, April, 1741, pp. 1-2.
70. *The London Magazine*, VIII (May, 1739), 239.
71. *Ibid.*, VIII (June, 1739), 285.
72. *Ibid.*, VIII (July, 1739), 342.
73. *Ibid.*, XXIX (October, 1760), 527-28.
74. *Ibid.*, XIV (December, 1745), 603.
75. *The Gentleman's Magazine*, IX (May, 1739), 239-42.
76. *Ibid.*, IX (August, 1739), 417.
77. *Ibid.*, XL (April, 1770), 160.
78. Hannah More, *An Estimate of the Religion of the Fashionable World* (London, 1791), p. 109.
79. In a letter to Gibbon, for which see Edward Gibbon, *The Memoirs of the Life of Edward Gibbon* (London, 1900), p. 197.
80. "On the Causes of Methodism," *The Round Table. The Complete Works*, ed. P. P. Howe (London and Toronto, 1930-34), IV, 61.
81. *Ibid.*, "On Thompson and Cowper," in *Lectures on the English Poets*, V, 94.
82. George Eliot, *Felix Holt* (New York, 1885), pp. 67-68.
83. Southey's *Espriella*, II, 358-59.
84. William Blake, *The Prophetic Writings of William Blake* (Oxford, 1926), I, 387-88.
85. John Greenleaf Whittier, "The Preacher," *Narrative and Legendary Poems* (Cambridge, 1888), p. 224.

A Chronology for
the Life of George Whitefield

The following chronology is supplied as an aid to the text. It is selective rather than comprehensive. Little is known about certain periods of Whitefield's life. The more significant events of his personal history are included.

1714	December 16	Born, Bell Inn, Gloucester, England
1726		Attends St. Mary de Crypt School
1732		Matriculates at Pembroke College, Oxford
1734		Meets the Wesley brothers
1735	Spring	Feels himself converted
	June 12	First mentions, in a letter, his new-birth pangs
1736	Spring	Decides for the ministry
		Prepares, by private study, for ordination
	June 20	Is ordained by Bishop Benson, at Gloucester
	June 27	Preaches first sermon, St. Mary de Crypt, Gloucester
	July	Receives Bachelor of Arts degree
	August 4	Goes to London: preaching and prison work
	December 22	Offers himself to the Wesleys as Georgia missionary
1737	Mid-January	First preaches without notes, in Bristol
	End of January	Visits Bath and preaches in the Cathedral

1737	*c.* March 1	Goes to London to wait on Oglethorpe and trustees of Georgia
	Mid-March	Already collecting funds for Georgia
	August 5	"New Birth" sermon is published
	End of August	Goes to London
	Mid-September	Is displeased over first publicity
	Early Fall	Encounters first opposition
	c. October	Delivers first extempore prayer
	November	*The Gentleman's Magazine* praises him in poem
	c. Christmas	Sits for first portrait
	December 30	Boards the "Whitaker" at Purfleet
1738	February 1	Receives advice from returning John Wesley against going to Georgia
	February 2	Finally departs from England
	February 19	Arrives at Gibraltar
	March 7	Sails on "Whitaker" for Savannah.
	May 7	Anchors near Tybee Island
	May 8	Begins public labor in Georgia
	August 24	Opens school at Highgate
	End of August	Arrives at Charleston, South Carolina; well received by Commissary Garden
	September 9	Embarks for England
	November 14	Anchors off coast of Ireland
	December 8	Arrives in London; meets with Moravians at Fetter Lane
	December 9	Is received favorably by Archbishop of Canterbury
	December 10	Discovers five London churches are closed to him
	December 12	Visits John Wesley
1739	January 5	Attends Oxford Conference at Islington where some matters are decided by lot
	January 14	Is ordained priest in Church of England
	Mid-January	Is given Georgia "Living" by Georgia trustees
	February 4	Preaches at St. Margaret's and is accused of usurping pulpit
	February 15	Preaches at Newgate prison

1739	February 17	Inaugurates field-preaching
	February 20	Is summoned by chancellor to answer charge of breaking canon law
	March 6	Goes to Wales
	March 12	Is forbidden to preach at Newgate
	March 14	Resolves on a future of field-preaching
	March 29	Rejoices that John Wesley is coming to carry on Bristol work
	April 2	Lays first stone for Kingswood school
	April 3	Goes to Wales
	April 29	Preaches at Moorfields and Kennington Common
	May 9	Visits Georgia trustees and receives grant of five hundred acres for Orphan-House
	May 12	Bargains for passage to America on the "Elizabeth"
	June 28-29	Preaches in brother's field at Gloucester to large congregations
	July 5	Leaves Gloucester; arrives at Chafford Common; preaches to ten thousand; receives admonition from Bishop Benson
	July 8	Preaches to ten thousand each at Bowling Green, Bristol, and Hannam Mount, and to twenty thousand at Rose Green
	July 15	Sees John Wesley for last time until 1741
	July 22	Receives invitation from Erskine to visit Scotland
	July 31	Preaches on original sin to twenty thousand at Newington near Hackney
	August 1	Is denounced in Bishop of London's "Pastoral Letter"
	August 11	Begins answer to Bishop of London's "Pastoral Letter"
	August 14	Embarks for America on the "Elizabeth"

1739	October 30	With William Seward leaves the "Elizabeth" at Lewis Town, one hundred miles from Philadelphia
	November 2	Arrives at Philadelphia
	November 10	Meets William Tennent, Sr.
	November 14	Arrives in New York; is delighted with Gilbert Tennent's preaching
	November 28	Preaches to throng in Philadelphia; learns from Franklin of success of published writings
	November 29	Sends party by boat to Georgia; departs by land for Georgia; rides to Chester
	By end of year	Has completed forty-six of the sixty-three sermons in official works
1740	January 10	Reaches Savannah
	January 11	Inspects site chosen by James Habersham for Orphan-House
	January 24	Takes possession of lot for Orphan-House; names it *Bethesda*
	February 25	Establishes school at Darien
	April 2	Departs for East with William Seward on sloop "Savannah"
	April 4	Writes letter of proposal to Elizabeth Delamotte
	April 22	Buys five thousand acres on fork of Delaware to establish school for Negroes and refuge for English friends
	April 29	Arrives in New York by noon; preaches outdoors to five thousand
	May 7	Arrives in Philadelphia; is guest of Benezet family
	May 15	Preaches to twelve thousand at Fagg's Manor; awakens many
	May 16	Boards the "Savannah," bound south
	Spring	Is attacked in letters published by Alexander Garden
	June 5	Arrives in Savannah
	July 2	Arrives in Charleston
	July 11	Is summoned to answer charges of breaking canon law

1740	July 15	Appears before court at St. Philip's Church; is granted request of twenty-four hours to secure legal information; preaches
	August 17	Boards "Savannah" to begin four-months preaching tour
	September 14	Lands at Newport, R. I.; is welcomed by Nathaniel Clap, dissenting minister
	September 18	Arrives in Boston; receives warm welcome
	September 24	Visits Harvard
	October 13	Bids farewell to Boston; departs in Governor Belcher's coach; arrives at Concord and preaches
	October 17	Arrives at Northampton; visits Jonathan Edwards
	November 8	Preaches at Trenton; proceeds to Philadelphia
	November 22	Preaches to many thousands at Fagg's Manor
	December 13	Arrives at Savannah
1741	January 16	Boards the "Minerva," bound for England
	March 11	Arrives in England
	March 25	Meets hostility in England; finds Seward dead, his publisher (Joseph Hutton) hostile, and his debts mounting
	Spring	Publishes letter attacking John Wesley's theology
	April 10	Appears before Parliament to report on Georgia
	April 19	Is using first Moorfields tabernacle by this date
	End of June	Leaves London to itinerate provinces
	July	Is "suspended" by Ecclesiastical Court
	July 24	Embarks at Gravesend for Scotland, sailing on "Mary and Ann"
	October 29	Leaves Edinburgh, bound for Wales
	November 14	Marries Mrs. Elizabeth James in Abergavenny

1741	December 4	Arrives in London after four months' absence
1742	February 5	Writes Gilbert Tennent he is discontinuing keeping a *Journal*
	June 3	Arrives with wife for second visit in Scotland
	July 11	Field preaching and communion service for twenty thousand at Cambuslang
	November 6	Arrives in London; begins stay of almost four months
1743	January 5	Elected moderator of conference of Calvinistic Methodists held at Waterford, South Wales
	April 6-7	Elected "life" moderator of Calvinistic Methodists at second conference
	April 9	Begins Welsh circuit, accompanied by Howell Harris; preaches at Cardiff and at Fonmon
	May 6	Is back in London
	October 4	His son, John Whitefield, is born
1744	February 8	Buries his infant son
	June 26	Is attacked and almost murdered in Plymouth
	August 7	Embarks with his wife from Plymouth for America
	October 26	Arrives in York, New England, desperately ill
1745	January through March	Preaches in vicinity of Boston
	September	Is offered eight hundred pounds annually to preach six months a year at Philadelphia
	c. November 6	Arrives with his wife at Charleston, S. C.
1746	May 1	On board the "Charlestown," bound from South Carolina to Philadelphia
1747	January 23	Is at Charleston, S. C., beginning preaching tour
	March 15	Reports from South Carolina the

1747		purchase of slaves and plantation in South Carolina
1748	February 28	Announces intention to return to England by way of the Bermudas; intends to leave his wife in America and rejoin her in the fall
	March 6	Is on board the "Ann," bound for the Bermudas
	March 15	Reaches the Bermudas and begins a stay of about two months
	June 2	Embarks for England on board the "Betsy"
	July 5	Arrives at London
	July 20	Moderates Association of Calvinistic Methodists meeting in London
	August 10	Is back in London after having visited in Wales
	August 22	Is engaged to preach at Lady Huntingdon's
	September 14	Arrives at Edinburgh for third visit to Scotland
	November 10	Is back in London by this time; is preaching daily, often to the "great and noble"
	November 12	Expresses a desire to make a college of the Orphan-House
	December 6	Writes trustees of Georgia in favor of legal slavery in colony
1749	*c.* January 24	With Howell Harris holds meeting of Association of Calvinistic Methodists
	May 15	Sets out for Wales
	c. June 26	His wife arrives from America
	c. July 1	Returns to London
	October 4	Is at Leeds; is visited by Wesley, whom he consoles over having lost the opportunity to marry Grace Murray
1750	January 12	Offers to assist Wesley in chapel work
	July 6	Arrives in Edinburgh for his fourth visit
	c. August 10	Is back in London
	December 17	Is ill in London

1751	May 24	Arrives in Dublin, having traveled five days by boat
	July 18	Arrives at Edinburgh for his fifth visit
	August 28	Is back in London by this time
	August 29	Boards the "Antelope," bound for America for his fourth visit; takes several destitute children with him
	November 20	Has arrived at Bethesda by this time
1752	January 1	Begins year with plans for spring preaching tour
	Early April	Makes sudden decision to return to England
	May 21	In Portsmouth (England) pleads Orphan-House business as excuse for early return
	May 26	Is back in London by this date
	c. September 7	Arrives at Edinburgh for his sixth visit; preaches twice a day for a fortnight
	November 10	Arrives at London
1753	Mid-May	Leaves London for tour of Wales
	June 7	Is in London by this date
	June 10	New tabernacle is opened
	July 20	Arrives at Edinburgh for his seventh visit
	September 25	Arrives at London
	December 25	Entertains Gilbert Tennent and Samuel Davies
1754	January-February	Prepares for another trip to America
	March 7	Embarks for America from Gravesend aboard the "Success"
	March 16-April 13	Is anchored at Lisbon; goes regularly to Roman Catholic lenten services
	May 26	Lands at Charleston, S. C.
	July 20	Is on board the "Deborah," bound for New York
	Late September	Receives M.A. degree from New Jersey College
	October 13	Is at Boston by this date; reports thousands attending and many turned away

1755	January 14	By this date is itinerating in Virginia on his way to Bethesda
	c. March 27	Embarks for England
	Mid-June	Ends a month of regular, successful preaching in London; leaves for three-week tour of Gloucester, Bristol, and the west of England
	August 9	Is at Norwich to reopen a tabernacle built for James Wheatley
	August 20	Is back in London by this time
1756	March 14	Is in Bristol to begin spring campaign
	March 25	Is subjected to organized rioting during preaching services
	June 4	Is back in London, having preached in Bristol, Bath, Westbury, Gloucester, Bradford, Frome, Warminster, Portsmouth, and other places
	August 20	Arrives at Edinburgh for his eighth visit; begins three-week period of preaching twice daily
	October 27	Is back in London by this date
	November 7	Tottenham Court Road Chapel is opened for worship
1757	May 11	Arrives at Edinburgh for his ninth visit
	End of June	Sets out for Ireland
	July 3-4	Suffers real persecution in Dublin
	August 28	Is back in London by this date
	November 26	Is suffering physically from preaching regularly to thousands in London
1758	Mid-May	Leaves winter quarters, bound for the west of England and Wales
	August 4	Arrives at Edinburgh for his tenth visit
	October 28	Is back in London by this date
1759	June 30	Arrives at Edinburgh for his eleventh visit
	August 30	Is again in London by this time
1760	March 14	Collects on this general fast day about four hundred pounds for sufferers in Brandenburg
	June	Is in Wales

1760	Early July	Is burlesqued in *The Minor*
1761	February 13	Collects almost six hundred pounds for German Protestants and victims of a Boston fire
	c. End of April	Begins a year of semi-invalidism
	November 9	Is in Edinburgh by this time, but does not preach
1762	June	Goes to Holland for his health
	August 10	Attends conference of Wesley and his itinerants at Leeds
	September 2	By this date is in Edinburgh for his twelfth preaching visit; has just returned from Glasgow
	October 15	Is in London by this date
1763	March 19	By this date has arrived at Edinburgh for his thirteenth visit; preaches frequently though seriously ill
	June 4	Embarks from Greenock on the "Fanny," bound for America
	September 1	Is in Virginia by this time
1764	February 20	Receives public thanks from Boston for charitable collections sent the city
	December 18	Is in Savannah; sends memorial to Governor James Wright in interest of making a college of Bethesda
	December 20	Receives concurring action from both houses of the Georgia Assembly
1765	June 9	Embarks from America
	July 7	Lands in England
	October 6	Participates in opening Lady Huntingdon's chapel at Bath
	October 26	Is back in London by this date; remains for the rest of the year
1766	Early January	Heals a breach in John Wesley's society at London
1767	*c.* January	Takes Cornelius Winter into his household
	March 4	Dines with John Wesley at a mutual friend's house
	March 20	Is in Brighton to participate in the

1767		reopening of Lady Huntingdon's chapel
	June 17	Is back in London by this date
	August 20-21	Meets in conference with John Wesley's ministers
	Early September	Starts preaching tour
	October 28	More popular than ever, preaches to six thousand at Moorfields tabernacle
1768	June 15	Is in Edinburgh for his last visit; is still tremendously popular
	August 9	His wife dies of fever
	August 24	Opens Lady Huntingdon's college at Trevecca
	September 1	Is in London by this date
1769	January	Continues in London for first three months of the year; suffers chronic ill health
	August 8	Boards the "Friendship," bound for America
	c. September 10	Is at Deal, where the "Friendship" is wind-bound for three weeks
	c. End of September	Finally departs from England
	November 30	Arrives at Charleston, S. C.
1770	January 28	Entertains Governor Wright and Savannah officials at Bethesda
	May 6	Arrives at Philadelphia
	June 14	Returns to Philadelphia after completing a circuit of 150 miles
	August 3	Arrives at New Port and begins a successful preaching tour
	September 21-22	Travels from Boston to Portsmouth though ill
	September 29	Preaches at Exeter
	September 30	Dies at Newbury Port

Selected Bibliography

Primary materials consulted in separate editions have been omitted from the bibliography when they are included in identical form in the official edition on Whitefield's *Works*.

A. Primary Materials

Whitefield, George. *The Almost Christian. A Sermon.* Edinburgh: Printed by W. Cheyne, 1741.

—— *A Continuation of the Reverend Mr. Whitefield's Journal, from His Arrival at Savannah, to His Return to London.* 2nd ed.; London: Printed by W. Strahan, 1739. (*Journal II*)

—— *A Continuation of the Reverend Mr. Whitefield's Journal, During the Time He Was Detained in England by the Embargo.* 3rd ed.; London: Printed by W. Strahan, 1739. (*Journal IV*)

—— *A Continuation of the Reverend Mr. Whitefield's Journal, from His Embarking After the Embargo, to His Arrival at Savannah in Georgia.* 2nd ed.; London: James Hutton, 1740. (*Journal V*)

—— *A Continuation of the Reverend Mr. Whitefield's Journal, After His Arrival at Georgia, to a Few Days After His Second Return Thither from Philadelphia.* London: James Hutton, 1741. (*Journal VI*)

—— *A Continuation of the Reverend Mr. Whitefield's Journal from His Arrival at London, to His Departure from Thence on His Way to Georgia.* 2nd ed.; London: Printed by W. Strahan, 1744. (*Journal III*)

—— *A Continuation of the Reverend Mr. Whitefield's Journal, from a Few Days after His Return to Georgia, to His Arrival at Falmouth, on the 11th of March, 1741.* 2nd ed.; London: Printed by W. Strahan, 1744. (*Journal VII*)

—— *Eighteen Sermons. . . . Taken Verbatim in Short-Hand, and Faithfully Transcribed by Joseph Gurney.* Revised Andrew Gifford. Newburyport: Printed by Edmund M. Blunt, 1797.

—— *An Extract of the Preface to the Reverend Mr. Whitefield's Account of the Orphan-House in Georgia. Together with an Extract of Some Letters Sent Him from the Superintendents of the Orphan-House, and from Some of the Children.* Edinburgh: Printed by T. Lumisden and J. Robertson, 1741.

—— *Fifteen Sermons, Preached on Various Important Subjects. . . . To Which Is Prefixed, a Sermon, on the Character, Preaching, &c. of the Rev. Mr.*

.*Whitefield*, by Joseph Smith, V. D. M. Philadelphia: Printed by Mathew Carey, 1794.

—— *The Indwelling of the Spirit, the Common Privilege of All Believers. A Sermon.* [n.p.], 1741.

—— *A Journal of a Voyage from London to Savannah in Georgia.* 6th ed.; London: The Author, 1743. (*Journal* I)

—— *A Letter from the Rev. Mr. Whitefield to the Religious Societies, Lately Set on Foot in Several Parts of England and Wales.* London: Printed by W. Strahan, 1740.

—— *The Nature and Necessity of Our New Birth in Christ Jesus, in Order to Salvation. A Sermon.* 3rd ed.; London: C. Rivington, 1737.

—— "Newly Discovered Letters of George Whitefield, 1745-46." Ed. John W. Christie. *Journal of the Presbyterian Historical Society*, XXXII, Nos. 2-4 (June-December, 1954), 69-90, 159-86, 241-70.

—— *The Prodigal Son. A Lecture.* Glasgow: Printed in the Gallowgate Printing-House, 1741.

—— *A Short Account of God's Dealings with the Reverend Mr. George Whitefield.* London: Printed by W. Strahan, 1740.

—— *The Two First Parts of His Life, with His Journals, Revised, Corrected, and Abridged.* London: Printed by W. Strahan, 1756.

—— *The Unbeliever Convicted. A Sermon.* Edinburgh: Printed by R. Drummond, 1742.

—— "An Unpublished Journal of George Whitefield." Ed. Earnest Edward Eells. *Church History*, VII, No. 4 (December, 1938), 297-345.

—— *Whitefield's Journals, to Which Is Prefixed His "Short Account" and "Further Account."* Ed. William Wale. London: Henry J. Drane [1905].

—— *The Works of the Reverend George Whitefield.* London: Edward and Charles Dilly, and Messrs. Kincaid and Bell, 1771-72. 6 vols.

B. Secondary Materials

Addison, Joseph; Steele, Richard, and others. *The Spectator.* Ed. G. Gregory Smith. New York: E. P. Dutton & Co., 1907 (reprinted, 1911). Vol I.

Allestree, Richard, supposed author. *The Whole Duty of Man.* London: Printed by William Pawlet, 1703.

Andrews, J. R. *George Whitefield.* 7th ed.; London: Sovereign Grace Union, 1930 (S.G.U. *Publication* No. 183).

Ashton, John. *Social Life in the Reign of Queen Anne.* New ed.; London: Chatto & Windus, 1897.

Ashton, Thomas Southcliffe, and Sykes, Joseph. *The Coal Industry of the Eighteenth Century.* Manchester: Manchester University Press, 1929.

Barbeau, A. *Life & Letters at Bath in the xviij th Century.* New York: Dodd, Mead & Co., 1904.

Bayne-Powell, Rosamond. *The English Child in the Eighteenth Century.* New York: E. P. Dutton & Co. [1939].

Beers, Henry A. *A History of English Romanticism in the Eighteenth Century.* New York: Henry Holt & Co., 1899.

Belcher, Joseph, ed. *George Whitefield.* New York: American Tract Society, 1857.

Belden, Albert David. *George Whitefield—the Awakener.* Nashville: Cokesbury Press, 1931.

Besant, Walter. *London in the Eighteenth Century.* New York: The Macmillan Co., 1903.

Billingsley, Amos Stevens. *The Life of the Great Preacher, Reverend George Whitefield.* Philadelphia: P. W. Ziegler, 1878.

Biographia Dramatica. London: Messrs. Rivington and others, 1782. 2 vols.

Biographia Dramatica. London: Longman, and others, 1812. 3 vols.

Blake, William. *The Prophetic Writings of William Blake.* Ed. D. J. Sloss and J. P. R. Wallis. London: Oxford University Press, 1926. 2 vols.

Bonney, T. G., ed. *Cathedrals, Abbeys and Churches of England and Wales.* Revised edition; London: Cassell & Co., 1898. 2 vols.

Boston Gazette (Boston, Mass.), 1737-42. Scattered nos. on film. Durham, N.C.: Duke University Library.

Boswell, James. *The Life of Samuel Johnson.* New ed., with notes by John Wilson Croker; London: John Murray, 1831. 5 vols.

Brown, John. *An Estimate of the Manners and the Principles of the Times.* 2nd ed.; London: L. Davis and C. Reymers, 1757.

Brown, R. *Memoirs of Augustus Hermann Francke.* Philadelphia: American Sunday School Union [1830].

Brown, Thomas. *The Works of Mr. Thomas Brown.* 4th ed.; London: Sam. Briscoe, 1715. 4 vols.

Butler, Dugald. *John Wesley and George Whitefield in Scotland.* Edinburgh and London: William Blackwood and Sons, 1898.

Caledonian Mercury (Edinburgh, Scotland), 1743. Scattered nos. in one vol. Durham, N.C.: Duke University Library.

Chauncy, Charles. *Enthusiasm Described and Caution'd Against. A Sermon.* Boston: S. Eliot and J. Blanchard, 1742.

———— *Seasonable Thoughts on the State of Religion in New England.* Boston: Samuel Eliot, 1743.

Chesterfield, P. D. S. *Letters of Lord Chesterfield to Lord Huntingdon.* Ed. Francis Steuart. London: The Medici Society, 1923.

Christ Riding in His Chariot of Salvation. A Letter from a Friend in Edinburgh to a Gentleman in the Country. Edinburgh: Printed by T. Lumisden and J. Robertson, 1742.

The Christian History . . . for the Year 1743. Boston: T. Prince, 1744-45. 2 vols.

Church of Scotland. *The Declaration of the True Presbyterians within the Kingdom of Scotland.* [n.p.] 1742.

Cowper, William. *The Poetical Works of William Cowper.* Notes by the Rev. George Gilfillan. Edinburgh: James Nichol, 1854. 2 vols.

Cross, Arthur Lyon. *The Anglican Episcopate and the American Colonies.* Cambridge, Mass.: Harvard University Press, 1924.

The Dictionary of National Biography. Ed. Leslie Stephen and Sidney Lee. London: Oxford University Press, 1937-38. 22 vols.

Eliot, George. *Felix Holt.* New York: John B. Alden, 1885.

Ellington, Edward. *The Reproach of Christ the Christian's Treasure.* London: E. and C. Dilly, 1771.

Fielding, Henry. *The Adventures of Joseph Andrews.* New York: Charles Scribner's Sons [1930]. (Modern Student's Library)

———— *The History of Tom Jones, a Foundling.* New York: Modern Library, 1931.

Foote, Samuel. *The Dramatic Works of Samuel Foote*. London: J. F. and C. Rivington and others, 1788. 4 vols.

Franklin, Benjamin. *The Life of Benjamin Franklin*. 5th ed.; Philadelphia: J. B. Lippincott [1916]. 3 vols.

———— *The Writings of Benjamin Franklin*. New York: The Macmillan Co., 1905-7. 10 vols.

Fries, Adelaide L. *The Moravians in Georgia, 1735-1740*. Raleigh, N.C.: The Author [1905].

Gamble, Thomas, Jr. *Bethesda*. Savannah, Ga.: Morning News Print., 1902.

Garden, Alexander. *Six Letters to the Rev. Mr. George Whitefield*. 2nd ed.; Boston: reprinted by T. Fleet, 1740.

Garrick, David. *The Private Correspondence of David Garrick*. London: Henry Colburn and Richard Bentley, 1781. 2 vols.

The Gentleman's Magazine, VII-XLI (1737-71).

Genuine and Secret Memoirs Relating to the Life and Adventures of that Arch Methodist, Mr. G. W - - fi - d. Oxford: The Author, 1742.

Gibbon, Edward. *The Memoirs of the Life of Edward Gibbon*. Ed. George Birkbeck Hill. London: Methuen & Co., 1900.

Gibson, E. *The Bishop of London's Three Pastoral Letters to the People of His Diocese*. London: Printed by S. Buckley, 1732.

Gillies, John. *Memoirs of the Life of the Reverend George Whitefield*. London: Edward and Charles Dilly; Edinburgh: Kincaid and Creech, 1772.

Gledstone, James Paterson. *George Whitefield*. 2nd ed.; New York: American Tract Society, 1901.

Graves, Richard. *The Spiritual Quixote*. 2nd ed.; London: J. Dodsley, 1774. 3 vols.

Haller, Mabel. *Early Moravian Education in Pennsylvania*. Nazareth, Pa.: Moravian Historical Society, 1953.

Harper, Charles G. *The Oxford, Gloucester and Milford Haven Road*. London: Chapman & Hall, 1905. 2 vols.

Harris, Thaddeus Mason. *Biographical Memorials of James Oglethorpe*. Boston: The Author, 1841.

Hazlitt, William. *The Complete Works*. Ed. P. P. Howe. Centenary ed.; London and Toronto: J. M. Dent & Sons, 1930-34. 21 vols.

Hobby, William. *An Enquiry into the Itineracy, and the Conduct of the Rev. Mr. George Whitefield*. Boston: Printed by Rogers and Fowle, 1745.

Hodge, Charles. *The Constitutional History of the Presbyterian Church in the United States of America*. Philadelphia: Presbyterian Board of Publication [1851]. 2 vols.

Hogarth, William. *The Works of William Hogarth*. London: Bell and Daldy, 1872. 2 vols.

Hutton, James. *Memoirs of James Hutton*. Ed. Daniel Benham. London: Hamilton, Adams, & Co., 1856.

Irving, William Henry. *John Gay's London*. Cambridge, Mass.: Harvard University Press, 1928.

Jackson, Thomas. *The Life of the Rev. Charles Wesley*. New York: G. Lane & P. P. Sandford, 1842.

Jay, William. *Memoirs of the Life and Character of the Late Rev. Cornelius Winter*. 1st American ed.; New York: Samuel Whiting, 1811.

Johnson, Amanda. *Georgia as Colony and State*. Atlanta: Walter W. Brown [1938].

Selected Bibliography

Johnson, Samuel. *A Dictionary of the English Language.* 4th ed.; London: Printed by W. Strahan, 1773. 2 vols.

—— *Lives of the English Poets.* Ed. George Birkbeck Hill. Oxford: Clarendon Press, 1905. Vol. II.

—— *The Works of Samuel Johnson.* New ed.; London: Nichols and Son, 1816. 12 vols.

Lam, George L., and Smith, Warren H. "Two Rival Editions of George Whitefield's *Journal*, London, 1738," *Studies in Philology* XLI, No. 1 (January, 1944), 86-93.

Lavington, George. *The Enthusiasm of Methodists and Papists, Compar'd.* London: J. and P. Knapton, 1749-51. 2 vols. (3 pts.)

Law, William. *A Serious Call to a Devout and Holy Life.* London: William Innys, 1729.

Lecky, William Edward Hartpole. *A History of England in the Eighteenth Century.* New York: D. Appleton & Co., 1888-91. 8 vols.

The London Chronicle, I-XXVIII (1757-70).

The London Magazine, 1739-52, 1756, 1760-62, 1764-70.

McCrady, Edward. *The History of South Carolina Under the Royal Government, 1719-1776.* New York: The Macmillan Co., 1901.

The Methodists, an Humorous Burlesque Poem. London: John Brett, 1739.

Miller, Perry. *Jonathan Edwards.* [New York]: William Sloane, Associates [1949]. (American Men of Letters Series)

Misson, François Maximilien. *Memoires et Observations Faites par un Voyageur en Engleterre.* La Haye: Henri van Bulderen, 1698.

Moore, Francis. *A Voyage to Georgia.* London: Jacob Robinson, 1744.

Moore, Robert Etheridge. *Hogarth's Literary Relationships.* Minneapolis: University of Minnesota Press, 1948.

More, Hannah. *An Estimate of the Religion of the Fashionable World.* 3rd ed.; London: T. Cadell, 1791.

Murray, James A. H., and others, eds. *A New English Dictionary on Historical Principles.* Oxford: Clarendon Press, 1888-1928. 10 vols. in 20.

The Nashville Christian Advocate, XXXI (March 4, 1871).

New, Alfred H., ed. *The Coronet & the Cross.* London: Partridge, 1857.

The New-England Historical & Genealogical Register and Antiquarian Journal, XXIV (1870); XXVII (1873).

Newell, Daniel. *The Life of Rev. George Whitefield.* New York: D. Newell [1846].

Nichols, John. *Biographical Anecdotes of William Hogarth.* 2nd ed.; London: J. Nichols, 1782.

—— *Literary Anecdotes of the Eighteenth Century.* London: The Author, 1812. 6 vols.

Ninde, Edward Summerfield. *George Whitefield.* New York: Abingdon Press, 1924.

"On Hearing George Whitefield at the New Building in Philadelphia," *The General Magazine and Historical Chronicle for All the British Plantations in America,* I, No. 1 (January 1741), 70.

Orphan-Letters. Glasgow: Printed in the Gallowgate Printing-House, 1741.

Overton, John H., and Relton, Frederic. *The English Church from the Accession of George I. to the End of the Eighteenth Century.* New York: The Macmillan Co., 1906. (*A History of the English Church,* Vol. VII)

Parrington, Vernon Louis. *Main Currents in American Thought*. New York: Harcourt, Brace & Co., 1930. 3 vols in one.

Pemberton, Ebenezer. *Heaven the Residence of the Saints. A Sermon*. Boston: Printed; London: Reprinted, E. and C. Dilly, 1771.

Pennsylvania Gazette (Philadelphia), 1739-70. Filmed by the Historical Society of Pennsylvania.

Philip, Robert. *The Life and Times of the Reverend George Whitefield*. London: George Virtue, 1837.

Pope, Alexander. *The Works of Alexander Pope*. London: B. Law, 1797. 9 vols.

Reed, Joseph. *The Register-Office*. New ed.; London: T. Davies and T. Becket, 1771.

Reichel, Levin Theodore. *The Early History of the Church of the United Brethren*. Nazareth, Pa.: Moravian Historical Society, 1888.

Remarks upon the Reverend Mr. Whitefield's Letter to the Vice-Chancellor of the University of Oxford. Oxford: J. Fletcher, 1768.

Roberts, Griffith T. *Howell Harris*. London: Epworth Press [1951]. (The Wesley Historical Society Lecture, No. 17, Sheffield Conference, 1951)

Rush, Benjamin. *The Autobiography of Benjamin Rush*. [Princeton, N. J.]: Princeton University Press, 1948. (American Philosophical Society *Memoirs*, Vol. 25)

The Scots Magazine, I-XCVI (1739-1825).

Seward, William. *Journal of a Voyage from Savannah to Philadelphia*. London: J. Oswald, 1740.

Seymour, Aaron. *The Life and Times of Selina, Countess of Huntingdon*. London: William Edward Painter, 1839-40. 2 vols.

Singleton, Mary, ed. *The Old Maid*. New ed.; London: A. Millar, 1764.

Sitwell, Edith. *Bath*. London: Faber & Faber [1932].

Smith, Josiah. *The Character, Preaching, &c. of the Reverend Mr. George Whitefield*. Boston: Printed; Glasgow: Reprinted, Sold by Robert Smith, 1741.

Smollett, Tobias. *The Expedition of Humphry Clinker*. Ed. George Saintsbury. London: Gibbings, 1895. 2 vols.

———— *The History of England*. New ed.; London: T. Cadell, 1790. 5 vols.

[Southey, Robert]. *Letters from England: by Don Manuel Alvarez Espriella*. 3rd ed.; London: Longman, Hurst, Rees, Orme, and Brown, 1814. 3 vols.

Southey, Robert. *The Life of Wesley*. 2nd ed.; London: Longman, Hurst, Rees, Orme, and Brown, 1820. 2 vols.

———— *Selections from the Letters of Robert Southey*. Ed. John Wood Warter. London: Longman, Brown, Green, and Longmans, 1856. 4 vols.

Sprague, William B. *Annals of the American Episcopal Pulpit*. New York: Robert Carter, 1859. (*Annals of the American Pulpit*, Vol. V)

Steele, Richard. *The Christian Hero*. Ed. Rae Blanchard. London: Oxford University Press, 1932.

Stephens, William. *A Journal of the Proceedings in Georgia*. London: W. Meadows, 1742. 2 vols.

Stevens, Abel. *The History of the Religious Movement of the Eighteenth Century, Called Methodism*. New York: Carlton & Porter [1858-61]. 3 vols.

Stoughton, John. *Religion in England Under Queen Anne and the Georges*. London: Hodder & Stoughton, 1878. 2 vols.

Sweet, William Warren. *Religion in Colonial America*. New York: Charles Scribner's Sons, 1942.

Tailfer, Patrick, and others. *A True and Historical Narrative of the Colony of Georgia in America*. Charles-Town, S.C.: The Authors, 1741.

Thomas, Gilbert. *William Cowper and the Eighteenth Century*. London: Ivor Nicholson & Watson, 1935.

Tillotson, John. *The Works of the Most Reverend Dr. John Tillotson*. London: R. Ware, 1743. 12 vols.

Tracy, Joseph. *The Great Awakening*. Boston: Tappan & Dennet, 1842.

Traill, H. D., ed. *Social England*. Vol. V: *From the Accession of George I. to the Battle of Waterloo*. New York: G. P. Putnam's Sons, 1902.

Trevelyan, G. M. *Illustrated English Social History*. Vol. 3: *The Eighteenth Century*. London: Longmans, Green & Co. [1951].

Trumbull, Benjamin. *A Complete History of Connecticut*. New-Haven, Conn.: Maltby, Goldsmith, and Samuel Wadsworth, 1818. 2 vols.

Turberville, A. S. *English Men and Manners in the Eighteenth Century*. London: Oxford University Press, 1926.

Tyerman, Luke. *The Life of the Rev. George Whitefield*. New York: Anson D. F. Randolph, 1877. 2 vols.

Union Society, Savannah, Ga. *Minutes of the Union Society*. Savannah: John M. Cooper, 1860.

Virginia Gazette (Williamsburg, Va.; founded by William Parks), 1737-72. Scattered nos. missing; filmed by the Institute of Early American Culture, Williamsburg, Va.

Virginia Gazette (Williamsburg, Va.; founded by William Rind), 1766-71. Scattered nos. Durham, N. C.: Duke University Library.

Wakeley, Joseph Beaumont. *The Prince of Pulpit Orators*. New York: Carlton & Lanahan, 1871.

Walker, George L. *Some Aspects of the Religious Life of New England with Special Reference to Congregationalists*. New York: Silver, Burdett and Company, 1897.

Walpole, Horace. *Correspondence with George Montagu*, I. New Haven, Conn.: Yale University Press, 1941. (Yale Edition of Walpole's *Correspondence,* Vol. 9)

—————— *Correspondence with Mary and Agnes Berry and Barbara Cecelia Seton,* 1. New Haven, Conn.: Yale University Press, 1944. (Yale Edition of Walpole's *Correspondence*. Vol. 11)

—————— *Correspondence with the Rev. William Cole,* I. New Haven, Conn.: Yale University Press, 1937. (Yale Edition of Walpole's *Correspondence,* Vol. 1)

—————— *Fugitive Verses*. Ed. W. S. Lewis. New York: Oxford University Press, 1931. (Miscellaneous Antiquities, No. 5)

Wesley, Charles. *An Elegy on the Late Reverend George Whitefield*. Bristol: Printed by William Pine, 1771.

Wesley, John. *The Journal of the Rev. John Wesley*. Ed. Nehemiah Curnock. London: Robert Culley [1909-16]. 8 vols.

—————— *A Sermon on the Death of the Rev. Mr. George Whitefield*. Atlanta: The Library, Emory University, 1953. (Emory University *Publications,* Sources & Reprints, ser. VIII, no. 2)

—————— *The Works of the Rev. John Wesley*. Ed. Thomas Jackson. 3rd ed.; London: Printed by John Mason, 1829-31. 14 vols.

The Wesleyan-Methodist Magazine, XLV-LXXII (1822-49). (Continuation of *The Methodist Magazine*)

Whitehead, John. *The Life of the Rev. John Wesley.* London: Printed by Stephen Couchman, 1793; Boston: Dow & Jackson, 1845.

Whittier, John Greenleaf. *Narrative and Legendary Poems.* Cambridge, Mass.: Printed at the Riverside Press, 1888. (*The Writings of John Greenleaf Whittier,* Vol. I)

Wilkinson, Tate. *The Wandering Patentee.* York: The Author, 1795. 4 vols.

Winslow, Ola Elizabeth. *Jonathan Edwards.* New York: The Macmillan Co., 1940.

Winsor, Justin, ed. *Narrative and Critical History of America.* Vol. V. Boston and New York: Houghton Mifflin Co., 1887.

Wood, George B. *Early History of the University of Pennsylvania from Its Origin to the Year 1827.* 3rd ed. with supplementary chapters; Philadelphia: 1896.

Woodforde, James. *The Diary of a Country Parson.* Ed. John Beresford. London: Oxford University Press, 1926. 2 vols.

Wright, Robert. *A Memoir of General James Oglethorpe.* London: Chapman and Hall, 1867.

Index

219